An Important Message to Our Readers

This book provides information and general advice about the law. But laws and procedures change frequently, and they can be interpreted differently by different people. For specific advice geared to your specific situation, consult an expert. No book, software or other published material is a substitute for personalized advice from a knowledgeable lawyer licensed to practice law in your state.

The information in this book is provided "as is" without any warranty of any kind, either expressed, implied, or statutory, including, but not limited to, any warranty that this information will conform to any specifications, any implied warranties of merchantability, fitness for a particular purpose, or any warranty that the information will be error free.

In no event shall the author or publisher, or the author's or publisher's contractors or subcontractors, be liable for any damages, including, but not limited to, direct, indirect, special or consequential damages, arising out of, resulting from, or in any way connected with this book, whether or not based upon warranty, contract, tort, or otherwise, and whether or not loss was sustained from, or arose out of the results of, or use of, the information contained in this book.

4th Edition

Patent Searching Made Easy

How to Do Patent Searches on the Internet and in the Library

by David Hitchcock

This book was last revised in: July 2007.

Fourth Edition

Front Cover Art   Copyright © Gina Miller, NanoGirl.com

Back Cover Photo   Copyright © Moller International, USA

Publisher's Cataloging-in-Publication data

Hitchcock, David, 1956-
    Patent searching made easy : how to do patent searches on the internet and in the library / by David Hitchcock.
    p. cm.
    4th edition.
    Includes index.
    ISBN 978-1-4303-2640-3
1. Patent searching. 2. Patent literature. 3. Patents--United States--Handbooks, manuals, etc. I. Title.

T210 .H58 2007
608.721--dc22   2007904966

Dedication

This book is dedicated to the independent inventors of the world, who toil endlessly in garages and basements in the hopes of making the world a better place through creativity.

This book is also dedicated to my wife Sylvia, who was always there when it mattered and to Jennifer, for putting up with a daddy who was constantly working in his office.

Acknowledgements

All screen shots from the USPTO website are courtesy of the United States Patent and Trademark Office. All screen shots from the EPO website are courtesy of the European Patent Office. All screen shots from the Defense Technical Information Center are courtesy of DTIC.

The dazzling front cover artwork was provided by Gina (NanoGirl) Miller and the back cover photograph is courtesy of Moller International, USA.

The author also gratefully acknowledges and thanks the Thomas Register, Google, Medical Informatics Engineering, the Intellectual Property Office of Singapore and the Microsoft Corporation for granting permission to use various screen shots in this book.

About the Author

David Hitchcock has degrees in physics and engineering, and has worked as a computer consultant on such diverse projects as the MX missile, the Milstar satellite program, advanced capability torpedoes and jet engine computer simulations for NASA. He has focused on patent searching and new technology for a number of years. Mr. Hitchcock holds one patent and is the author of a training video on patent searching.

Table of Contents

Introduction

Part 1: The Basics

1. Introduction to Patents and Patent Searching   1

2. Tools and Resources   17

Part 2: Internet-Based Patent Searching 23

3. Patent Searching at the PTO Website 25

4. Advanced Patent Searching at the PTO Website 53

Appendices

A. Patent and Trademark Depository Libraries

B. Forms
Classification Search Sheet
Class Finder Tool

C. Summary of Searcher's Secrets

Glossary

Index

Preface

This fourth edition of *Patent Searching Made Easy* has been completely updated to include the latest changes at the PTO's patent searching website and the latest resources available at the Patent and Trademark Depository Library system. The chapter covering the European Patent Office has also been updated. A new chapter covering Google's patent searching capability and the resources of the Intellectual Property Office of Singapore has been added.

It is my sincerest hope that you find this guide informative, easy to use and helpful in your invention development efforts.

David Hitchcock
July 2007

Introduction

If you are an inventor or owner of a business engaged in research and development, this book shows you how to:

- quickly "check out" any new idea, to see if anyone else has already patented it

- verify the patent status of ideas submitted to you for development (if you are a potential developer)

- save lots of money in legal fees, and

- avoid reinventing the wheel.

A. Check out New Ideas

You come up with what seems like a new way to solve a problem or accomplish a task. But you wonder if somebody has already trod this ground before you, and either succeeded in obtaining a patent or proved that your idea is not feasible?

You have been told that to answer these questions you will need to have a patent search performed by a lawyer or professional patent searcher at a cost of $500.00 or more—possibly much more. You know you can't afford to spend that much money on an idea that someone else may

well have thought of already. Maybe you should just forget about it.

Well, think again. The fact is you can do your own patent search in your spare time, and with only a reasonable amount of effort. Even better, you can do this without spending more than a few dollars. If it turns out that your idea has never before been addressed in a patent, it may be that its time for a patent has come. And depending on what you do with that patent, you may gain a new amount of independence and ability to fulfill your life goals.

As we explain in Chapter 1, an invention must be judged both novel and unobvious (surprising in light of prior developments) to receive a patent. The novelty of your idea will be judged not only against all previously issued patents, but also against all previous developments in the same field, whether or not they were ever patented. For instance, the grooves in an automobile steering wheel were deemed to be a non-patentable invention because of the traditional use of grooves in sword handles. This rule means that to be absolutely sure that your idea is patentable you will have to go beyond the patent database and examine all written references to similar developments and all real-life items that may embody your idea. But that type of comprehensive search can wait until later.

For now, a search of the U.S. patent database is a good place to start. If someone has thought of your idea before, and deemed it valuable, chances are the idea will show up in one or more patents. Keep in mind, however, that pending patent applications (patent applications that have already been submitted, but for which no patent has yet been issued) are kept confidential for 18 months and cannot be searched until that time has been exceeded. (See Chapter 11 for further discussion on pending patent applications.)

What is the Patent Database?

The U.S. patent database contains all of the patents issued by the United States Patent and Trademark Office (PTO) from the beginning of the country. Individual patents are stored in patent file folders at the PTO in Virginia. Additionally, the PTO has created a computer database of patent images and text.

The traditional method of searching the patent database is to hire a search professional to travel to the U.S. Patent and Trademark Office in Virginia and conduct the search there. While very effective, this process is also very expensive. However, you can save yourself some money by performing a preliminary search yourself. If your search reveals that your idea has already been described in one or more previous patents, you will have saved yourself the expense of hiring a search professional.

You don't have to go to Virginia to perform your preliminary search. Instead, you can use the World Wide Web. The PTO provides an online database where you simply type in words which describe your

invention—called keywords—to search for patents as far back as 1971 that contain those same words. Pre-1971 patents can also be searched on a much more limited basis.

Another great resource for patent searching is a network of special libraries called Patent and Trademark Depository Libraries (PTDL's—see Appendix A for a list). At a PTDL you can perform computer searches of the PTO's electronic database.

As you learn how to search for patents, you also will learn how to think about your ideas in the same way that the patent office would were you to apply for a patent on them. This knowledge will enable you to search for ideas that are not only the same as yours, but similar to yours. This process will allow you to determine not only if your invention is the first, but also whether it is the best. And if it is not, the search may inspire you to refine your idea in ways that will qualify it for a patent.

Key to assessing the patentability of your new idea is understanding what previous developments—known in the trade as prior art—the patent office will consider when deciding whether to issue a patent on your idea. This book will help you to:

• understand how the patent office classifies different types of inventions

• assign your idea to the right class

• compare your idea to other similar ideas in the same class, and

• tentatively conclude whether your idea is new enough to qualify for a patent.

By doing your own preliminary patent search, you will become educated about the true nature of your idea. Strangely enough, many people who come up with new ideas—including full time inventors—often do not fully understand what they have invented. They may dwell on one particular aspect of their invention, and miss a much more valuable general concept that is revealed to them in the course of their patent search.

For example, suppose you want to invent a system to deploy a banner from a hot air balloon. For airplanes, banners simply need to be dragged behind the airplane. The speed of the aircraft, combined with the wake of the plane, will then cause the banner to be unfurled.

However, balloons travel much more slowly than airplanes. If you want to deploy a banner in the horizontal direction, you will need to insert a retractable rod into one side of the banner. You design an air cylinder and rod system, using compressed gas to deploy the rod. Since weight and cost are considerations, you use nitrogen as your compressed gas.

As an after thought, you check the U.S. patent database for similar designs. You find out that no one has patented a retractable banner system for balloons using compressed nitrogen and a rod. Your search reveals that compressed nitrogen has been used to inflate air bags, but not banners. But wait, inflating air bags with compressed nitrogen makes you to realize that the rod itself could be eliminated from your design. Compressed nitrogen alone could be used to inflate an inner chamber in the banner. This will greatly simplify the design. Hold on, why limit yourself to nitrogen when you could use any compressed fluid? You now have a much more general deployment system that can be used in several applications.

Performing patent searches is a great way to get familiar with patent terminology. This will come in handy during all aspects of the patent search as well as the patent application process itself. In particular,

when dealing directly with the patent examiner who is reviewing your application, it helps if you are both speaking the same language.

B. Check Product Submissions

So far we have addressed you as if you are an inventor, whether formal or informal. But this book can also be of great benefit if you are a business owner who, because of the nature of your business, tends to be approached by people who want you to manufacture or distribute their new invention. The outside inventor wants you to invest thousands of dollars in special tooling, and related manufacturing or marketing costs. The idea seems good. It looks like it will enhance your existing product line. But how do you know that another company is not making the same, or a similar product? If another company is manufacturing a similar product, you need to know about this before investing time, money and effort on the submitted idea. This does not necessarily preclude the submission, but gives you a warning flag to seek an expert opinion before proceeding.

Business owners often spend thousands of dollars on professional patent searchers to verify the uniqueness of new product submissions. This cost can add up quickly. As a business owner, you can save yourself considerable amounts of money by performing some of this searching yourself. Additionally, with the cost savings you realize, you will be able to evaluate more new products. This can be an especially valuable benefit if your business has a tight operating budget.

This book can help you "check out" new product ideas. You can also monitor new patents issued for devices in your line of business. By doing so, you can help your company advance with the leading edge of technology. You will also see what patents are owned by your competitors. This will help reduce the chances of having a nasty surprise product turn up on the shelves—a product which does everything that yours does, but at half the cost.

C. Save Time and Money

Performing your own preliminary patent search can save you a lot of money and time. If you want the patent office to grant you a patent on a particular invention, you will have to file what is known as a patent application. It is essential to perform a patent search before filing. Why? Because, filing a patent application, with its associated specification, drawings and fees, is an expensive, time consuming process— often costing up to $10000 or more, if you have it done by a patent attorney. You can, however, do it yourself for far less money with the help of *Patent It Yourself* by David Pressman (Nolo). Either way, before setting out to file a patent application, you will want to be reasonably sure, at the very least, that your idea has not been trumped by a previous patent.

As mentioned, the average cost of a single preliminary patent search performed by a patent search professional is around $500.00. By using the techniques in this book, you will be able to do most, if not all, of this work yourself. If you have lots of ideas and you are trying to select the best one to patent, you can save some really serious money. This is because a professional patent searcher will charge you separately for each invention. For example, if you want four ideas searched, the cost

easily could be $2000. Even if you ultimately decide to use a professional patent searcher, you can perform some of the preliminary searching yourself. This may save you a portion of the search fees and make you a more knowledgeable client.

D. Avoid Reinventing the Wheel

By checking the U.S. patent database first, you can avoid spending a lot of time tweaking your invention, only to find out later that you have reinvented the wheel. For example, suppose that your favorite hobby is amateur astronomy. You love to spend endless hours under the night sky with your telescope. One problem you have is reading the sky charts and comparing them with what you see through the eyepiece of the telescope. You purchased a red light nightlight because the red light does not interfere with your night vision. But you keep losing the nightlight or you have to hold the nightlight and fumble with the chart while switching your vision back and forth between the eyepiece and the chart.

Then it hits you. You will invent a special attachment for the nightlight; an attachment that will allow you to clip it to whatever is handy. Over the next several days you spend hours coming up with several designs; nightlights with clips, nightlights with screws, and nightlights with rubber bands. Finally, you have it. The best solution is a nightlight with a flexible housing that can be wrapped around any convenient nearby structure. You've invented the flexible astronomy nightlight! Wrong, you've reinvented the snake light.

E. How to Use "Patent Searching Made Easy"

> **ICON KEY**
>
> → Skip Ahead
>
> 📖 More Information

These icons are used throughout this book.

This book is arranged in four parts:

- Part One: The Basics
- Part Two: Internet-Based Patent Searching
- Part Three: PDTL-Based Patent Searching
- Part Four: Where Do I Go from Here?

Part one gives you your basic training. Here, we help you come up with words to describe your invention. These are known as keywords or search words. Once you come up with these words, you can use your computer to search the U.S. patent database for patents that contain these words. In addition to searching for isolated occurrences of your individual search terms, you can also search for combinations of search terms. Often, the use of words in combination will produce much more targeted or specific search results. For your information, the rules of logic that control how we combine keywords are known as Boolean logic. In Chapter 1, we will review Boolean logic in detail, and show how you use it to get the best possible search results. In Chapter 2, we will cover the required hardware, software and windows skills necessary for doing patent searches on the Internet.

In Part Two, you will perform simple and advanced patent searches using the Internet. You will use different keywords and vary their combinations with Boolean logic. We will also introduce you to the USPTO's classification system. These are the categories that the PTO uses to classify or sort the various types of inventions. Here we will help you discover what category the USPTO will most likely use for your invention. Once we identify these categories, we will show you how to search for other patents within the same category. This will tell you what patents have issued for inventions similar to yours.

Part Two also covers:

- Searching at the European Patent Office (EPO)
- Use a translation service to translate foreign language patents.
- Searching non-patent resources

In Part three we cover the resources available at the nationwide network of Patent and Trademark Depository Libraries (PTDLs). These resources include:

- Using the following printed manuals: the *Index to the U.S. Patent Classification*, *Manual of Classification* and *Classification Definitions*.
- Using the Classification And Search Support Information System (CASSIS) computer system.

In Part four we will help you assess the results of your search in terms of their effect on the patentability of your invention.

Part 1

The Basics

In this part of the book, we introduce you to the tools and techniques used to perform a basic preliminary patent search. In Chapter 1, we discuss what a patent is and how word-based patent searches work. In Chapter 2, the computer hardware, software and Windows skills that you will need are reviewed. Chapter 2 also introduces us to the resources available at the Patent and Trademark Depository Library (PTDL).

Chapter

1

Introduction to Patents and Patent Searching

A. What is a patent, and what does it do for me?

A patent is a right, granted by the government, to a person or legal entity (partnership or corporation). A patent gives its holder the right to exclude others from making, using or selling the invention "claimed" in the patent deed for twenty years from the date of filing (For patents issued before June 8, 1995, seventeen years from the date the patent was issued by the U.S. Patent and Trademark Office). Once the patent expires, the invention covered by the patent enters the public domain and can be used by anyone. The scope of a U.S. patent is limited to the borders of the United States and its territories.

The right of exclusion given to a patent owner can best be thought of as an offensive legal right. This right of exclusion allows the patent owner to file a lawsuit in federal court against an infringer (anyone who violates the right of exclusion). Because the right of exclusion is not a defensive legal right, the patent owner can't rely on law enforcement agencies to automatically prosecute someone that infringes (copies) his or her patented invention.

Patent Application Process

When you submit your completed patent application and filing fee to the PTO, you will be assigned a filing date. After a six- to 18- month waiting period, a patent examiner will review the application. While it is possible that your application will be allowed as is, this is usually not the case. More often than not, the patent examiner will object to one or more of your claims, or require changes to your patent drawings or specifications. This results in what is known as an "Office Action." The office action is an official communication (letter) from the patent office, outlining the objections to your original patent application. You then have the choice of either modifying the application or convincing the examiner that he/she was in error.

After you successfully respond to the office action the patent examiner will allow your application and you will have to pay an issue fee. After a few more months' delay, your patent will finally issue. The entire process, from initial patent application submission to issued patent, usually takes from 1.5 to three years.

📖 *For more information about how to complete and file a patent application, see* Patent It Yourself, *by David Pressman (Nolo).*

In the sense that a patent gives the patent holder the right to sue anyone who tries to develop, use or manufacture the invention covered by the patent, the patent can be a valuable commodity. It can be sold outright or licensed in exchange for a royalty. Additionally, the patent owner may choose to manufacture and distribute the invention, thereby keeping all the proceeds for him or herself.

📖 *For more information about licensing inventions, see* License Your Invention, *by Richard Stim (Nolo).*

Patents as a Type of Intellectual Property

A patent falls under the larger category of Intellectual Property. Other forms of intellectual property are Trademarks, Trade Secrets and Copyrights. Depending on the type of invention, one of these other forms of intellectual property may give you greater offensive legal rights. For example, a trademark would be appropriate if your innovation is a new type of symbol, or word associated with a particular product, or a family of products. Examples of popular trademarks are Diet Coke, and Mr. Coffee. A trade secret would generally be described as any information that, by being kept a secret, gives its owner a competitive business advantage. The formula for Kentucky Fried Chicken is one of the best known examples. Copyright law is used to protect the expressive works of authors, computer programmers, movie producers and other artistic creators.

📖 *For more information about trademarks, trade secrets and copyrights, consult the following resources:* Trademark: Legal Care For Your Business & Product Name, *by Kate McGrath and Stephen Elias (Nolo),* Patent, Copyright & Trademark, *by Stephen Elias (Nolo), and* The Copyright Handbook, *by Stephen Fishman (Nolo).*

1. Categories of Patents

There are three main types of patents: utility patents, design patents and plant patents. In this book, we will focus on utility patents because they are more common. Not surprisingly, a utility patent covers the functional aspects of an invention. As an example, assume that the hammer hasn't been invented yet. Ivan Inventor conceives of the hammer as an invention after he accidentally smashes his thumb with a rock he was using to pound a square peg into a round hole. If Ivan applies for a patent and his patent application describes his hammer invention in general enough terms, the patent would cover all variations of the hammer as a utilitarian device. It would cover common household hammers, sledge hammers, rubber hammers and the like. Perhaps even hydraulic hammers could be covered.

A design patent only covers the appearance of an invention. In our example, Ivan might apply for a design patent for a hammer with a horsehead etched into the shaft of the hammer. Removal of the horsehead would not affect the utility or functioning of the hammer. Design patents are easy to work around. A competitor could design a hammer with a slightly different horsehead, (longer mane or bigger eyes) and the new hammer design most likely would not infringe on the original design patent.

Plant patents are for new types of plants. Because plant patents are uncommon we don't cover them in this book.

2. Patent Eligibility Requirements

In order to get a utility patent (as opposed to a design patent), your patent application has to satisfy four legal criterion. (Novelty, unobviousness and other patent requirements are discussed in greater detail in Chapter 11.)

1. Your invention has to fit into an established Statutory Class.
2. Your invention must have some Utility. In other words, it has to be useful.
3. Your invention must have some Novelty. It must have some physical difference from any similar inventions in the past.
4. Your invention must be Unobvious to someone who is skilled in the appropriate field.

In order to fit within an established Statutory Class (the first legal criterion), your invention must be either a Process, a Machine, an Article of Manufacture, a Composition of Matter or a New Use invention.

- A Process is just the performance of a series of operations on something.

- A Machine is a device consisting of a series of fixed or moving parts that direct mechanical energy towards a specific task.

- An Article of Manufacture can be made by hand or machine. As opposed to machines, Articles of Manufacture are inventions that are relatively simple, with few or no moving parts.

- A Composition of Matter is a unique arrangement of items. Chemical compositions such as glue and plastics are good examples of compositions of matter.

- A New Use process is simply a new way of using an invention that fits in one of the first four statutory classes.

The second criterion your patent application has to satisfy is that it must be useful. Fortunately, any new use will satisfy this requirement. In general if your invention is operable (if it functions), it will satisfy this requirement.

The next requirement is Novelty. To get a patent, your invention must be somehow different from all previous inventions documented in the prior art. Generally, there are three types of difference categories.

1. Physical differences between your invention and previous inventions.
2. New combinations made by using previous aspects of two or more different inventions.
3. A new use of a previous invention.

As mentioned, your invention will also have to be deemed unobvious. This is the toughest of the patent requirements. Essentially, what it means is that your new concept must be a significant step forward in the field of the invention. In other words, if a skilled worker who is thoroughly familiar with developments in the area of your invention would consider the idea obvious, you would fail this test.

3. The Patent Document

In one sense a patent is an abstract notion. The PTO issues a patent. The patent gives you certain affirmative rights. The patent expires in 20 years. You can sell or license your patent. In all these uses, the term patent is an abstraction. In reality, the terms of a patent are spelled out in a document called a patent deed that is produced by the PTO. More commonly, the patent document is simply referred to as a patent or patent reference. The patent database consists of hardcopy, microfiche or electronic copies of patent documents.

Every utility patent document, which we'll simply refer to as a patent from this point on, has several identifiable fields or sections. Understanding the different parts of the patent will be especially important when we cover computer searching. This is because we will conduct our search in

TABLE OF PATENT SECTIONS

Patent Section	Description
Title	Patent title.
Inventor information	Inventor's name and address.
Patent number	The number assigned to the issued patent.
Patent filing date	The date that the patent application was filed with the PTO.
Patent issue date	The date that the patent was issued by the PTO.
Classification	Class and subclass information. These are the categories that the PTO uses to classify or sort the various types of inventions.
Referenced patents	The patent numbers of previous patents referred to in the patent application, along with their classes and subclasses.
Abstract	Usually one concise paragraph that summarizes the invention in plain English. Appears on the front page of the issued patent. This is the most frequently referenced section of the patent.
Drawings	Drawings of the invention from different perspectives.
Background of the invention	Discussion of any previous inventions that were related to this invention. This is known as "prior art".
Summary of the invention	A discussion of the invention that captures its essential functions and features.
Brief description of drawings	A one-sentence description of each patent drawing figure.
Detailed description of the preferred version of the invention	An in-depth discussion of the various aspects of the invention. Painstaking references to the patent drawings are made.
Claims	This section defines the legal scope of the patent (like a deed describes the boundaries of real estate).

certain sub-sections of the patent, and it helps to know what sort of information to expect to find there.

Above is a table showing the typical sections that appear in a patent, along with a brief description of what is in each one. Our table introduces us to several terms commonly used in the patent world. "Class" and "subclass" refer to the complex system used by the PTO to categorize each and every patent that it issues. Conceptually, the system is similar to an alphabetical library index file. For example, to search a library for a book about baseball, one would first go to the subject card index. In the file drawer for subjects beginning with the letter S, you would most likely find a Sports section. Under the sports section, you would go to the subsection for Baseball. There you would find the titles of several books related to baseball. The PTO currently has over 100,000 classes and subclasses.

An "abstract" is simply a summary of the most important features of the invention covered by the patent. The abstract appears on the front page of the issued patent. Patent searchers consult the abstract to get a quick overview of the invention. This in turn helps them decide whether it is worthwhile to review the entire patent. The abstract is the searcher's way to separate the wheat from the chaff. A typical abstract is shown below. This is from patent # 5,712,618, an automatic turn signaling device for vehicles.

no. 1,466,559 - Exercising Device

ABSTRACT

An automatic signaling device for a vehicle which automatically initiates a method and apparatus for an automatic signaling device warning signal to pedestrians and to other vehicles in connection with lane changes and upon turns. The present invention is activated and deactivated automatically providing significant safety advantages for all of those using the roads and highways.

15 Claims, 2 Drawing Figures

The "background of the invention" is a discussion of previous inventions that are related in some way to the current invention. These inventions are known as the prior art of the current invention. These previous inventions may embody some of the same or similar elements as the current invention. For example, sprinkler systems and fireproof blankets are two vastly different products. However, they are both related by the fact that they are fire suppressant devices. So, if you invented a modern-day fire suppression device (for instance one using nanotechnology —tiny microscopic machines—to deprive the fire of oxygen), both sprinkler systems and fireproof blankets would be considered prior art related to your invention.

The first two paragraphs from the background section of patent number 5,712,618 are shown on the following page. The first paragraph is a general summary of the background of the invention. The next paragraph begins the discussion of the advantages of the current invention over previously patented inventions.

BACKGROUND OF THE INVENTION

The invention disclosed herein relates to preferred methods and apparatuses for an automatic signaling device which automatically activates a warning signal. The following patents form a background for the instant invention. None of the cited publications is believed to detract from the patentability of the claimed invention.

U.S. Pat. No. 3,771,096 issued to Walter on Nov. 6, 1973, discloses a lane changing signaling device for vehicles employing a rotary electrical connector joined to the steering wheel. The principal disadvantage of the device is that it fails to measure the angle of rotation of the steering wheel.

Prior art is not limited to inventions patented in the U.S. Patents issued in other countries are considered valid prior art, and, if you apply for a patent, will be compared against your invention. Also, any other published information, from any corner of the globe, can prevent a patent from being granted. Even unpublished works, such as a Masters thesis, can be considered valid prior art. In Chapter 11 we explain how to evaluate your invention in light of the relevant prior art.

The "detailed description of the preferred version of the invention" (*embodiment* in patent terms) is a detailed description of an actual, "nuts and bolts" version of the current invention. It is essentially the inventor's best-guess (preferred embodiment) description of the product, at the time the patent application is written. By reading the detailed description, a person who is familiar with similar products should be able to build and operate

the current invention. It is important to note that the legal scope of the patent is not defined (the language of patents calls it "limited") by the details of the description of the preferred embodiment. Rather, the scope of the patent is determined by the "claims" (see below).

The first paragraph of the detailed description of the preferred embodiment for patent number 5,462,805; a fire safety glass panel, is shown below. Reading through the description we see that specific numbered elements of figure number 1 (from patent 5,462,805) are referenced. This figure is shown as figure 1 below. Here we have a glass plate (element 10), another glass plate (element 11), an intermediate resin layer (element 12), and first and second adhesive layers (elements 13 and 14). By following

DESCRIPTION OF THE PREFERRED EMBODIMENT

Referring to **FIG. 1**, a fire-protection and safety glass panel according to a preferred embodiment of this invention comprises a first glass plate **10**, a second glass plate **11** opposite to the first glass plate, and an intermediate resin layer between the first and second glass plates **10** and **11**. At least one of the first and the second glass plates **10** and **11** is a heat-resistant glass plate. The intermediate resin layer comprises a polyethylene terephthalate film (namely, a PET film) **12** and first and second adhesive agent layers **13** and **14** and has a thickness which is not greater than 200 um. The first adhesive agent layer **13** adheres the PET film **12** to the first glass plate **10**. The second adhesive agent layer **14** adheres the

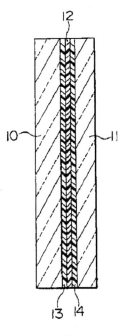

Figure 1

susceptible to being ruled invalid if the patent holder ever finds it necessary to bring an infringement case.

The first claim from the fire safety glass patent (5,462,805) is shown below. While calling out the same elements of the invention as described in the preferred embodiment, the specific element references have been omitted. This is because the claim is meant to be general enough to include different designs based upon the same invention concept.

Also, note that here the glass plates are referred to as "low-expansion crystallized glass." This is broad enough to include many types of glass that do not readily expand when exposed to heat. If a specific type of low-expansion glass were claimed,

along with the detailed description, and matching the numbered elements of the description with the labeled elements of the drawing, a person familiar with fire safety glass would be able to construct this invention.

The "claims" of the patent are a series of tersely worded statements that precisely describe and define the underlying invention. As we suggest in the chart, patent claims operate in much the same way as do real estate deeds—they precisely delimit the scope of the patent in the same way as the real estate deed describes the precise location of the property.

From the patent applicant's viewpoint, the claims should be as broad as possible, thus covering many possible versions of the same basic invention. Broad claims make it difficult for someone to defeat the patent by making a minor change to the invention. On the flip side, if patent claims are too broad, there is always the possibility of someone finding a previous invention (prior art reference) that falls within the patent's scope. This could make the patent

CLAIMS

What is claimed is:
1. A fire-protection and safety glass panel comprising a first glass plate, a second glass plate opposite to said first glass plate, and an intermediate resin layer between said first and said second glass plates, at least one of said first and said second glass plates being a low-expansion crystallized glass plate of a low-expansion crystallized glass, wherein said intermediate resin layer comprises a polyethylene terephthalate film, a first adhesive agent layer for adhering said polyethylene terephthalate film to said first glass plate, and a second adhesive agent layer for adhering said polyethylene terephthalate film to said second glass plate, said intermediate resin layer having a thickness which is not greater than 200 um.

then the patent could be "worked around" by simply claiming a different type of low-expansion glass.

B. Understanding Patent Databases

In order to get the most benefit from a word-based computer search, it is useful to first understand how searchable databases are put together. Creating a computer database is basically a two step process. First, the information has to be entered into the computer. Then, the information has to be processed by a special kind of computer program so that the information can be easily retrieved in a meaningful form.

There are generally two ways to get information into a computer (not including voice recognition hardware and software, which is still not commonly used). Someone can physically type the data in at the keyboard, or a person can make use of a device called a scanner. A scanner is similar to the everyday copy machine. A page is placed on a surface and a machine records an image of what's on the page. However, when a scanner is connected to a computer, it is possible to capture an image of a document and store that image on the hard disk of the computer.

When a document is scanned into a computer, it may take one of two forms:

- an image, or
- text that has been extracted from the scanned document by software known as OCR (Optical Character Recognition).

For the purpose of searching by computer, there is a big difference between an image of a document that hasn't been subjected to OCR software and the text that an OCR scan produces. If, for example, a patent is scanned into a computerized database without OCR treatment, the contents of the image can't be searched; after all, it's just a picture. The computer has no way of knowing what the picture contains. You can pull up the patent on your computer screen the same as any other graphical image, but you can't search for the patent according to the words contained in it. However, if the text in the patent document is read by an OCR program before it makes its way into the database, the database will be able to index the text and pull up the patent document according to the words contained in a keyword search.

The database that gets created as a result of OCR processing (or of text that is manually entered or already in computer-readable form) is essentially a huge lookup table. The program that builds this table searches through all the entered text and extracts all the meaningful words. Then, these words, along with a link to the original document they were found in, are placed into the lookup table.

When you use a computer program to perform a word-based search, the program matches the search words you type in with words stored in its lookup table. The search words that you enter are called "keywords" and the search process is called a keyword search. If the computer finds a match, the program will report back to you the document in which the word was found and, in some cases, the location of the word within the document.

The lookup table ("database" in computer talk) is similar to indexes found in the back of many books. In book indexes, words are listed alphabetically, along with a comma-separated list of each page in the book where the word was used.

C. Understanding Keyword Searching

When you use a computer program to search for patents, you often must search for them by entering words into a "query" box and asking the search program to match your words with words stored in its database.

As you might expect, performing keyword searches is a skill with a learning curve. Sure, anyone can put one or two words into a box and pull up all the patents with those words. No skill there. But the overall number of patents you pull up is likely to be huge and the number of the patents that are relevant to your search is likely to be low. To pull up a manageable number of patents and to assure that most of them will have some relevance to your own invention, you will need to know at least some of the basic techniques for choosing your search terms and combining them into meaningful search queries.

1. The Role of Wildcards in Keyword Searching

One powerful tool that is often used during keyword searching is called the wildcard. A wildcard is a special character inserted into your keyword. This character tells the computer search program to do something special with the keyword within which it's used. The two most often used wildcard symbols are the dollar sign '$', and the question mark '?'.

The dollar sign wildcard is used at the end of a word root to take the place of any number of additional letters that may come after that root. For example, assume you

have invented a new type of dance shoe. The shoe can be used for ballroom, ballet and tap dancing. In addition to the keywords "ballroom," "ballet" and "tap," you will certainly want to search for the word "dance." But there are several variations of the word "dance," such as, "dancing," "dancer," "danced," and even "danceable." By using "danc$" as your keyword, the dollar sign replaces any other possible characters that would follow the four letters, "danc."

Figure 2, below, contains the search results from searching the titles of U.S. patents issued in the years 1997-1998 for the word "dance." The patent titles that have the word "dance" in them are listed and numbered. As you can see, there are four patents that have the word "dance" in the title. The first title relates to a dance practice slipper, the second title concerns the sole of a dance shoe, the third title relates to a type of dance and the fourth title relates to a portable dance floor.

| Refine Search |

| ISD/1/1/1997->12/31/1998 and ttl/dance |

PAT. NO.	Title
1 D388,592	**T** Dance practice slipper
2 5,682,685	**T** Dance shoe sole
3 PP9,938	**T** Peach tree "Snow Dance"
4 5,634,309	**T** Portable dance floor

Figure 2 (Source: USPTO Website)

Figure 3, below, contains the search results from searching the titles of U.S. patents issued in the years 1997-1998 for the word "danc$." As you can see, we now have nine patents listed. The first patent listed (patent number 5,827,107) contains the word "dancing" as opposed to "dance."

Refine Search	ISD/1/1/1997->12/31/1998 and ttl/danc$

PAT. NO.   Title

1 5,827,107 **T** Spinning dancing top

2 D388,592 **T** Dance practice slipper

3 5,682,685 **T** Dance shoe sole

4 5,669,117 **T** Buckle for line dancing

5 D382,902 **T** Unit for teaching dancing

6 5,659,229 **T** Controlling web tension by actively controlling velocity of dancer roll

7 PP9,938 **T** Peach tree "Snow Dance"

8 5,634,309 **T** Portable dance floor

9 5,602,747 **T** Controlling web tension by actively controlling velocity of dancer roll

Figure 3 (Source: USPTO Website)

The first four letters (danc) are the same as in the word "dance," but the wildcard ($) was used for the letters "ing." The next two titles are the same ones that we obtained before. However, title numbers 4 and 5 also contain the word "dancing" as opposed to "dance." Similarly, title numbers 6 and 9, contain the word "dancer," as opposed to "dance." Here, the wildcard ($) was used for the letters "er."

The question mark (?) wildcard can be used to replace any single character in a word. Continuing with our dancing example, the words "foot" or "feet" could be searched by using "f??t" as our keyword. Obviously, you would not want to use the keyword "f$", as this would return every word that started with the letter "f." By using "f??t," every four-letter word that starts with "f" and ends with "t" would be searched for by the computer. For example, along with the words "feet" and "foot", the words "flat" and "fast" would also be reported to you in the search results.

In Figure 4 below, we show the search results obtained from searching the titles of U.S. patents issued on 12/9/1997 for the word "f??t." The first two patents listed (Pat. Nos. 5696609 and 5696529), contain the word "flat" in the title. The next two patents listed (Pat. Nos. 5696435 and 5695530) contain the word "fast" in the title. The fifth and sixth patents listed (Pat. Nos. 5695527 and 5695526), contain the word 'foot' in the title. The seventh, eighth, ninth and tenth patents listed (Pat. Nos. 5695,360, 5695,359, 5,694,834 and 5695792), contain the word "flat" in the title. Finally, the eleventh patent listed (Design Pat. No. D387,428), contains the word "foot" in the title.

| Refine Search | ISD/12/9/1997->12/9/1997 and ttl/f??t |

PAT. NO.   Title
1 5,696,609 **T** Illumination system for a flat-bed scanning system
2 5,696,529 **T** Flat panel monitor combining direct view with overhead projection capability
3 5,696,435 **T** Fast battery charger for a device having a varying electrical load during recharging
4 5,695,530 **T** Method for making high charging efficiency and fast oxygen recombination rechargeable hydride batteries
5 5,695,527 **T** Coil prosthetic foot
6 5,695,526 **T** One-piece mechanically differentiated prosthetic foot and associated ankle joint with syme modification
7 5,695,360 **T** Zero insertion force electrical connector for flat cable
8 5,695,359 **T** Zero insertion force electrical connector for flat cable
9 5,694,834 **T** Device for forming in series flat objects of adjustable shape and thickness by deposition of a relatively fluid substance on a support
10 5,694,792 **T** Needle selection device of flat knitting machine
11 D387,428 **T** Transparent x-ray film cassette holder for x-ray of a foot and ankle

Figure 4 (Source: USPTO Website)

2. The Role of Boolean Logic in Keyword Patent Searching

A search technique known as Boolean logic can be used to combine individual keywords into powerful searches. Boolean logic uses a total of four words (called "logical operators") to define the search: AND, OR, XOR, and ANDNOT. The AND operator is by far the most useful. A graphical representation known as a Venn diagram will help you to understand how these operators work.

In Figure 5 below, we have a circle that has been shaded. The area inside the circle represents all of the patents that contain the keyword represented by the letter A. The area outside the circle represents all the other patents that do not contain the keyword represented by A. In other words, if we were to search a database of patents for all the occurrences of the keyword A, our search results would be contained in the shaded circle above.

In Figure 6, below, we have two keywords represented by the circles A and B. Searching for individual occurrences of the keywords A or B would result in a lot of search results. It would take a long time to review these results and most of them would be irrelevant.

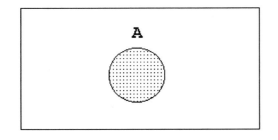

Figure 5

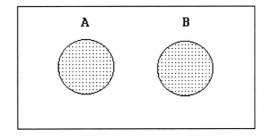

Figure 6

For example, let's suppose we have an invention idea for a new type of telephone cable. A search for the keyword telephone would return numerous references to different types of telephones. Similarly, a keyword search for the word cable would return patents related to cable television, bridge support cables, cable cars, and so on. What we need is a way to search for both the keywords telephone and cable within the same patent. This is where Boolean operators come into the picture.

3. The AND Boolean Operator

In Figure 7 below, we have used the Boolean operator AND to combine the keywords A and B. The shaded area where the circles overlap represents the search results that contain both keywords A and B. As you can see, the AND operator is a great way to narrow the scope of the search.

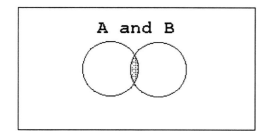

Figure 7

When a match is found between a keyword (or a combination of keywords) and a patent, the result is called a "Hit." When patent searches are conducted, the number of hits, or occurrences, of a keyword match is usually reported to the user. By using the AND operator, the user reduces the quantity of hits that need to be reviewed.

For example, let's suppose that you have invented a new type of steam engine. A steam engine is a machine for converting the

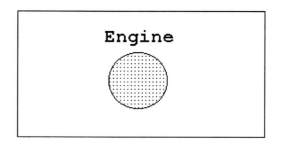

Figure 8

heat energy in steam into mechanical energy by means of a piston moving in a cylinder.

The search results using the keyword Engine are shown in Figure 8 above. The shaded circle represents all of the patents that contain the word Engine. This could be quite an extensive list. For example, all the various types of internal combustion engines would be included in this list. A steam-powered vehicle is an external combustion device; the steam is usually obtained from an external boiler. However, if we only searched for the word Engine, we would have to review search results that contained references to gasoline-powered engines for cars, trucks, trains and all other engine-powered devices.

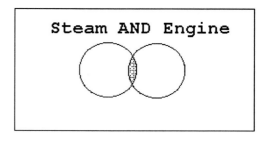

Figure 9

Figure 9 above, shows the search result obtained when using the Boolean AND operator to combine the keywords Steam and Engine. The resulting number of hits is represented by the small shaded area in the diagram, where the two circles overlap. We can see at once why AND is the most often

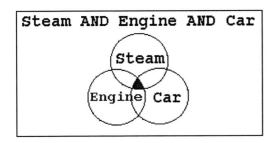

Figure 10

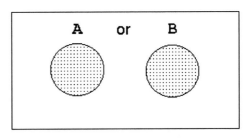

Figure 11

used Boolean operator. It allows the searcher to narrow the scope of the search and obtain more meaningful results.

In Figure 10 above, we see the results of a search using the keywords Steam, Engine and Car. In this case the overlapping area is even more precisely defined. It would be necessary for a patent to contain all three keywords before being reported as a match.

Throughout this book, we will identify critical concepts used for effective patent searching. We have labeled these concepts; *Searcher's Secrets.* The use of the AND operator brings us to Searcher's Secret #1.

Searcher's Secret Number 1

The more keywords used with the AND operator, the smaller the number of matches obtained and the more meaningful each match is to the searcher.

4. The OR Boolean Operator

In Figure 11 above, we have used the Boolean operator OR to combine the keywords represented by the letters A and B. The shaded area within the circle labeled A represents

all of the patents that contain the keyword represented by the letter A. Similarly, the shaded area within the circle labeled B represents all of the patents that contain the keyword represented by the letter B. When you use the Boolean OR operator, you can't tell from your search results whether a particular reference contains just one of your key words or both. Using our Venn diagrams to represent one possible set of search results, we see that in Figure 11, above, there were no hits that contained both of the keywords represented by the letters A and B. If the search results did have some patents that contained both keywords, the resulting Venn diagram would look like Figure 12 below.

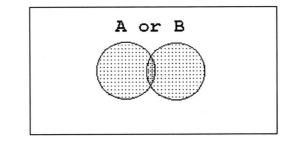

Figure 12

In Figure 12 above, we have the two circles A and B, with a small overlapping area. The lightly shaded areas of A and B, that do not overlap represent patents that contain only one of our keywords. The

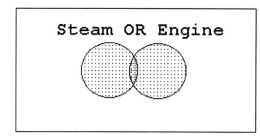

Figure 13

heavily shaded, overlapping area represents patents that contain both keywords.

Returning to our steam engine example, Figure 13 above, represents the number of hits returned when we use "Steam OR Engine" to search the patent database. What this means is that any patent that contained the word Steam or the word Engine, would be returned as a match. The lightly shaded areas of the circles represent patents that contain the keyword Steam or the keyword Engine, but not both. The heavily shaded area where the two circles overlap, represent patents that contain both keywords. Remember, however, that you couldn't tell this from your research results; the Venn diagrams are only being used to explain what happens in fact. Use of the OR operator brings us to our next Searcher's Secret.

Searcher's Secret Number 2

The OR operator is used to widen the scope of the search results.

5. The XOR Boolean Operator

The exclusive or operator is symbolized by the XOR letters. This operator is very

similar to the OR operator, but with one important difference. The overlapping area is not included in the search results. So, if we used "Steam XOR Engine" to search our database, we would obtain a list of patents that contained the word Steam, or the word Engine, but not both.

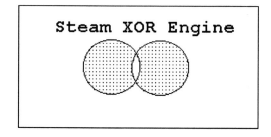

Figure 14

This brings us to our third Searcher's Secret.

Searcher's Secret Number 3

One, and only one, of the keywords combined with the XOR operator will appear in each of the patents in the search results.

6. The ANDNOT Boolean Operator

The final Boolean operator we will be reviewing is the ANDNOT operator. The ANDNOT operator is actually a combination of the AND and NOT operators. The NOT operator, by itself, simply finds all the patents that do not contain the keyword used. The reason the NOT operator is combined with the AND operator can be seen in Figure 15, below. If

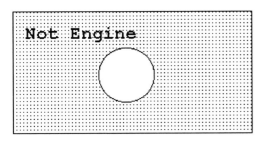

Figure 15

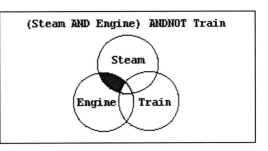

Figure 16

you were to use the NOT operator, by itself, with just the keyword Engine, your search results would include all the patents that do not contain the word Engine—a very large search result indeed.

An example of the correct use of the ANDNOT operator is shown below. If you wanted to search for steam engines used in all devices except trains, you could compose a query like:

(steam AND engine) ANDNOT train

This would return patents concerning steam engines in cars, boats, etc. However, any patent containing the word Train would be excluded. This is true, even if the words Steam and Engine were contained within the train-related patent. Figure 16 shows the search result obtained when using the above query. The resulting number of hits is again represented by the small shaded area in the diagram where the circles representing the keywords Steam and Engine overlap. However, a small section of that overlapping area has been excluded. This excluded area represents the patents that contain the keyword Train.

Use of the ANDNOT operator brings us to our next Searcher's Secret.

Searcher's Secret Number 4

The ANDNOT operator is used to exclude specific keywords from the search results.

7. Use of Parentheses

Also, notice that we have made use of left and right parenthesis—( )—around the words Steam and Engine. This means that the words within the parenthesis are evaluated first, then the ANDNOT condition is applied.

You can also combine wildcards with Boolean operators. To return to our dance shoe example, we can combine the keyword "danc$", with the keyword "Shoe", and exclude the keyword "Tap" with the following query.

(Danc$ AND shoe) ANDNOT tap

The resulting patents would have the words "shoe" and one or more words like "dancing", "dancer" or "dance," but not the word "tap."

Summary

What is a patent, and what does it do for me?

- A patent is a right of exclusion, granted by the government, for a term of years. It is a document as well as an abstract right.
- A utility patent covers the functional aspects of the invention. A design patent only covers the appearance of an invention.

How keyword searches work

- A computer program matches the words you type in (keywords), with words stored in its database.

How Wildcards work

- The dollar sign ($) wildcard can take the place of any number of letters following it's location in the word.
- The question mark (?) wildcard can be used to replace any single character in a word.

Boolean Logic

- Use Boolean logic to combine keywords into powerful searches.
- The more keywords used with the AND operator, the smaller the number of matches obtained and the more meaningful each match is to the searcher.
- The OR operator is used to widen the scope of the search results.
- The ANDNOT operator is used to exclude keywords from the search results.
- Left and right parenthesis—( )—are used in complex Boolean logic to determine which terms are evaluated first.
- You can also combine wildcards with Boolean operators.

Chapter

2

Tools and Resources

Here we introduce you to the tools you'll need to use this book and the resources that will help you carry out your preliminary patent search.

→ *You can skip ahead to Section F of this chapter if you already have a computer and Internet browser and a basic understanding of how the Internet works.*

A. What is the Internet?

The Internet is commonly described as a network of computers joined together by telephone lines, cables and satellite links. Not so. The Internet is actually a network of computer networks. The Internet is an international "web" of interconnected government, business, university, and scientific computer networks. Every day, hundreds of millions of people, from all over the world, tie into this 'web' of networks. Using the Internet gives us access to thousands of databases all over the world. Almost every subject is covered to some extent.

Where did the Internet come From?

The Internet had its beginning as one computer network called the ARPANET (Advanced Research Projects Agency NETwork). The ARPANET was created by the U.S. government in 1969. The ARPANET allowed computer resources to be shared by multiple users. In the 1960's and 70's, computer hardware was much more expensive than it is today. Sharing resources was an effective method of cost reduction.

The ARPANET split into two networks in the early 1980's, the ARPANET and Milnet (a non-classified, military network). Connections between the two networks were established and references to this pair of connected networks referred to them as, the 'Internet'. In the years since, other computer networks were created. Then, additional connections were made between these new networks and the Internet. With the creation of user friendly software in the mid-1990s, the Internet began growing rapidly.

B. How Does the Internet Work?

Without getting too technical, information on the Internet is broken down into chunks of data called packets. A computer image (such as a patent drawing), or a document (such as a patent abstract), will be divided into several data packets. These packets of information are sent from the source computer, over the various interconnected networks, to the destination computer. In addition to the image, or document data, each data packet contains some header information. This header information contains the address of the sending and receiving computer, and the order (or sequence) in which the packets must be assembled to produce the finished document.

An analogy would be moving a building from New Mexico to Florida. You could take the building apart, label all the pieces, and ship everything out. You may use more than one common carrier. For the medium weight sections, you could use trucks. For the heavier sections, you may choose railroad. Some of the building parts would arrive at their destination out of order. The roof may arrive before the walls; the second floor may arrive before the first, and so on. But, none of this makes any difference. With careful labeling of all the components, you will know which section goes first, which section goes second, and so on. In a similar fashion, the receiving computer on the Internet knows how to read the header information of each arriving data packet. These packets are then assembled into a finished document for your viewing pleasure.

C. Computer Hardware Requirements for Using the Internet

Almost every modern off-the-shelf computer comes equipped with sufficient memory and graphics display capability to effectively use the Internet. What you need in addition to a computer is a Modem. The word modem is actually a contraction of the words **MO**dulator and **DEM**odulator. A modem can transmit digital data to another computer over telephone lines. The modem does this by converting digital computer data into analog data (the modulate function), and then sending it out. A modem can also receive analog data from another computer and convert it back into digital data (the demodulate function).

Broadband Internet access uses (Digital Subscriber Lines) DSL, (Integrated Services Digital Networks) ISDN or existing cable television networks. Additional computer equipment (special cable ready modems and network cards) is required. However, the increase in speed can be up to 100 times greater than with a residential telephone line.

Once you have your computer system squared away, you will need to find an Internet Service Provider (ISP). An Internet service provider is a company that provides you with access to the Internet. There are several well known ISP's like; America OnLine (AOL), CompuServe and Netcom. Adelphia is an example of a cable company offering Broadband Internet access. There are also many smaller, local companies that can provide Internet access. Check your local Yellow Pages, newspapers, magazines and television ads for listings of these companies.

For telephone access, make sure your ISP have a local telephone number available. This is the telephone number that your modem will dial to access the Internet. When you have a local dialup number, every time you access the Internet, you are simply making a local phone call. It makes no difference if you are accessing information from an Internet site in Australia, England, or Bora Bora. It's still a local telephone call. If your ISP does not have a local dialup number, you will have to pay an extra charge every time your access the Internet.

The current average cost for unlimited Internet dialup access is around $20/month. For Broadband this figure usually jumps to around $40/month. For this fee, you should be able to use the Internet for as long as you want, at any time of the day, seven days a week.

D. Computer Software Requirements

In addition to your computer system setup and your local ISP connection, you will need some computer software to perform Internet patent searches. In this book, we will assume that you are using the Microsoft Windows operating system. Typically, when you purchase a new computer, Windows is already installed on the system.

1. Browser Programs

In order to view information on the Internet, you will also need computer software that provides an easy way of looking at information on the World Wide Web (WWW). This software is called a "browser." What is the WWW and how does it differ from the Internet? Well, the WWW is just one part of the Internet. The WWW consists of a world wide series of computers and computer networks that adhere to the same strict software protocols. These computers allow public access to information stored on their respective hard disks. By following the same software protocols, different computers from all over the world can transmit and receive data from each other. The World Wide Web uses the HyperText Transfer Protocol (http), which allows you to click your way from one site or document to another.

A browser handles all of these details for you, so you don't have to think about them. A browser program allows you to visit what is known as a website. A website is a specific location on the WWW. The browser program reads the information at the website, and displays it for you on your computer monitor. Each website on the WWW has a specific address, which defines its location of the WWW. We will discuss addressing in detail, when we visit some of the various websites that provide patent search resources.

There are other computers on the Internet that do not use the protocols necessary for the WWW. However, due to the lack of a browser type of program, access to these machines is not as easy. As a result, the vast majority of Internet users limit their activities to the WWW. All of the Internet resources that we will be using in this book are available on the WWW.

Currently, the most popular browser programs are Microsoft's Internet Explorer and the Netscape Navigator. In order to follow the examples in this book, you will need one of these programs installed on your computer. If your computer system was purchased with Windows installed, Internet Explorer should also be installed.

Since Microsoft's Internet Explorer is currently the most widely used browser program, we will use it in most of the examples given in this book. However, the presentation differs insignificantly from Netscape Navigator.

2. Word Processing Programs

Although not essential for patent searches, you should have a professional word processing program installed on your system. Later in this book, we will be using a word processor to assemble a summary of our patent search results. Although, small word processing programs, such as Notepad and Wordpad, usually ship with Windows, these programs lack the tools that a full-blown, word processing application has. We recommend installing Word for Windows or WordPerfect. Both of these programs have spell check capability and a thesaurus. A thesaurus comes in handy when you trying to think of words that describe your invention.

Another, very useful program is the Adobe Reader. As we shall see later in this book, the adobe format is widely used in the European Patent Office (EPO) website. The Adobe Reader can be freely downloaded from the following Internet address:

www.adobe.com

E. Windows Skills

There are only a couple of basic Windows skills that are essential for Internet-based patent searches. At a minimum, you need to be able to enter search words with the keyboard and you need to be able to use the mouse. For those of you that have never used a mouse before don't worry. There are only a couple of essential mouse skills that you need, namely, the "click" and the "double click." A click means simply pressing the left mouse button down once, and then releasing it. A double click means pressing the left mouse button down and releasing it twice, in rapid succession.

F. What's Available at the PTDL?

As an alternative to using the Internet, if you happen to live near Alexandria, Virginia, you can perform patent searches at the U.S. Patent and Trademark Office (PTO) itself. The patent search room is located at: Madison East, 1st Floor, 600 Dulany Street, Alexandria Virginia, 22314. The hours of business are: weekdays (except holidays) from 8:00 a.m. to 8:00 p.m. For information, call: (571) 272-3275.

For the rest of us there is the Patent and Trademark Depository Library (PTDL) System. A network of over 80 PTDL's are located in 49 states, the District of Columbia, and Puerto Rico. (See Appendix A for a list of PTDLs, showing locations and telephone numbers.) The PTDL system provides access to many of the same products and services offered at the PTO in Arlington Virginia. The scope of the various patent collections, the hours of operations and available services vary from location to location.

➔ *In Part 3 of this book we show you how to use the PTDL and its many useful resources.*

Summary

What is the Internet?
- The Internet is a worldwide web of interconnected government, business, university and scientific computer networks.
- Hundreds of Millions of individual users tie into this 'web' of networks everyday. Most users connect to the Internet via a personal computer, modem, telephone line or cable, and some software.
- Using the Internet gives us access to thousands of databases all over the world. Almost every subject is covered to some extent.

Computer Hardware Requirements for Using the Internet
- You will need to find an Internet Service Provider (ISP).
- You will need a Cable Modem for high speed access via cable or a telephone modem for dialup access.

Computer Software Requirements
- An Internet Browser. These are typically bundled into the operating system of your computer.
- A Word Processing program such as Word for Windows or Wordperfect.
- The Adobe reader program.

Windows Skills
- Keyboard entry and mouse skills are the essential skills needed for performing patent searches using the computer. The most important mouse skills are the "click" and the "double click." Understanding the various parts of a window (maximize / minimize button, title bar, etc.) would be a plus.

Part 2

Internet-Based Patent Searches

In this part of the book, we use the patent searching tools and techniques discussed in Part 1. This part consists of five chapters. The first two chapters—Chapters 3 and 4—explain how to perform preliminary patent searches at the PTO website. Chapter 5 covers the European Patent Office (EPO) website. Chapter 6 is new to the 4th edition and covers Google's patent search engine and the patent searching capabilities available at the Intellectual Property Office of Singapore. Finally, Chapter 7 explores some other important prior art search resources such as Internet search engines and government websites.

Chapter

3

Patent Searching at the PTO Website

A. Simple Keyword Searches at the PTO's Website

Now that you have a pretty good idea what a patent consists of, and you understand the mechanics of a keyword search, it's time to try some actual patent searches at the U.S. Patent and Trademark Office's patent search website (a different website from the general website maintained by the PTO at www.uspto.gov). The PTO's patent search website allows you to search the full text and drawings of all patents issued since 1976. The full page images of patents since 1790 are also available for viewing. Furthermore, you can search patent applications published since March 15th, 2001.

1. Connecting to the PTO's Website

In order to get to the PTO's patent searching website, you need to type the following address in the address window of your web browser:

www.uspto.gov/patft

After a slight delay (depending on Internet traffic and the speed of your Internet connection), you should see the homepage for the PTO's patent searching site, as shown in Figure 1, below.

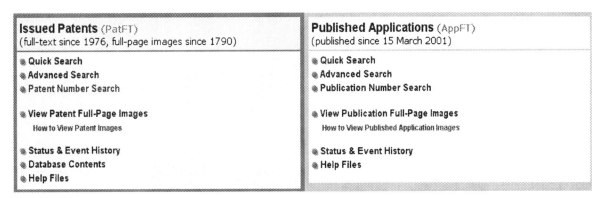

Figure 1 (Source: USPTO Website)

There are two databases available for searching at the PTO's Patent Search Website, the PatFT (Patent Full Text) database and the AppFT (Patent Applications Full Text). In this chapter we will be dealing with the PatFT database. The PatFT database is actually a combination of two separate databases; one, which lets you search the full-text of patents issued since 1976, and another, which lets you search the full-page images of patents issued from 1790 through 1975.

2. Understanding the PTO's Quick Search Page

To perform a Quick Search of the PatFT database, click on the "Quick Search" link illustrated in Figure 1. You will then be presented with the webpage shown in Figure 2, below.

As you can see from Figure 2, there are several fields that can be filled in. We will discuss them one at a time.

The first area that we want to address is the "Select years" pull-down menu. This is located in the lower left of Figure 2. To make a selection, click with your left mouse button on the down-arrow (v). The result is shown in Figure 3, below. There are two selections to choose from:

- 1976 to present [full-text]
- 1790 to present [entire database]

The current selection is set to "1976 to present [full-text]." Using this setting will allow you to search through every word contained in every patent issued since January 1st 1976.

The second selection, "1790 to present [entire database]," will allow you to search through the full-text of patents since 1976 and the images of patents from 1790 through 1975.

Note that for patent image data from 1790 through 1975 only three fields can be searched. These three fields are the Issue Date (ISD), Patent Number (PN) and the Current Classification (CCL). Issue date can be in the form of Month/Day/Year. Patent numbers must be seven characters in length, excluding commas, which are optional.

What this effectively means is that your keyword search for this range of years will only be applied to the Current Classification field.

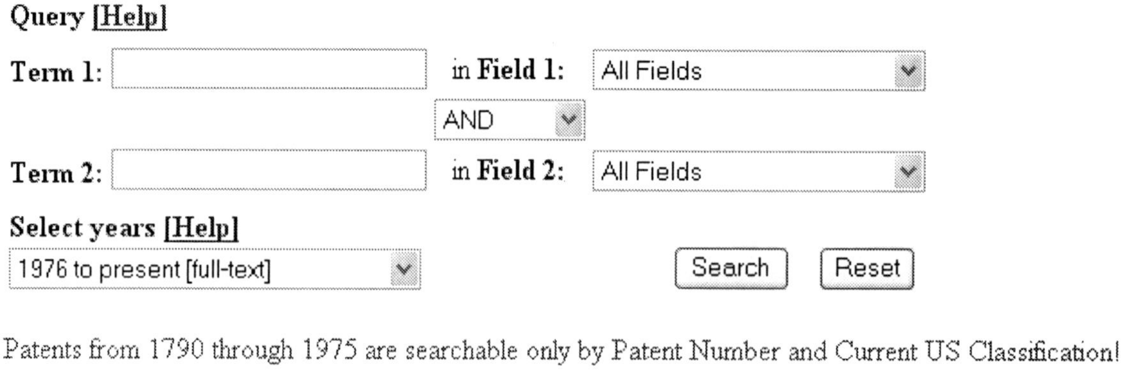

Query [Help]

Term 1:	[ ]	in **Field 1:**	All Fields ▾
		AND ▾	
Term 2:	[ ]	in **Field 2:**	All Fields ▾

Select years [Help]

| 1976 to present [full-text] ▾ | Search | Reset |

Patents from 1790 through 1975 are searchable only by Patent Number and Current US Classification!

Figure 2 (Source: USPTO Website)

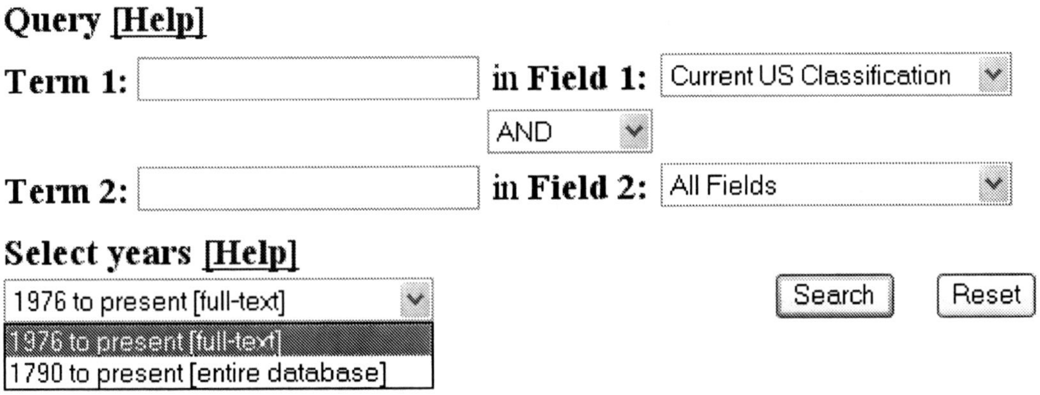

Query [Help]

Term 1: [_____] in **Field 1:** [Current US Classification ▾]

[AND ▾]

Term 2: [_____] in **Field 2:** [All Fields ▾]

Select years [Help]

[1976 to present [full-text] ▾]   [Search] [Reset]

| 1976 to present [full-text] |
| 1790 to present [entire database] |

Figure 3 (Source: USPTO Website)

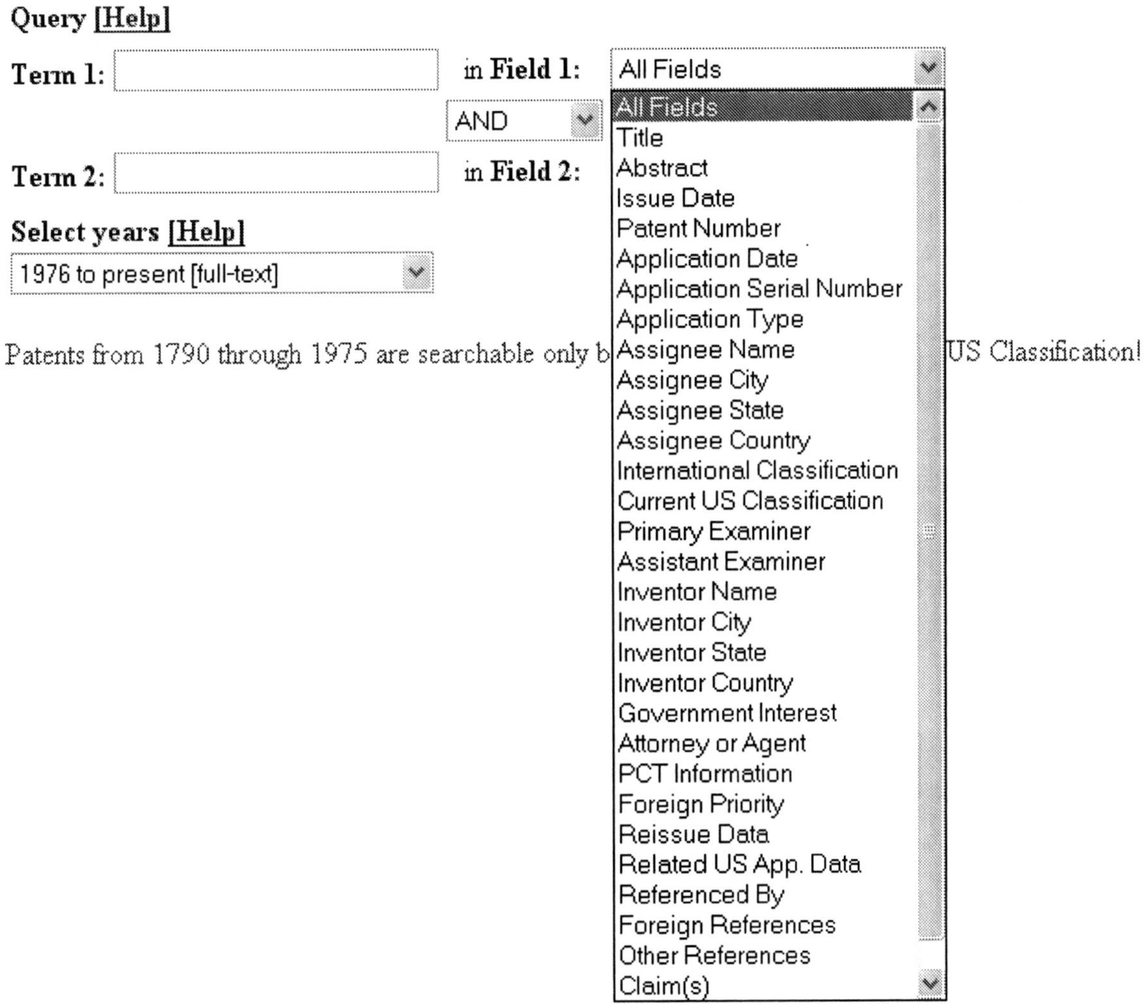

Query [Help]

Term 1: [_____] in **Field 1:** [All Fields ▾]

[AND ▾]

| All Fields |
| Title |
| Abstract |

Term 2: [_____] in **Field 2:**

| Issue Date |
| Patent Number |
| Application Date |
| Application Serial Number |
| Application Type |

Select years [Help]

[1976 to present [full-text] ▾]

| Assignee Name |
| Assignee City |
| Assignee State |
| Assignee Country |
| International Classification |
| Current US Classification |
| Primary Examiner |
| Assistant Examiner |
| Inventor Name |
| Inventor City |
| Inventor State |
| Inventor Country |
| Government Interest |
| Attorney or Agent |
| PCT Information |
| Foreign Priority |
| Reissue Data |
| Related US App. Data |
| Referenced By |
| Foreign References |
| Other References |
| Claim(s) |

Patents from 1790 through 1975 are searchable only b   US Classification!

Figure 4 (Source: USPTO Website)

To the right of Figure 3, above, are two Field selection pull-down menus. By positioning your mouse over the down arrow and clicking once, you can see all of the searchable fields of the patent database that are available. This action is shown in Figure 4, above.

With field selections you can limit the scope of your search to a particular section of the issued patent. For example, if you only wish to search the abstract of the patent, you can scroll down (move the mouse over) to that entry point, the item will be highlighted, and then click with the mouse to select it.

To search the entire text of all the issued patents, in the years 1976 to the present, select the entry 'All Fields' (as shown in Figure 4) and leave the Select year pull-down set to the default selection, "1976 to present [full-text]."

Limiting your search to certain sections of the issued patent has several advantages. Chief among them is to precisely define your search in order to find just the patents you are looking for and nothing extra.

To the left of the field pull-down menus of Figure 4, is the Operator selection pull-down. To see the available Boolean operators that can be used to combine your search keywords, click on this pull-down.

This action is shown in Figure 5, below. By selecting the down arrow, you will be able to chose among the three Boolean operators; (AND, OR, and ANDNOT) that we discussed in Chapter 1. For the purposes of this first search, let's select the AND operator, which is the default.

3. Doing the Search

To the left of the Operator selection pull-down in Figure 5, below, are the Search term entry boxes. Here is where you enter your search words (keywords). For example, let's suppose that your invention is related to a device that is involved in fire protection. You could type in "fire" for the first search term, select the logical operator AND, and enter "protection" for the second search term. The Field selections could be set to All Fields and the Select years pull-down set to 1976 to present. This is shown in Figure 6 below.

Now we are ready to begin our search. The search program will search for the terms "fire" and "protection" in all the fields of all the patents issued between the years 1976 to the present. To start the search, click on the

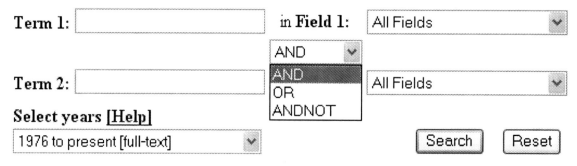

Figure 5 (Source: USPTO Website)

Query [Help]

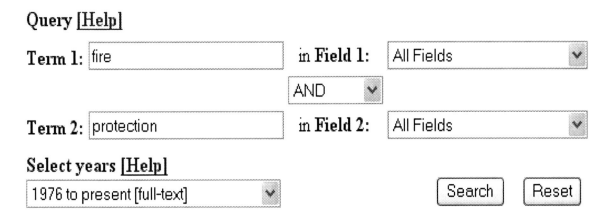

Term 1: fire   in Field 1: All Fields

                                                AND

Term 2: protection   in Field 2: All Fields

Select years [Help]

1976 to present [full-text]   Search   Reset

Figure 6 (Source: USPTO Website)

button labeled Search, located at the lower right of the screen (as shown in Figure 6). Adjacent to the Search button is the Reset button. Clicking on this button will clear all of the entries and selections that you have made. This comes in handy when starting a new search.

The time it takes the PTO's search engine to complete its task will depend on several factors: The number of persons using the system at a given time, the Internet traffic returning the information to your site, and in particular, if you specified all fields for your search. In any case, the time delay should seldom be longer than 30 seconds.

4. Understanding the Search Results

The results of our search are shown in Figure 7 below. Under the heading Results of Search in 1976 to present db for: fire AND protection, the system has reported 21,593 "hits" or patents in which our two

search terms were found. Remember, that with the use of the AND Boolean operator, both search terms "fire" and "protection" must be present for the system to report a match.

Why so many hits? The reason is that because of the All Fields selection in our Field setting, the search terms "fire" and "protection" can occur *anywhere* in the issued patent to generate a hit.

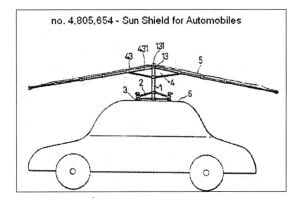

no. 4,805,654 - Sun Shield for Automobiles

Results of Search in US Patent Collection db for:
fire AND protection: 21593 patents.
*Hits **1** through **50** out of **21593***

[Next 50 Hits]

[Jump To] [   ]

[Refine Search] | fire AND protection |

PAT. NO.		Title
1	7,197,514 T	Managing information relating to firestopping systems
2	7,197,465 T	Apparatus, systems and methods for printing dimensionally accurate symbologies on laser printers configured with remote client computer devices
3	7,197,234 T	System and method for processing subpicture data
4	7,197,167 T	Registration apparatus and method, as for voting
5	7,196,885 T	Appliance leakage current interrupter and nightlight combination
6	7,196,661 T	Security system including a method and system for acquiring GPS satellite position
7	7,196,657 T	Radar system using RF noise
8	7,196,655 T	System and method for highly directional electronic identification and communication and combat identification system employing the same
9	7,196,631 T	Method of utilizing existing fire alarm systems and existing smoke detectors to detect aerolized radioactive material
10	7,196,295 T	Two-wire layered heater system
11	7,196,271 T	Twisted pair cable with cable separator
12	7,196,245 T	Polynucleotides and polypeptides that confer increased biomass and tolerance to cold, water deprivation and low nitrogen to plants

Figure 7 (Source: USPTO Website)

Figure 7 illustrates a major source of frustration for novice patent searchers. How do you search through such a large number of patents? But, this frustration can quickly be eliminated with a more focused search. In Figure 8 we have changed the All Fields settings to Title. The results of our new search are shown in Figure 9. Here we see that by limiting our keyword search to the title field only, the number of hits has been reduced from 21,593 to 227.

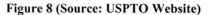

Query [Help]

Term 1: | fire | in Field 1: | Title ▼ |

| AND ▼ |

Term 2: | protection | in Field 2: | Title ▼ |

Select years [Help]

| 1976 to present [full-text] ▼ | [Search] [Reset]

Figure 8 (Source: USPTO Website)

Results of Search in US Patent Collection db for:
TTL/fire AND TTL/protection: 227 patents.
Hits 1 through 50 out of 227

Next 50 Hits

Jump To

Refine Search   TTL/fire AND TTL/protection

PAT. NO.	Title
1 7,185,711	**T** Fire protection system
2 7,165,822	**T** Fire protection cabinet assembly
3 7,165,624	**T** Early suppression fast response fire protection sprinkler
4 7,144,527	**T** Fire-protection coating
5 7,140,471	**T** Elevator shaft closure and method of fulfilling fire protection requirements of an elevator shaft closure and of mounting the same
6 7,104,334	**T** Deployable automatic foaming fire protection system

Figure 9 (Source: USPTO Website)

Reading the search summary, we see that hits 1 through 50 of 227 are listed. Looking below the "PAT. NO." and "Title" headings in the middle of Figure 9, we see the matching patents. Notice that the patent numbers start with the most recently issued (highest number) patent first, and then proceed backward in time.

Each of these listed patent numbers is accompanied by a patent title. If you don't find what you are looking for in the first 50 hits, you can select the Next 50 Hits button (shown at the top of Figure 9), to see the next 50 matches. Note that only the first seven patents are shown in Figure 9.

5. Saving and Printing the Search Results

You can get a printout of the displayed patent numbers and titles by using your browser's print feature. Simply move your mouse to the File menu item at the upper left corner of your browser screen display and click once. Then scroll down to the Print function. This action is demonstrated in Figure 10 below.

Figure 10

Microsoft product screen shot(s) reprinted with permission from Microsoft Corporation

When you select the Print function, a printer control window similar to Figure 11, below, will open up. On our computer, the default printer is an HP Photosmart 3300 (yours may be different). The down arrow next to the printer name will allow you to select from among any installed printers that you have. To obtain your printout, just click the OK button at the bottom of the window.

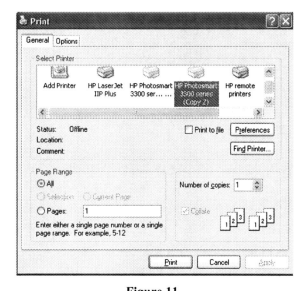

Figure 11

Microsoft product screen shot(s) reprinted with permission from Microsoft Corporation

When you find a patent whose title seems appropriate to your search, you can view the entire text of that patent, by simply clicking on that title. This is because, the search results listing is actually a list of hypertext links. Let's suppose that after selecting the Next 50 Hits button a couple of times, we see that patent number 5,462,805 is one that we are interested in. This is item number 122 as shown in Figure 12 below. To view the front page of this patent, just select the link with the mouse and click once.

The full-text of the patent will then be displayed, as shown in Figure 13. Here, you can review the inventors name, patent issue date and patent abstract. By scrolling down the page, you can see the current classification of this patent. This is shown in Figure 14, below. Scrolling down further, we see a list of referenced patents (Figure 15). These are the patents that were determined to be the prior art for patent number 5,462,805.

117 <u>5,524,616</u> **T** <u>Method of air filtration for fire fighter emergency smoke inhalation protection</u>

118 <u>5,518,638</u> **T** <u>Fire extinguishing and protection agent</u>

119 <u>5,505,383</u> **T** <u>Fire protection nozzle</u>

120 <u>5,495,894</u> **T** <u>Fire protection filter</u>

121 <u>5,467,923</u> **T** <u>Method and device for the monolithic application of a thermal-insulation and/or fire-protection compound to a surface</u>

122 <u>5,462,805</u> **T** <u>Fire-protection and safety glass panel</u>

123 <u>5,433,991</u> **T** <u>Reinforcement system for mastic intumescent fire protection coatings comprising a hybrid mesh fabric</u>

124 <u>5,423,150</u> **T** <u>Automated exterior fire protection system for building structures</u>

125 <u>5,396,715</u> **T** <u>Microwave clothes dryer and method with fire protection</u>

126 <u>5,392,993</u> **T** <u>Fire protection nozzle</u>

127 <u>5,378,530</u> **T** <u>Device for protection against fire, made of endothermic flexible material</u>

Figure 12 (Source: USPTO Website)

USPTO PATENT FULL-TEXT AND IMAGE DATABASE

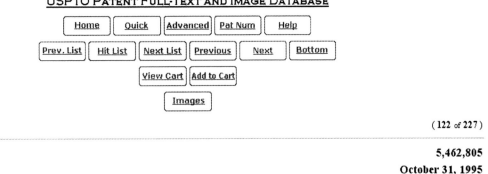

| Home | Quick | Advanced | Pat Num | Help |

| Prev. List | Hit List | Next List | Previous | Next | Bottom |

| View Cart | Add to Cart |

| Images |

(122 of 227)

United States Patent   **5,462,805**
Sakamoto , et al.   **October 31, 1995**

Fire-protection and safety glass panel

Abstract

In a fire-protection and safety glass panel having a transparent appearance and dual functions as a fire protection glass for shutting out flame and smoke for a long period of time upon occurrence of fire and as a safety glass which is neither shattered into pieces and nor forms any through hole if it is broken in an ordinary life, a PET (polyethylene terephthalate) film (12) is arranged between a first glass plate (10) and a second glass plate (11). The first and the second glass plates (10 and 11) and the PET film (12) are adhered through transparent acrylic adhesive agent layers (13 and 14), respectively. An intermediate resin layer comprises the PET film (12) and the adhesive agent layers (13 and 14) and has a thickness between 75 and 200 .mu.m.

Figure 13 (Source: USPTO Website)

The full-text of recently issued, referenced patents can be viewed by clicking on the patent number. Images of older referenced patents (patent number 3,900,673) are also available.

The first thing to do to determine if this patent represents relevant prior art is to read the abstract of the patent. If it is germane to your invention, then you will want to save this information. (Chapter 11 helps you to evaluate the relevance of the patents you uncover during your preliminary search.) Again, you can obtain a hardcopy printout, as discussed above. However, you can also save an electronic copy. To do this, we again move our mouse to the File menu item at the upper left corner of our Browser and click once. Then we scroll down to the Save As... selection, as shown in Figure 16 below.

Inventors: **Sakamoto; Akihiko** (Shiga, JP); **Takahashi; Tadashi** (Shiga, JP); **Ninomiya; Masayuki** (Shiga, JP)
Assignee: **Nippon Electric Glass Co., Ltd.** (Otsu, JP)
Appl. No.:   **099226**
Filed: **July 29, 1993**

Foreign Application Priority Data

Jul 30, 1992[JP]   4-223470

Current U.S. Class: **428/430**; 428/215; 428/410; 428/426; 428/480; 428/911; 428/913; 428/920
Intern'l Class: B32B 009/00
Field of Search: 428/458,432,437,141,524,480,215,412,410,426,911,913,920 526/87

Figure 14 (Source: USPTO Website)

References Cited [Referenced By]			
U.S. Patent Documents			
3900673	Aug., 1975	Mattimoe et al.	428/339.
4358329	Nov., 1982	Masuda	156/106.
4382996	May., 1983	Mori et al.	428/442.
4910074	Mar., 1990	Fukawa et al.	428/215.
4911984	Mar., 1990	Parker	428/428.
4952460	Aug., 1990	Beckmann et al.	428/429.
5002820	Mar., 1991	Bolton et al.	428/215.
5091258	Feb., 1992	Moran	428/437.
5091487	Feb., 1992	Hori et al.	526/87.
5145746	Sep., 1992	Tomoyuki	428/458.
5219630	Jun., 1993	Hickman	428/38.
5230954	Jul., 1993	Sakamoto et al.	428/332.
Foreign Patent Documents			
684017	Jul., 1966	BE.	
1905619	Aug., 1970	DE.	
480276	Dec., 1969	CH.	

Primary Examiner: Ryan; Patrick J.
Assistant Examiner: Krynski; William A.
Attorney, Agent or Firm: Hopgood, Calimafde, Kalil & Judlowe

Figure 15 (Source: USPTO Website)

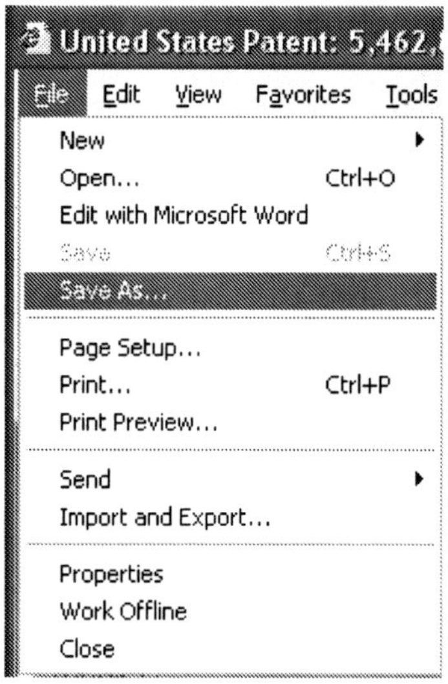

Figure 16

Microsoft product screen shot(s) reprinted with permission from Microsoft Corporation

When you click Save As… you will have a choice of whether to save the file as an *HTML* document or a *TXT* document. An HTML document has special codes in it that allow browser programs to display and link the document with other documents on the Internet. Saving the document in HTML format will preserve the hypertext links. However, you will most likely not need these links since you will be assembling your patent search results in a word processor. Therefore, you should save the file in a TXT format. A TXT format is a common format that any word processor can read.

In addition to the patent abstract, you can determine the class and subclass of the patent from Figure 14. The PTO uses classifications to group patents according to their subject matter. In short order, we will see how to use this classification system to jump-start your patent search.

The class and subclasses of the referenced patents are shown in Figure 15. These are arranged in columns. From left to right, the columns represent patent number, issue date, inventor, and major Class/Sub-class. For referenced patent number 5,230,954, also by Sakamoto, class 428 and subclass 332 are listed. Class 428 is also shown in Figure 14 as the current classification for this patent.

B. Searching the Manual of Classification

In the previous section you searched the full-text of recently issued patents. You may have gathered information about patented inventions that were similar to your invention idea. This information includes the one-paragraph abstract (or description) of the patent, the class/subclass that the patent was filed under, the claims of the patent and a detailed description of the patent. But how do you know that you found all of the relevant classes and patents? The search results that you obtained so far depended entirely on the keywords that you used. Suppose other inventors used different words to describe similar, patented inventions. In that case, you may have missed entire classes of related patents. One way to help prevent this from happening is to search for patents according to how they've been grouped by the PTO (that is, by class and subclass).

The document that summarizes all the classes used by the PTO is called the Manual of Classification. To search this document you need to type the following address in the address window of your web browser:

www.uspto.gov/go/classification

After a few seconds' delay you should see the webpage shown in Figure 17, below.

A. Access Classification Info by Class/Subclass HELP

1. Enter a US Patent Classification...

    428 /

    Class (required)/Subclass (optional)
    e.g., 704/1 or 482/1

2. Select what you want...
    ○ Class Schedule (HTML)
    ○ Printable Version of Class Schedule (PDF)
    ◉ Class Definition (HTML)
    ○ Printable Version of Class Definition (PDF)
    ○ US-to-IPC8 Concordance (HTML)
    ○ US-to-IPC8 Concordance (PDF)
    ○ US-to-Locarno Concordance

3. Submit   Reset

C. Classification Information
  • Information on E-Subclasses
  • Documents and Reports Related to the Manual of Classification
  • Classification Orders New!

B. Search

Can't find what you want? Try...

Search for:

Search FirstGov Search Tips

Figure 17 (Source: USPTO Website)

In the previous section, we discovered that the current classification of the Sakamoto patent (patent number 5,462,805) was Class 428. In section A of Figure 17, under item 1 (Enter a USPC Classification), we have entered 428 into the Class text entry box. Under item 2 (of Section A) we have selected the third Radio button (Class Definition HTML). This will allow us to view the Class definition for class 428 as an interactive HTML document in a browser window. To view the Manual of Classification entry for Class 428, click the Submit button under item 3 (of Section A). The results are shown in Figure 18 below.

Figure 18 shows the very top of a lengthy document which describes the types of inventions that are classified under class 428. If you were to print out this class description, it would consume over 200 pages of printout. That's a lot of pages to print and read! In the next section we will show you how to use the Find feature of your web browser to greatly simplify this task.

One of the reasons for the length of the class description is the large number of subclasses contained in Class 428. However, we already know that the current classification of the Sakamoto patent is Class 428, Subclass 430. Therefore, we can quickly locate the description for Subclass 430 by entering 430 into the Subclass text entry box shown in Figure 19.

After clicking the Submit button shown in Figure 19 (lower left), the class/subclass description shown in Figure 20 will be displayed. This class description is quite brief, but special notation is made that the subclass is actually indented under a broader subclass numbered 426. In your browser window, this notation of subclass 426 is actually a hypertext link. To see this subclass description, click on the link. The results are shown in Figure 21 below. Reading this further description we can clearly see that subclass 426 is germane to the Sakamoto fire-resistant glass patent.

Webpage Locations

The Internet is dynamic and the PTO is no exception. The location and content of the PTO's webpages often changes. The web address of the Manual of Classification is current as of the publication date of this text. However, by the time you read this the address may have changed. One way to keep abreast of these changes is to go to the main PTO website at:

www.uspto.gov

and look for a link called Site Index. This is usually an updated listing of the location of the PTO's online resources.

◪ CLASS 428, STOCK MATERIAL OR MISCELLANEOUS ARTICLES
Click here for a printable version of this file

SECTION I - CLASS DEFINITION

This class accommodates certain products of manufacture which are not provided for in classes devoted primarily to manufacturing methods and apparatus. The bulk of the documents are directed to stock material composites, that is, materials having two or more distinct components which are more ordered than a mere random mixture of ingredients.

Certain finished articles, generally of an ornamental or readily disposable nature, are placed herein when this class specifically provides for them. Unfinished articles, e.g., blanks requiring further significant shaping to be suitable for ultimate use, and stock materials from which an indefinite number of usable portions may be cut, are placed herein unless specifically provided for elsewhere. The determination whether a product is a finished article or a stock material is made on the basis of the amount of structure included in the body of the claims.

Figure 18 (Source: USPTO Website)

A. Access Classification Info by Class/Subclass

1. Enter a USPC Classification...

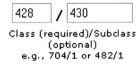

Class (required)/Subclass
(optional)
e.g., 704/1 or 482/1

2. Select what you want...

○ Class Schedule (HTML)

○ Printable Version of Class Schedule (PDF)

◉ Class Definition (HTML)

○ Printable Version of Class Definition (PDF)

○ US-to-IPC Concordance

○ US-to-Locarno Concordance

3. [Submit]   [Reset]

Figure 19 (Source: USPTO Website)

430 Next to polyester (e.g., alkyd)

This subclass is indented under subclass 426. Product in which a layer contiguous with quartz or glass contains polyester*.

Figure 20 (Source: USPTO Website)

426   Of quartz or glass

This subclass is indented under subclass 411.1. Product in which at least one layer contains fused silica (i.e., quartz), or a mixture of (1) fused silica, and (2) alkali and alkaline silicates, commonly known as glass.

(1) Note. The glass may be in the form of fibers or as a fiber glass mat.

(2) Note. Such materials as waterglass, isinglass and plexiglass are not considered as glass.

(3) Note. Vitreous enamel or vitreous ceramic, per se, is considered to be glass.

SEE OR SEARCH THIS CLASS, SUBCLASS:

38,	for stained glass elements in an aperture or frame.
49,	for a unilayer of plural glass sections extending in both lateral and longitudinal directions.
174+,	for corrugated fiber glass web or sheet.
312,	317, 325, 392, 406+, 415, and 417, as appropriately entitled, for other products containing glass, in the form of particles, a layer, foam, or fibers.

Figure 21 (Source: USPTO Website)

1. Browsing the U.S. Patent Classes

At the top of the PTO's Manual of Classification webpage,
www.uspto.gov/go/classification
above the Section A entries we used for Class and Subclass searching, are a series of navigation aids. To browse through the various major patent classifications click on the link labeled "Class Numbers & Titles" shown at the top of Figure 22. You will then be presented with the webpage illustrated in Figure 23.

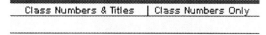

A. Access Classification Info by Class/Subclass

1. Enter a USPC Classification...

Figure 22 (Source: USPTO Website)

	Class Number and Title
Go	002 Apparel
Go	004 Baths, closets, sinks, and spittoons
Go	005 Beds
Go	007 Compound tools

Figure 23 (Source: USPTO Website)

Adjacent to each class number within the listing of Figure 23 is a Go button. These buttons are actually hypertext links to a description of the referenced class. By scrolling down this webpage, you could read the titles of the various classes until you encountered one or more relevant classes. But, as we explain below, there are more efficient methods.

Before continuing, let's stop and ask: What good will this classification information do us?

Suppose you came up with a new idea for a nightlight. Since many nightlights are used in bathrooms, you reason that shining a light off the reflective surfaces of porcelain fixtures (sinks and toilet bowls) would help light up the bathroom. You design your bathroom nightlight to mount to a wall fixture. In order to have the nightlight shine at the appropriate angle, you position the bulb at the end of a flexible support.

It seems simple enough to search for a classification called "lights" or "light." You would think that the PTO should have a huge listing of subclasses under the class "light." To check this assumption, we will use the "find" feature of our browser.

To activate the find feature, just click on the "Find" menu item at the top of the browser display. This action is shown in Figure 24 below.

After clicking on Find (on This Page) shown in the Figure below, the little window shown in Figure 25 below, will pop up. This utility will allow you to search for any word occurring in the list of class titles.

To search for the word "light" in the title of any of the classes, enter the word "light" into the find box, as shown in Figure 25. Make sure the direction radio button is set to "down", and click "Find Next." Each time the find function encounters the word "light" in a class title, the word will be highlighted. After viewing each occurrence of the word "light" in a classification title, you can proceed to the next occurrence by clicking "Find Next."

Figure 24

Figure 25

Microsoft product screen shot(s) reprinted with permission from Microsoft Corporation

You may be surprised to learn that while there are classifications for lasers (Class 372 Coherent Light Generators) and lights used in Surgery (Class 607 Light Surgery), there is no major classification using the word "light." How can this be? Isn't the light bulb the universal symbol for a new idea, or invention? The case of the word "light" should serve as a warning that the PTO may use a term you don't expect to see for a class title. First-time patent searchers often make the mistake of searching for obvious keywords only. This has a serious impact on the reliability of their patent search results. In this case, common sense tells us that all of the patents related to lights must be classified somewhere else. This is where a thesaurus comes in handy. Use a thesaurus to find alternatives for the keywords you used the first time.

This brings us to our next Searcher's Secret.

Searcher's Secret Number 5

The PTO may use a term you don't expect for a class/subclass title. Use a thesaurus as necessary to find alternative descriptive words for your class titles.

One alternative form of the word "light" is "illumination." Trying our search again with the word "illumination" inserted into the search box, as shown in Figure 26, we eventually get to class number 362. This is shown in Figure 27, below. (When conducting a new search, reposition yourself at the top of the document again. Be sure to select the proper search direction with the radio buttons shown in Figure 26.)

Figure 26

Microsoft product screen shot(s) reprinted with permission from Microsoft Corporation

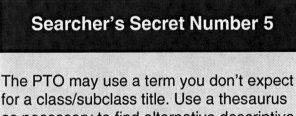

	360	Dynamic magnetic information storage or retrieval
Go	361	Electricity: electrical systems and devices
	Class Number and Title	
Go	362	Illumination
Go	363	Electric power conversion systems
Go	365	Static information storage and retrieval
Go	366	Agitating

Figure 27 (Source: USPTO Website)

Adjacent to each class number within the listing of Figure 27 is a Go button. As previously stated, these buttons are actually hypertext links to a description of the referenced class. Therefore, to view a description of the class 362: Illumination, just click on the adjacent Go button. The result is shown in Figure 28 below.

▣ Class 362 ILLUMINATION

Click here for a printable version of this file

▣	1	**DAYLIGHT LIGHTING**
▣	2	·　Including selected wavelength modifier (e.g., filter)
▣	3	**PHOTOGRAPHIC LIGHTING**
▣	4	·　Light responsive
▣	5	·　Measuring or indicating
▣	6	·　Heat responsive or control
▣	7	·　Convertible
▣	8	·　Combined
▣	9	··　With battery support means
▣	10	·　Safety or interlocks
▣	11	·　Plural light sources or light source supports
▣	12	··　Diverse type or size
▣	13	··　Lamp substitution or selection
▣	14	···　Indexing (i.e., dynamic)
▣	15	····　With electrical ignition
▣	16	·　Including specific light modifier

Figure 28 (Source: USPTO Website)

This webpage shows an indented list of all the sub-classes that can be found under class 362. Reading this entire webpage to see if there is a subclass title that might pertain to your invention could be very time consuming. Instead, we will again make use of your browser's Find feature.

Recall that besides having a light, another feature of our invention was the use of a flexible support. Might there be a subclass, under the class "illumination," that refers to lights with flexible supports? To find out, we will use our search window as in Figures 25 and 26, but this time we will use the word "flex." This will find all the derivatives of the word ("flexible," "flexing," and others). Here, we don't have to use a wildcard such as the dollar sign ($), as we do with Boolean searching.

Eventually, our find function will bring us to

subclass number 198, as shown in Figure 29 below. This is the subclass titled, "flexibly or extensibly mounted lamp bulb or lamp support." This certainly sounds like what we are looking for. To read a description of this sub-class, click on the link to the left of Figure 29, labeled "198". This will load the webpage description for the entire class 362 and position you at the exact location of the subclass 198 description. This is shown in Figure 30 below.

At this point we seem to have identified one of the primary classes and subclasses of our invention, namely, Class 362, subclass 198. Wouldn't it be nice to be able to get a comprehensive list of all the patents issued in this class/subclass combination? Well, we can, by using the Quick search page.

194	·	Battery supported separable lamp assembly
195	··	Battery terminal sole support of lamp
196	·	Mating-halves type flashlight casing
197	·	Lamp bulb or lamp support axis adjustable or angularly fixed relative to axis of flashlight casing
198	··	Flexibly or extensibly mounted lamp bulb or lamp support
199	··	Separate lamp housing or lamp support pivoed to flashlight casing
200	·	Flat flashlight casing
201	··	Lamp terminal directly contacts a battery terminal

Figure 29 (Source: USPTO Website)

198 Flexibly or extensibly mounted lamp bulb or lamp support
This subclass is indented under subclass 197. Subject matter wherein the light source or light source support is connected to the casing by a means which is movable to permit the light source or light source support to be moved to various locations consistent with the length of the means or by an electric cord of such length to permit the light source or light source support to be moved to various locations consistent with the length of the cord.

(1) Note. The means of this subclass type may be, for example, telescopic, flexible, and sectional pivoted members.

Figure 30 (Source: USPTO Website)

2. Finding All the Patents under a Particular Class and Subclass

You will recall that the PTO's patent searching website is at the following web address:

www.uspto.gov/patft

To perform our Class/Subclass search, first select the "Quick Search" link (illustrated at the beginning of this chapter in Figure 1).

To search for all the patents in a particular class and subclass, we select the down arrow for Field number 1, and change the setting from "Any Field" to "Current US Class." In the Term 1 entry box, we need to type "362/198". That is, the class 362, followed by a slash, and then the subclass 198. Next we need to specify a range of years to search. In this case, for the "Select years" pull-down menu, let's select "1790 to present" to search the entire patent database. Note that since we are searching the patent classification we can also search through the collection of patent images that are searchable

by classification and patent number. These selections and entries are shown in Figure 31 below.

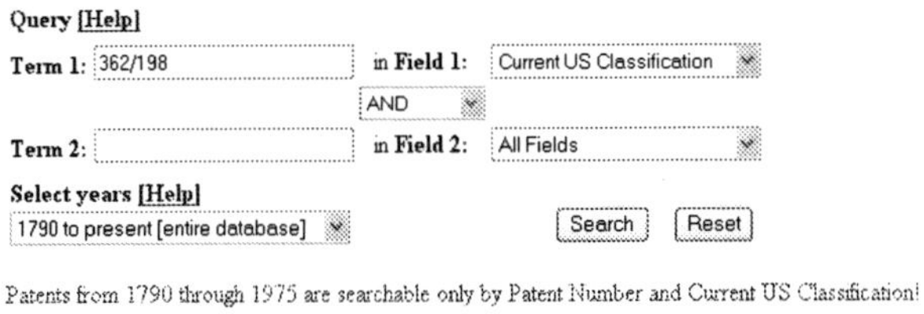

Query [Help]

Term 1: 362/198   in Field 1: Current US Classification
                  AND
Term 2:   in Field 2: All Fields

Select years [Help]
1790 to present [entire database]   [Search] [Reset]

Patents from 1790 through 1975 are searchable only by Patent Number and Current US Classification!

Figure 31 (Source: USPTO Website)

After selecting the search button, the list of patents shown in Figure 32 (first three patents only) will be returned. As shown in the figure, there were 104 patents issued between the years 1790 and the present (as of the time of printing of this book), in the class 362, subclass 198. These are patents issued for inventions that involve a light with a flexible support. Recall that our invention involves a nightlight for the bathroom that casts reflections off the porcelain fixtures. In scanning the list of patents (after selecting Next 50 Hits), we seen that item number 92, patent number 5,136,476, toilet bowl illuminator, sounds similar to our idea. See Figure 33.

90	5,154,483	T	Flashlight with flexible extension
91	5,136,477	T	Miniature battery-powered lighting device
92	5,136,476	T	Toilet bowl illuminator
93	5,012,394	T	Hand portable light with extendable lamp housing
94	4,931,913	T	Portable sirening and illumination device
95	4,870,543	T	Extensible safety light

Figure 33 (Source: USPTO Website)

Results of Search in US Patent Collection db for:
CCL/362/198: 104 patents.
Hits 1 through 50 out of 104

[Next 50 Hits]

[Jump To] [   ]

[Refine Search] CCL/362/198 [   ]

PAT. NO.   Title
1 7,188,969 T Emergency flashlight
2 7,175,295 T Adjustable flashlight supportable about a user's neck
3 7,165,869 T Internally illuminated elastomeric novelty device with external projections

Figure 32 (Source: USPTO Website)

To get a listing of the text of this patent, just click on the patent number or title. We are then presented with the text of patent number 5,136,476, issued to D. Horn on Aug. 4, 1992. By reading the patent abstract, as shown in Figure 34, we see that some aspects of our idea have been anticipated by the Horn patent. Clearly, patent number 5,136,476 requires further study.

(85 of 149)

United States Patent	5,136,476
Horn	August 4, 1992

Toilet bowl illuminator

Abstract

An easily-installed, portable illuminator for the illuminating of toilet bowls is disclosed. More specifically, the illuminator of this disclosure hangs on the rim of a toilet bowl by a tubular conduit through which electrical conductors carry current from a battery pack or other power source external to the bowl and to a light source suspended within the bowl. Light-sensitive and manual switches and current-regulating circuitry are options on advanced embodiments.

Figure 34 (Source: USPTO Website)

3. Searching with a Keyword Query

Another method of finding relevant classes for our invention is to directly search the class descriptions. You can accomplish this by searching the Manual of Classification. You will recall that the web address for the Manual of Classification is:

www.uspto.gov/go/classification

Section B of this website is shown in Figure 35 below. This section allows us to search for keywords within the class descriptions. To search for occurrences of the word illumination within the various class descriptions, just type the word illumination into the query box, as shown in the figure, and click on the Search Now button.

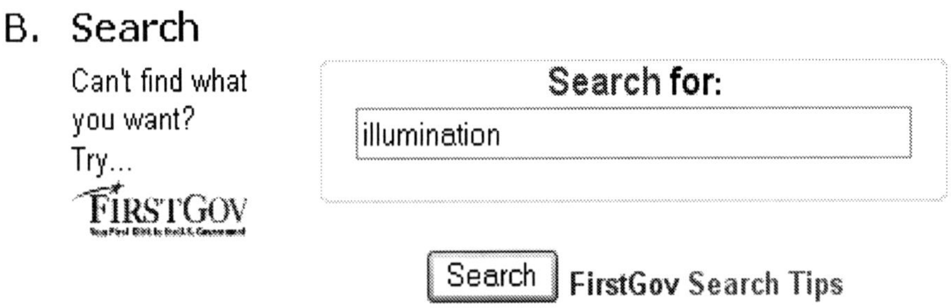

B. Search

Can't find what
you want?
Try...

FIRSTGOV

Search for:

illumination

[Search] FirstGov Search Tips

Figure 35 (Source: USPTO Website)

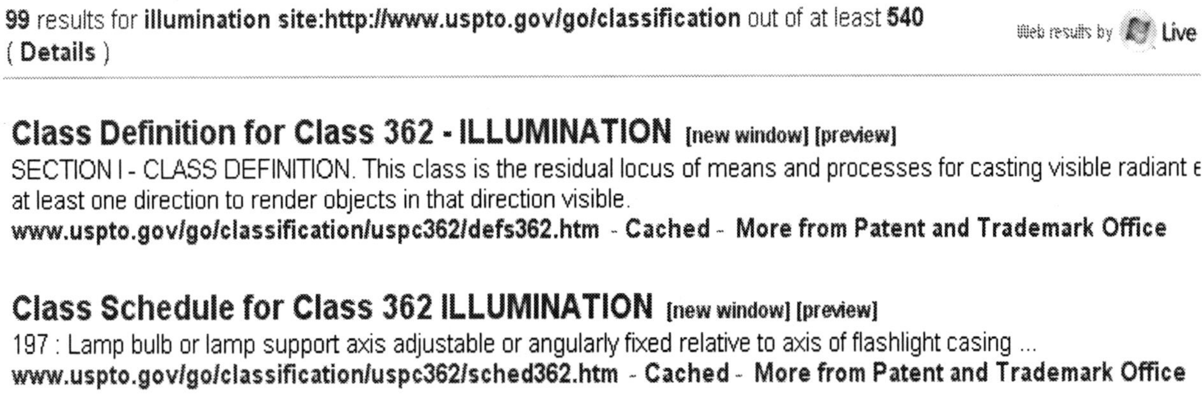

99 results for **illumination site:http://www.uspto.gov/go/classification** out of at least **540**
(**Details**)

Web results by 🔵 Live

Class Definition for Class 362 - ILLUMINATION [new window] [preview]
SECTION I - CLASS DEFINITION. This class is the residual locus of means and processes for casting visible radiant ε
at least one direction to render objects in that direction visible.
www.uspto.gov/go/classification/uspc362/defs362.htm - **Cached** - **More from Patent and Trademark Office**

Class Schedule for Class 362 ILLUMINATION [new window] [preview]
197 : Lamp bulb or lamp support axis adjustable or angularly fixed relative to axis of flashlight casing ...
www.uspto.gov/go/classification/uspc362/sched362.htm - **Cached** - **More from Patent and Trademark Office**

Figure 36 (Source: USPTO Website)

A portion of the results are shown in Figure 36 above. After you have collected the most relevant classes, you can return to the Quick Search page, and search for all the patents within those classes.

C. Search by Patent Number

Let's suppose that you have a patent number and wish to quickly look up a description of that patent. This can come in handy for sudden inspirations or for detailed product research. For example, suppose you are doing some interior decorating and you are working with a stud

finder. Stud finders are used to find the wooden studs hidden behind plasterboard on interior walls. It's important to drive support nails into the wooden studs when hanging heavy wall decorations.

After missing a stud and driving a nail through the wall, you decide that there has to be a better design for a stud finder. A quick look at the back of the device you are using reveals a patent number in raised plastic. Wouldn't it be great if you could review a patent document just by typing in a patent number?

The PTO provides just such a feature. Here's how it works. After returning to the main PTO patent search webpage

Issued Patents (PatFT)
(full-text since 1976, full-page images since 1790)

🔵 Quick Search
🔵 Advanced Search
🔵 Patent Number Search

🔵 View Patent Full-Page Images
　　How to View Patent Images

🔵 Status & Event History
🔵 Database Contents
🔵 Help Files

Figure 37 (Source: USPTO Website)

Enter the patent numbers you are searching for in the box below.

Query [Help]

| 5,148,108 | | [Search] [Reset] |

All patent numbers must be seven characters in length, excluding commas, which are optional. Examples:

Utility -- 5,146,634 6923014 0000001
Design -- D339,456 D321987 D000152
Plant -- PP08,901 PP07514 PP00003
Reissue -- RE35,312 RE12345 RE00007
Defensive Publication -- T109,201 T855019 T100001
Statutory Invention Registration -- H001,523 H001234 H000001
Re-examination -- RX29,194 RE29183 RE00125
Additional Improvement -- AI00,002 AI000318 AI00007

Figure 38 (Source: USPTO Website)

(www.uspto.gov /patft), you will see the links shown in Figure 37, above. To search by patent number, select the Patent Number Search link.

You will then be presented with the webpage shown in Figure 38 below. To review a particular patent, just enter the patent number into the query box, as shown in the figure, and click on Search. The results are shown in Figure 39 below.

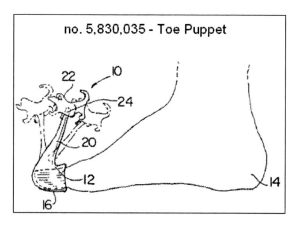
no. 5,830,035 - Toe Puppet

United States Patent
Dufour

5,148,108
September 15, 1992

Stud finder with level indicator

Abstract

A stud finder includes a magnetic subassembly for detecting the presence of a ferrous metal object, such as the head of a nail or screw, in a wall, with the magnetic subassembly being mounted at one end of a base member. A level vial is mounted at the other end of the base member, and a slot is formed in the base member between the magnetic subassembly and the level vial. When the base member is placed against a wall and the presence of a stud is detected by the magnetic subassembly, the base member is moved to a position in which the level vial indicates level. The slot has its longitudinal axis oriented perpendicular to the longitudinal axis of the level vial, so that the user can place a vertical mark on the wall through the slot. The slot is oriented so as to be in vertical alignment with the nail or screw head, when the base member is moved such that the magnetic subassembly is directly over the nail or screw head. With this arrangement, the mark made on the wall by the user is vertically aligned with the nail or screw head.

Figure 39 (Source: USPTO Website)

D. Patent Images

In addition to searching through the full text of all patents issued since January 1, 1976, you can look at images of each page. What's the advantage of looking at scanned images of a patent page? After all, recalling the discussion of Optical Character Recognition in Chapter 1, Section B, an image can't be searched. The big advantage is that viewing scanned images of issued patents allows you to review the patent drawings. The detailed descriptions of patents contain painstaking references to the patent drawings. By reading the detailed description and referring to each of the numbered elements of the patent drawings, a reviewer can gain a detailed understanding of the patent.

1. Loading the Image Viewer

The first step to viewing patent images on the PTO's website is to load a separate image viewer program into your computer. The good news is that the program is free and can be downloaded over the Internet. At the main PTO patent search webpage (www.uspto.gov/patft), below the links to the Issued Patents database (PatFT) and the Published Applications database (AppFT), is a link to an online patent image viewer program. This link is labeled:

"View Patent Full-Page Images." See Figure 40.

● View Patent Full-Page Images
How to View Patent Images

Figure 40 (Source: USPTO Website)

By clicking on this link, you will be presented with a webpage that provides some background information about PTO compatible image viewer programs. Currently, there are two freely available image viewer programs that will work with the PTO's online database. By scrolling down the above mentioned webpage you will see links to these programs. These links are shown in Figure 41, below.

The image viewer we will be installing is the Medical Informatics Engineering "AlternaTIFF" program. To gain access to this program, click on the link labeled "AlternaTIFF' shown in the center of Figure 41, below. You will then be presented a webpage that will allow you to download the actual Image Viewer program. The actual link that you want to click on is about halfway down the webpage (see Figure 42 below).

The only free, unlimited time TIFF plug-ins offering full-size, unimpeded patent viewing and printing unimpeded by any advertising on **Windows® x86 PCs** of which we are aware are:

- AlternaTIFF: http://www.alternatiff.com/ (tested: IE, Netscape, Opera)
- interneTIFF: http://www.internetiff.com/ (tested: IE, Netscape)

Figure 41 (Source: USPTO Website)

1. ActiveX control, auto-install
For Internet Explorer 4.x and higher.

<**Click here to go to the installation page**>

Figure 42 (Source: USPTO Website)

After clicking this link you should see the AlternaTIFF installation webpage shown in Figure 43 below. To install the viewer, click on the "Auto-install AlternaTIFF ActiveX control" link shown at the bottom of Figure 43.

AlternaTIFF ActiveX auto-installation for Internet Explorer

*Before you install: AlternaTIFF will configure itself to be Internet Explorer's default TIFF file viewer, but it cannot prevent other applications from changing that setting in the future. If **QuickTime**, or some other ActiveX TIFF viewer, is installed on your computer, your best bet is to turn off TIFF support in that application before installing AlternaTIFF. Here are instructions about QuickTime. Most other imaging applications do not include an ActiveX control for Internet Explorer, and therefore do not need to be reconfigured.*

To install, click this link: **Auto-install AlternaTIFF ActiveX control**.
You may wish to scroll down and read the rest of this page first.

Figure 43 (Copyright Medical Informatics Engineering – reprinted with permission)

After clicking on the Auto-install link shown in Figure 43, you should see a small pop-up warning window similar to Figure 44, below.

Click on the Install button to install the viewer. If the AlternaTIFF viewer is properly installed on your computer, you should see a confirmation message similar to the one shown in Figure 45.

Internet Explorer - Security Warning

Do you want to install this software?

Name: alttiff.cab
Publisher: **Medical Informatics Engineering**

More options | Install | Don't Install

While files from the Internet can be useful, this file type can potentially harm your computer. Only install software from publishers you trust. What's the risk?

Figure 44

Microsoft product screen shot(s) reprinted with permission from Microsoft Corporation

If you can read this,
the AlternaTIFF ActiveX control is installed in your browser.

(click here)

Figure 45 (Copyright Medical Informatics Engineering – reprinted with permission)

2. Using the Image Viewer

After successfully installing the AlternaTIFF image viewer, we can return to the PTO's patent search website and view the scanned images of each page of our relevant patents. At the PTO patent search homepage, click on Patent Number Search (See Figure 37). For example, let's look at the scanned images of patent number 5,462,805, the fire-protection and safety glass panel. After entering the patent number and clicking on Search (See section C to refresh your memory on how to do this), you will see the webpage shown in Figure 46, below.

Figure 46 shows the Abstract of patent number 5,462,805. Note that, across the top of Figure 46 are several navigation buttons. The center button labeled "Images" is an activation button for our patent image viewer program. To start the viewer, click on the Images button. You will then see the webpage shown in Figure 47, below.

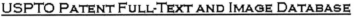

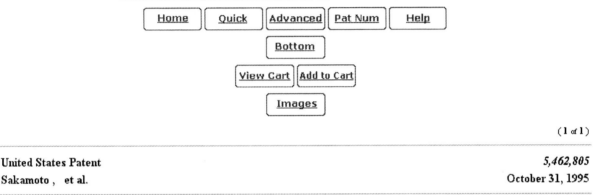

(1 of 1)

United States Patent   **5,462,805**

Sakamoto , et al.   October 31, 1995

Fire-protection and safety glass panel

Abstract

In a fire-protection and safety glass panel having a transparent appearance and dual functions as a fire protection glass for shutting out flame and smoke for a long period of time upon occurrence of fire and as a safety glass which is neither shattered into pieces and nor forms any through hole if it is broken in an ordinary life, a PET (polyethylene terephthalate) film (12) is arranged between a first glass plate (10) and a second glass plate (11). The first and the second glass plates (10 and 11) and the PET film (12) are adhered through transparent acrylic adhesive agent layers (13 and 14), respectively. An intermediate resin layer comprises the PET film (12) and the adhesive agent layers (13 and 14) and has a thickness between 75 and 200 .mu.m.

Figure 46 (Source: USPTO Website)

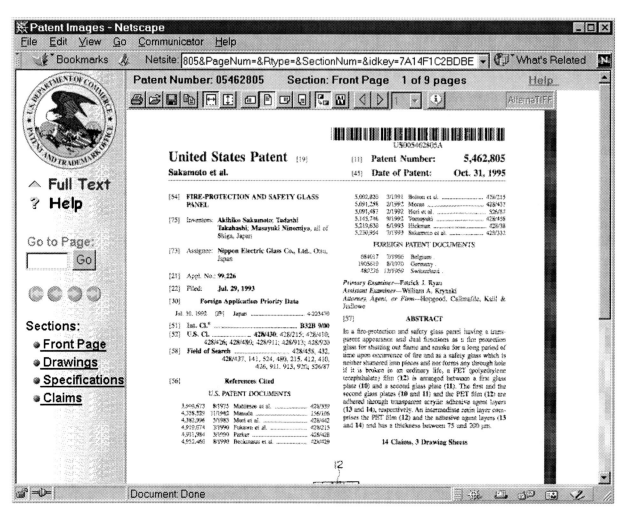

Figure 47 (Source: USPTO Website)

Figure 47 shows the image viewer program with the first page of patent 5,462,805 already loaded. The left side of Figure 47 shows several controls for the image viewer. We will discuss these one by one.

Towards the center left of Figure 47 there is an entry box labeled "Go to Page." You can make the image viewer display any selected page of patent 5,462,805 by typing in the page number and clicking on the small button labeled Go immediately to the right.

Below the "Go to Page" box are a series of arrows. They work in a similar fashion to the indicators on a tape recorder. The left-most arrow will rewind the image viewer to the beginning, or first page of the patent. The next arrow reduces the page number of the current

display, one page at a time. Similarly, the third arrow from the left advances the displayed patent page, one page at a time. Finally, the forth arrow advances the displayed page to the last page of the patent.

Below the arrows, hypertext links have been setup for the major sections of the displayed patent. As shown in the figure, these sections are the Front Page, Drawings, Specifications and Claims. Clicking on any of these links will cause the respective section of the patent to be immediately displayed in the viewer. This can come in handy if, for example, you want to jump directly to the patent specifications section. This way you don't have to search for it by advancing one page at a time through the entire patent.

One of the primary reasons for using the image viewer is to review the patent drawings. Figure 48 shows the image viewer display after the "Drawings" link has been selected. As you can see from the top of the display, this particular patent has three drawing pages. The image viewer has jumped to the first drawing page.

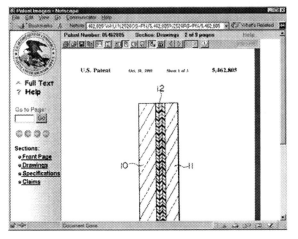

Figure 48 (Source: USPTO Website)

Enlarged images of the patent drawings can be displayed by moving the mouse cursor over the displayed area. The shape of the cursor will change from an arrow to a magnifying glass. An enlarged display of a section of a patent drawing can be obtained by positioning the cursor over the selected area and clicking once. An enlarged display of the top area of patent drawing number 1 is shown in Figure 49. This clearly shows where drawing element 12 is used in this patent. The image is returned to normal size by clicking once again, with the mouse.

Oct. 31, 1995   Sheet 1 of 3

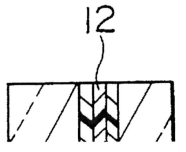

Figure 49 (Source: USPTO Website)

3. Printing and Saving Patent Images

Images of any displayed patent page can be printed or saved to hard disk for future reference. To print the currently displayed page, just click on the button with the small image of the printer. This is shown in the top left of Figure 47. A close-up view is shown below, in Figure 50.

To save the displayed patent page to the hard disk, click on the second button from the left. This is the button with the small image of a floppy disk shown in Figure 50.

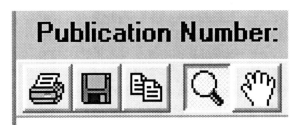

Figure 50 (Source: USPTO Website)

E. An Effective Strategy for Basic Patent Searches

When searching the patent database, there are two goals that you must keep clearly in mind. The first goal is to find the most relevant classes and sub-classes for your invention. Relevancy is determined by reading the class descriptions and applying them to your invention. The second goal is to review all of the issued patents within those classes and determine if your idea has been anticipated by the prior art. Anticipation means that all the main aspects of your idea have been documented in previously issued patents or other sources of prior art. We explain anticipation in more detail in Chapter 11.

Searcher's Secret Number 6

Find the most relevant classes and subclasses for your invention. Then review all of the issued patents within those classes.

You can approach this problem in one of two ways. First, as shown in Section B, you start from a keyword search of the patent classes. By reviewing the class descriptions, you determine where your invention might fit in. Then you review all of the issued patents within those classes. Alternately, as shown in Section A, you can start from keyword searches of the patents themselves, and after reviewing the matching patents, extract the relevant patent numbers and classes.

Starting from a keyword search of the classes first is usually more efficient. However, we recommend using both methods. That way,

you are less likely to miss an important prior art reference. Figure 51 shows a flowchart for searching the patent classes. Notice that you can start from keyword searches of the

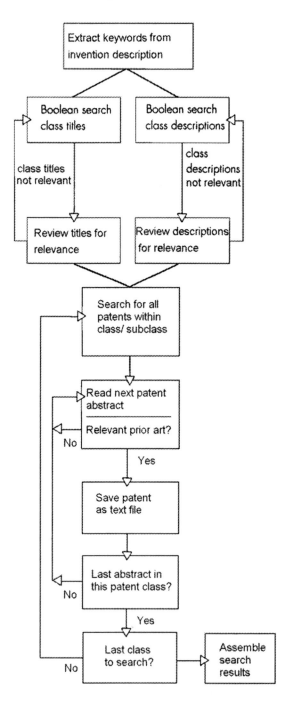

Figure 51

class titles or of the class descriptions. Figure 52 shows a flowchart for searching the text of the patents themselves.

This is what we would call a one-level-deep search. In other words, you have made one pass of your keywords through the Internet PTO database and hopefully extracted some relevant prior art; you have probably found two or three classes and several patents that speak to different aspects of your invention.

After saving the text of all relevant prior art patents, you can assemble these documents into a quick search results report. For example, using the "Insert..File" function of the Word for Windows word processor (see Figure 53), we can insert each of our saved patents into a single document.

After inserting all of the patents into your new document, just use "File..Save As" command (see Figure 54), with a new file name.

Use the patent image viewer to print out and save images of each page of the pre-1976 relevant patents.

In order to do a reasonably thorough patent search, you should make a second-level pass through your results. This means reviewing the referenced patents listed on the front of each of those prior art patents. This action is shown in Figure 55. This can lead to a lot of reading. For example, if you found ten patents related to yours, and each of these referenced ten older patents, then you have an additional one hundred patents to review. It's worth the effort, however, because this may lead you to an important class or patent that you might have otherwise overlooked.

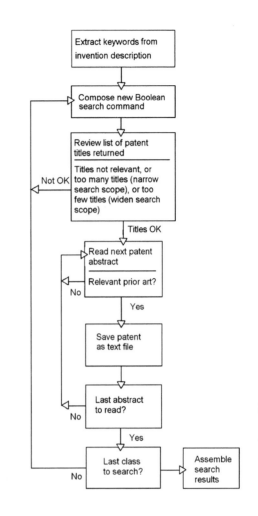

Figure 52

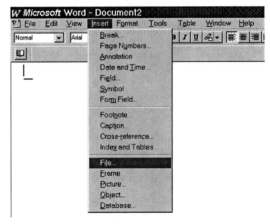

Figure 53

Microsoft product screen shot(s) reprinted with permission from Microsoft Corporation

Figure 54

Microsoft product screen shot(s) reprinted with permission from Microsoft Corporation

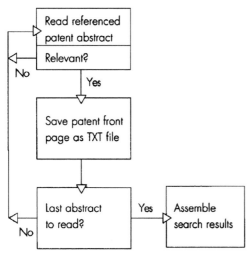

Figure 55

Summary

Simple Keyword Searches
- Perform keyword searches of the PTO's Internet database using simple Boolean logic.
- Review abstracts and descriptions of matching patents for relevance.
- Use the "File..Save" command to save your results.

Searching the Manual of Classification
- Perform keyword searches of classification titles using the Find function.
- Perform keyword searches of classification descriptions using the PTO's search function.
- Be aware that the PTO may use different words than you would expect to describe a given class of patents.
- Search for all patents issued within a class using the PTO's Boolean search function.

Patent Number Searches.
- Use the Patent Number Search feature to review the text of a given patent number.

Patent Images
- Load the image viewer onto your computer.
- Install the viewer.
- Use the image viewer to review, save, and print each page of prior art patents.

An Effective Strategy for Basic Patent Searches
- Perform keyword searches of classes first, then find all patents issued within those classes. Save the text of relevant patents.
- Perform keyword searches of the text of issued patents. Save any relevant results.
- Use the Patent Number search feature to review the text of each relevant patent your uncovered.
- Review the referenced patents of your results for further prior art.
- Assemble results into a quick search report.

Chapter 4

Advanced Patent Searching at the PTO Website

This chapter introduces you to advanced Boolean search commands at the PTO Internet site. Before attempting these techniques, it is necessary to have a good understanding of basic Boolean logic (Chapter 1). Also, before starting this section, you will be best served by understanding the basic keyword searching methods used at the PTO Internet site (Chapter 3).

A. Advanced Patent Searching at the PTO's Website

In Chapters 1 and 3, we explained the basics of Boolean searching and using the PTO website to search for patents. That information was enough to get you started. Now that you grasp the basics, it's time to improve your searching skills.

1. Using Multiple Boolean Operators

Simple Boolean expressions are generally understood to mean the use of two keywords connected by a single Boolean operator. For example:

Fire AND Protection
or
Building OR Structure

The first query would return all of the patents that contained both of the words Fire and Protection. By requiring both of the keywords to be present, we reduce the size of our search results. The second query would return all of the patents that contained the word Building or the word Structure. By requiring only one of the keywords to be present, we enlarge the size of our search results.

An advanced Boolean query involves the use of more than one operator and sometimes the use of parenthesis. For example:

Fire AND Protection AND (Building OR Structure)

This Boolean search command would return only patents that contained the words Fire, Protection, and the word Building or the word Structure. The first two keywords use a logical AND operation to narrow the search results. Then the logical AND operation is applied to the expression contained within the parentheses. The use of the parenthesis around the keywords "Building OR Structure" means that patents are searched for either of these words (this widens the size of the search results, because either keyword can cause a hit). However, the result of the search for the keywords "Building OR Structure" is then further narrowed because these two words must occur in combination with the words Fire and Protection. The flow chart of Figure 1 illustrates this process. The correct placement of parenthesis is important because this determines how the keywords are combined.

Let's try some advanced search commands at the PTO website and examine the results. As shown in Chapter 3, to get to the PTO patent search website, you need the following address (you can also get to the patent search site through the PTO's homepage at www.uspto.gov):

www.uspto.gov/patft

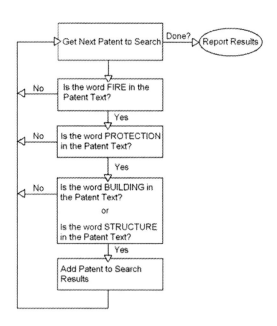

Figure 1

To get to the advanced search page, click on the Advanced Search link shown in Figure 2, below.

Figure 2 (Source: USPTO Website)

The advanced search page is shown in Figure 3 below. There are several similarities to the Boolean search page discussed in Chapter 3. The "Select years" pull-down menu gives you the same two ranges as the Quick Search page. These selections are:

- 1976 to present [full-text]
- 1790 to present [entire database]

For the present we will use the default selection, which is "1976 to present [full-text]." Using this setting will allow us to search through every word contained in every patent issued since January 1st 1976.

The query box of the advanced search page is quite different from the Boolean search page. We no longer have the two keyword entry fields separated by a Boolean operator field, as shown in Chapter 3, Figure 6. Instead, we are faced only with a challenging blank box. It is here that we enter our advanced Boolean expressions. Let's type in the search command "Fire AND Protection AND (Building OR

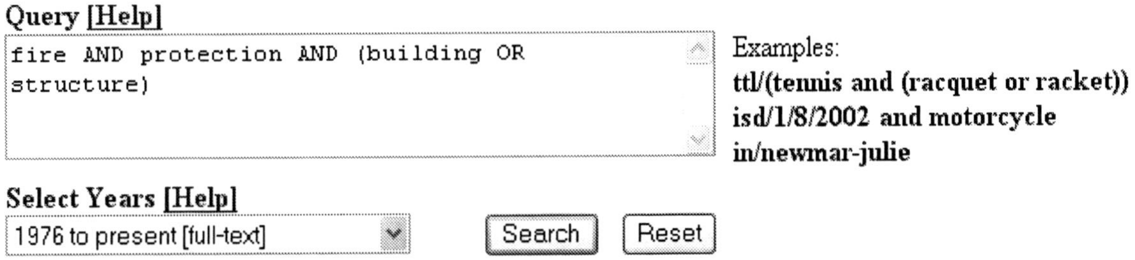

Query [Help]

```
fire AND protection AND (building OR
structure)
```

Examples:
ttl/(tennis and (racquet or racket))
isd/1/8/2002 and motorcycle
in/newmar-julie

Select Years [Help]

| 1976 to present [full-text]   ▼ | [Search]   [Reset]

Figure 3 (Source: USPTO Website)

Structure)," as shown in the Figure. To start the search, just click on the Search button shown in the lower right of Figure 3.

First note in the Search Summary section in Figure 4, below, that your search query was modified slightly by the search engine to enclose your first two search terms in parentheses. It also enclosed your entire query in parentheses. Below, we explain what these parentheses mean and when you can use the same approach to perform your search.

In Chapter 3 we executed the simple Boolean search command "Fire AND Protection" for patents issued in the years 1976 to the present. The results we obtained (Figure 7 of Chapter 3) show that 21593 hits were found. Now, by using a more complex Boolean expression, we were able to add the requirement for the keywords Building or Structure. The results of our new search are shown in Figure 4 below. From the figure, you can see that the number of matching patents has been reduced from 21593 to 14099.

Why so many hits? Recall that we are searching through the entire text of every patent issued from the year 1976 to the present for a match to our search query. In Section 3 we will show you how to greatly narrow your search results by the use of Field Codes.

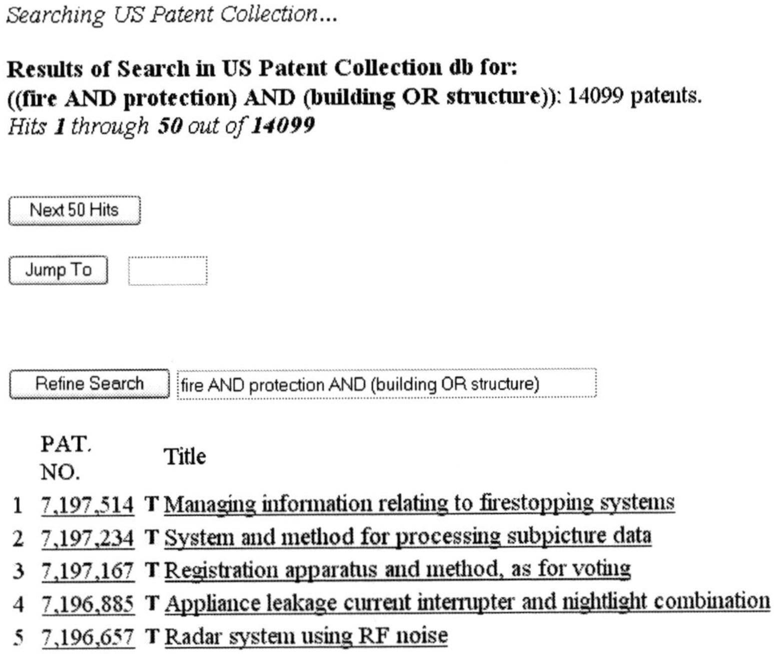

Searching US Patent Collection...

Results of Search in US Patent Collection db for:
((fire AND protection) AND (building OR structure)): 14099 patents.
*Hits **1** through **50** out of **14099***

[Next 50 Hits]

[Jump To]   [   ]

[Refine Search] | fire AND protection AND (building OR structure) |

PAT. NO.	Title
1 7,197,514	**T** Managing information relating to firestopping systems
2 7,197,234	**T** System and method for processing subpicture data
3 7,197,167	**T** Registration apparatus and method, as for voting
4 7,196,885	**T** Appliance leakage current interrupter and nightlight combination
5 7,196,657	**T** Radar system using RF noise

Figure 4 (Source: USPTO Website)

The query entry box of the advanced search page will allow you to type in any valid Boolean search command. This provides you with the ability to precisely define your search requirements. It means that your search results will be more relevant and that there will be less material to read over. Of course, the down side to the advanced query box is that if you are too narrow in your search requirements, you may overlook patents that are relevant. For example, instead of the words Building or Structure, a relevant patent may contain the words edifice, palace or skyscraper.

As always, to read the text of any patent reported as a hit (or to view images of the patent with an image viewer as in Chapter 3, Section D) just click on the patent number or title. To return to the advanced search page, just click on the back arrow of your browser.

As explained in Chapter 1, another import Boolean operator is the ANDNOT operator. As you may recall, the ANDNOT operator allows you to exclude certain keywords from the search results. Let's suppose that our invention is a fire protective device used in various buildings, but does not involve sprinklers. To exclude sprinklers from the search results we add "ANDNOT sprinkler" to our search command and compose the following query (shown in Figure 5):

Fire AND Protection AND (Building OR Structure) ANDNOT Sprinkler

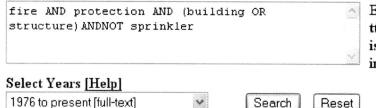

Figure 5 (Source: USPTO Website)

2. Using Parentheses to Organize Your Search Query

When using multiple Boolean operators, it's important to keep in mind which terms are evaluated first. Proceeding from left to right in the above command, the AND operator will first be used to combine the two terms Fire AND Protection. The next term encountered is the word Building. But this word is enclosed in parentheses with the OR operator and the word Structure. This forces the expression within the parentheses (Building OR Structure) to be evaluated

first. Then the AND operator is used to combine the result of the first two words. Finally, the ANDNOT operator will be used to exclude the term Sprinkler.

If you are in doubt about the order of evaluation of a complex Boolean expression, you can always add more parentheses. For example, in the expression shown below:

((Fire AND Protection) AND (Building OR Structure)) ANDNOT Sprinkler

First, the inner parentheses around Fire AND Protection causes these two terms to be AND'ed together. Then, the parentheses around Building OR Structure causes these two terms to be OR'ed together. Finally, the outer parentheses causes the results of both operations to be AND'ed together.

In fact, the PTO's patent search server will automatically add parentheses to your search command and display it at the top of your search results. In this way, you can check to see that the executed search command matches what you intended.

Figure 6 shows the results of our search that excludes Sprinklers. Notice that the executed search command is displayed at the top of the search results. Namely:

(((Fire AND Protection) AND (Building OR Structure)) ANDNOT Sprinkler)

Here, we can see that Fire AND Protection will be evaluated first. Then Building will be OR'ed with Structure. Then

the results of these two operations will be AND'ed together. Finally, the ANDNOT Sprinkler operation will be applied to all of the above. The total number of resulting hits has been further reduced from 14099 to 13516.

Searcher's Secret Number 7

When in doubt about the order of evaluation in complex patent search commands, use parentheses to explicitly set the order. Then check the output command at the top of the results report.

Searching US Patent Collection...

Results of Search in US Patent Collection db for:
(((**fire AND protection) AND (building OR structure)) ANDNOT sprinkler**): 13516 patents.
Hits 1 through 50 out of 13516

| Next 50 Hits |

| Jump To | |

| Refine Search | fire AND protection AND (building OR structure) ANDN |

PAT. NO.	Title
1 7,197,514	T Managing information relating to firestopping systems
2 7,197,234	T System and method for processing subpicture data
3 7,197,167	T Registration apparatus and method, as for voting
4 7,196,885	T Appliance leakage current interrupter and nightlight combination

Figure 6 (Source: USPTO Website)

3. Using Field Codes to Narrow Your Search

So far we have been searching the entire text of issued patents with the advanced search mode of the PTO's patent search database. We can however, limit our searches to certain sections of the issued patent through the use of Field Codes. Why limit your search to only selected sections? Why not always search through the maximum amount of patent text available? The answer is that by always searching through the maximum amount of patent text, you will often get thousands of matching patents that don't really have any bearing on your invention. Selected keywords like Fire and Protection can occur in many contexts. They are used in literally thousands of different types of

inventions. Constructing queries that blindly look for any use of these keywords will often return many irrelevant hits. This fact is well illustrated by the results shown in Figure 6, where 13516 hits were returned.

At the bottom of the advanced search page is a table showing all the available field codes. This is shown in Figure 7 below. Next to the field codes is the name of the field. You may recognize by now that this name is actually a hypertext link. To get a further description of any particular field code, just select its name. For example, to read a description of the Patent Abstract field code (ABST), just click on Abstract (forth from the top on the left-most column) shown in Figure 7. The resulting description is shown in Figure 8.

Field Code	Field Name	Field Code	Field Name
PN	Patent Number	IN	Inventor Name
ISD	Issue Date	IC	Inventor City
TTL	Title	IS	Inventor State
ABST	Abstract	ICN	Inventor Country
ACLM	Claim(s)	LREP	Attorney or Agent
SPEC	Description/Specification	AN	Assignee Name
CCL	Current US Classification	AC	Assignee City
ICL	International Classification	AS	Assignee State
APN	Application Serial Number	ACN	Assignee Country
APD	Application Date	EXP	Primary Examiner
PARN	Parent Case Information	EXA	Assistant Examiner
RLAP	Related US App. Data	REF	Referenced By
REIS	Reissue Data	FREF	Foreign References
PRIR	Foreign Priority	OREF	Other References
PCT	PCT Information	GOVT	Government Interest
APT	Application Type		

Figure 7 (Source: USPTO Website)

Abstract (ABST)
This field contains a brief summary of the patented invention.

TIP: The abstract contains many of the relevant words of a patent.

Figure 8 (Source: USPTO Website)

As the description says, the patent abstract is a brief summary of the patented invention that contains many of the relevant words of a patent. As a learning exercise in how to use field codes to improve the relevancy of our search results, let's limit our patent search to the patent abstract only. We would then use the ABST field code shown in Figure 7. Let's further suppose that we wish to search for the words Fire and Protection, or the words Safety and Glass in the abstracts of issued patents. We would then compose the query shown in Figure 9 below.

Notice how each keyword is preceded by the characters "ABST/." This tells the patent search program to look for that keyword, in the patent abstract only.

The results of our search are shown in Figure 10 below. The reduction in the number of reported hits is quite dramatic. Comparing Figure 6 with Figure 10 we see that the number of reported hits has been reduced from 13516 to a much more manageable 76 patents.

Query [Help]

```
(ABST/Fire AND ABST/Protection) AND
(ABST/Building OR ABST/Structure) ANDNOT
ABST/Sprinkler
```

Figure 9 (Source: USPTO Website)

Searching US Patent Collection...

Results of Search in US Patent Collection db for:
(((ABST/fire AND ABST/protection) AND (ABST/building OR ABST/structure)) ANDNOT ABST/sprinkler): 76 patents.
Hits 1 through 50 out of 76

[Final 26 Hits]

[Jump To] [   ]

[Refine Search] [ABST/fire AND ABST/protection AND (ABST/building]

PAT. NO.	Title
1 7,140,471	T Elevator shaft closure and method of fulfilling fire protection requirements of an elevator shaft closure and of mounting the same
2 6,992,027	T Composite panel with fire resistant face sheets
3 6,980,978	T Site integration management system for operational support service in an internet data center
4 6,918,447	T Fire protection apparatus and method

Figure 10 (Source: USPTO Website)

There is actually a shorthand way of composing the above query. When you are using parentheses you can place the field code characters (in this case "ABST") outside the parenthesis. The patent search program will then apply the field code to entire contained expression. In this case, we can re-compose our query to what is shown in Figure 11, below, and obtain the same result.

Searcher's Secret Number 8

By placing a Field Code outside a set of parentheses in complex Boolean queries, you apply that field code to every keyword in the contained expression.

Query [Help]

```
ABST/(((Fire AND Protection) AND (Building OR
Structure)) ANDNOT Sprinkler)
```

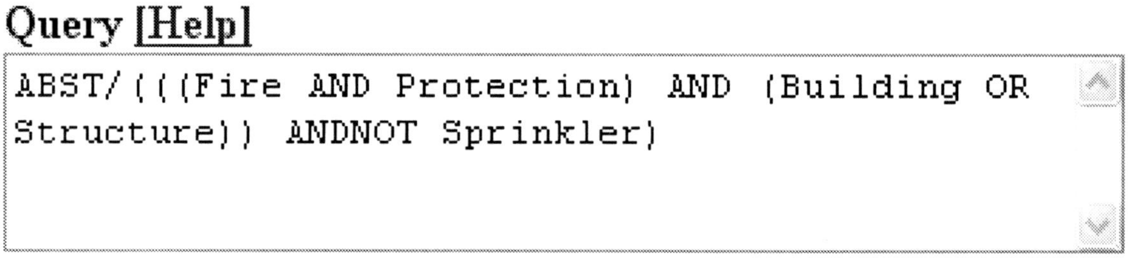

Figure 11 (Source: USPTO Website)

4. Searching for a Phrase

Another way that we can use the advanced search page is through the use of a quoted phrase. Specific words are often adjacent to each other in certain fields of endeavor. For example, in the field of Biotechnology, the phrase "Absorption Spectroscopy" is often encountered. Absorption Spectroscopy is the use of a Spectrophotometer to determine the ability of solutes to absorb light through a range of specified wavelengths. To search for this phrase just enclose the words in double quotes as shown in Figure 12 below. Then select the search button. The results are shown in Figure 13 below.

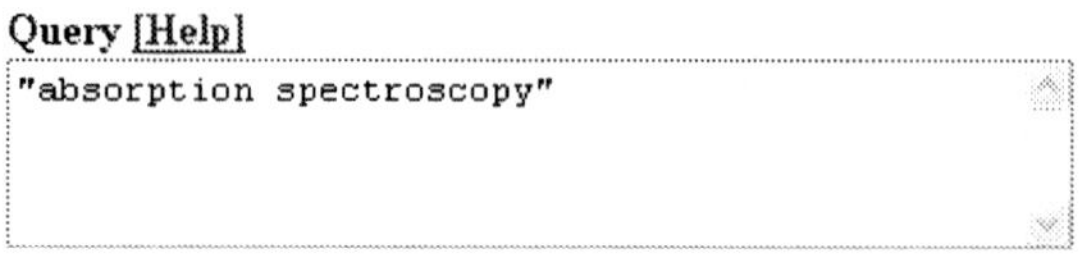

Here we see that there have been 4759 patents issued since 1976 that have the phrase "Absorption Spectroscopy" in them. Care should be exercised with the use of phrases. If the sequence of words does not exactly match their use in the patent text to be searched, you won't get a match, and you could miss a relevant prior art patent.

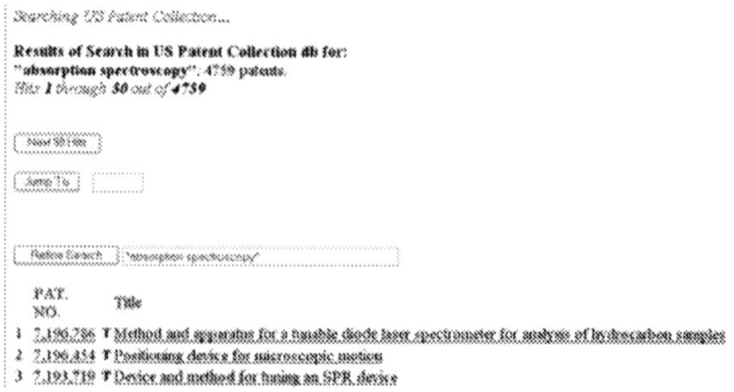

Query [Help]

```
"absorption spectroscopy"
```

Figure 12 (Source: USPTO Website)

Searching US Patent Collection...

Results of Search in US Patent Collection db for:
"absorption spectroscopy": 4759 patents.
Hits 1 through 50 out of 4759

Refine Search   "absorption spectroscopy"

PAT.
NO.   Title
1 7,196,786 Method and apparatus for a tunable diode laser spectrometer for analysis of hydrocarbon samples
2 7,196,454 Positioning device for microscopic motion
3 7,193,719 Device and method for tuning an SPR device

Figure 13 (Source: USPTO Website)

5. Limiting the Range of Years Searched

In Figure 13, above, 4759 hits resulted from our search query. That's an awful lot of results to read through. We could reduce this number by limiting our search to specific sections of the issued patent; specifically the abstract. But what if we missed a relevant prior art reference?

Our search for Absorption Spectroscopy leads us to another important way of refining our search queries. The Select Years pull-down menus on both the Quick Search and Advanced Search web pages at the PTO's Internet site only allow for two selections. Namely:

- 1976 to present [full-text]
- 1790 to present [entire database]

Often, it is desirable to limit the range of years searched to a smaller value. For example, suppose that you are a Biotechnology researcher and you have come up with an improvement to a Spectrophotometer. The improvement is not only limited to the field of Absorption Spectroscopy, but also depends of recent technological developments. Therefore, you could reasonably assume that any relevant patents would have been issued quite recently; say, in the past three years. But how do you limit the range of years to be searched?

In Figure 7, above, one of the specified field codes is the Issue Date (ISD). This code is used to search for a patent that was issued on a specific date. We can use this code and a special operator, to apply our patent search query to a discrete range of dates.

In Figure 14, below, we have composed the following query:

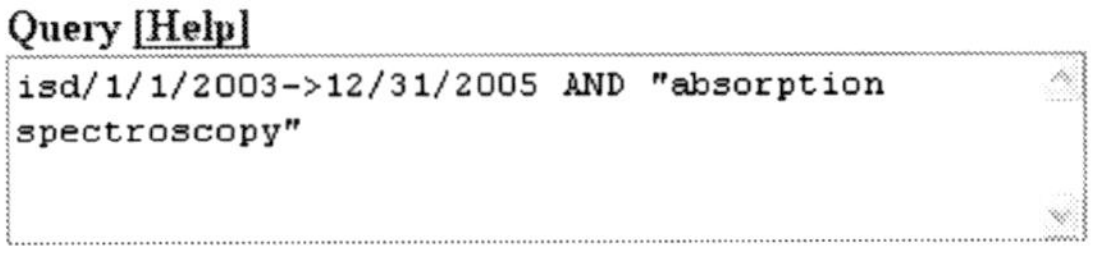

Query [Help]

```
isd/1/1/2003->12/31/2005 AND "absorption
spectroscopy"
```

Figure 14 (Source: USPTO Website)

ISD/1/1/2003->12/31/2005 AND
"absorption spectroscopy"

To apply the Issue Date field code (ISD) to a range of dates we use the (->) operator, that is; a dash character (-), immediately followed by a greater than character (>). One gathers that the intent of the -> operator is to resemble an arrow.

In Figure 14 we have combined the range of years with our search phrase using the Boolean AND operator. The results are shown in Figure 15, below.

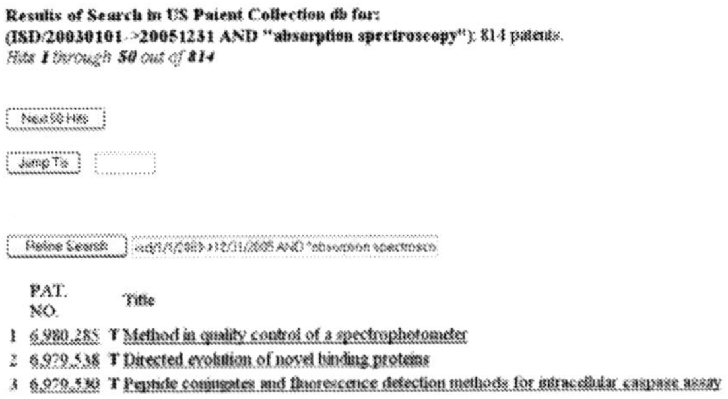

Results of Search in US Patent Collection db for:
(ISD/20030101->20051231 AND "absorption spectroscopy"): 814 patents.
Hits 1 through 50 out of 814

[Next 50 Hits]

[Jump To] [   ]

[Refine Search] isd/1/1/2003->12/31/2005 AND "absorption spectrosc

PAT. NO.	Title
1	6,980,285 T Method in quality control of a spectrophotometer
2	6,979,538 T Directed evolution of novel binding proteins
3	6,979,530 T Peptide conjugates and fluorescence detection methods for intracellular caspase assay

Figure 15 (Source: USPTO Website)

Comparing Figures 13 and 15, we can see that the number of hits has been reduced from 4759 to 814.

Searcher's Secret Number 9

To apply the Issue Date field code (ISD) to a range of dates use the (->) operator. For example:

ISD/1/1/2003->12/31/2005

6. Navigating the Search Results

One of the most interesting inventors that I have ever met is a man named Dr. Robert L. Forward. Dr. Forward has a Ph.D. in gravity physics (for his Doctoral Thesis, Dr. Forward built the world's first bar gravitational radiation detector - now on display at the Smithsonian), and worked at Hughes Research Labs for over 30 years. During his time at Hughes and since retiring, Dr. Forward has been granted several patents. To search for all of the patents issued to Dr. Forward since 1976 we compose the following query:

IN/Forward-Robert-L

Here we have used the inventor name field code; IN, followed by the name of the inventor, last name first. Also note the placement of a dash (-) between the last and first name, and between the first name and the middle initial. This search command is shown in Figure 16 below.

Query [Help]

```
IN/Forward-Robert-L
```

Figure 16 (Source: USPTO Website)

The results of our search are shown in Figure 17 below. Here we see a list of patents issued to Dr. Forward, since 1976. To see the text of the first patent, just click on it with the mouse. This is shown in Figure 18.

Results of Search in 1976 to present db for:
IN/Forward-Robert-L: 20 patents.
Hits 1 through 20 out of 20

Jump To

Refine Search   IN/Forward-Robert-L

PAT. NO.	Title
1	6,431,497 **T** Failure resistant multiline tether
2	6,419,191 **T** Electrodynamic tether control
3	6,386,484 **T** Failure resistant multiline tether
4	6,290,186 **T** Planar hoytether failure resistant multiline tether
5	6,286,788 **T** Alternate interconnection hoytether failure resistant multiline tether
6	6,260,807 **T** Failure resistant multiline tether
7	6,173,922 **T** Failure resistant multiline tether
8	6,116,544 **T** Electrodynamic tether and method of use
9	5,183,225 **T** Statite: spacecraft that utilizes sight pressure and method of use

Figure 17 (Source: USPTO Website)

At the top Figure 18 are a series of buttons or quick links. Calling your attention to the second row from the top, you will see three buttons. These are labeled Hit List, Next and Bottom. These buttons allow you to quickly navigate through a list of patents. After you have finished reading the text of patent number 6,431,497, you can immediately jump to the next patent on the list of returned patent hits by clicking on the button labeled "Next." This saves you the extra step involved in going back to the patent list, and then selecting the next patent title. The patent search results are listed chronologically, from the most recent to the oldest patent on the list.

United States Patent   6,431,497

Hoyt , et al.   August 13, 2002

Failure resistant multiline tether

Abstract

A tether having the special technical feature of multiple primary load-bearing lines and normally slack secondary lines. These primary and secondary lines are connected together with knotless, slipless interconnections so the tether maintains high strength and some of the lines can be cut without failure of the tether when it is operated near the ultimate failure load of the material from which it is constructed. This tether can safely carry load hundreds of times longer than prior art tethers in harsh environments where a single-line tether experiences a substantial risk of failure. The specific industrial applications of an electrodynamic tether system to deorbit satellites and a low Earth orbit to lunar surface tether transport system are all part of the general innovative concept of the invention.

Figure 18 (Source: USPTO Website)

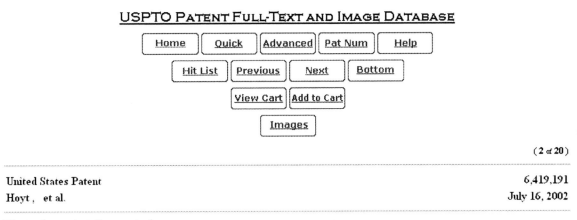

United States Patent   6,419,191

Hoyt , et al.   July 16, 2002

Electrodynamic tether control

Abstract

The present invention comprises apparatus and methods for using and controlling electrodynamic tethers. The apparatus taught by the present invention uses an interconnected multiwire (compared to the long, narrow single wires of the prior art) conductive tether whose

Figure 19 (Source: USPTO Website)

After clicking on the Next button, you are presented with patent number 6,419,191 as shown in Figure 19. Now an extra directional button has appeared in the second row of links at the top of Figure 19. This button is labeled "Previous." As you might guess, clicking on this link allows you to immediately jump to the previous patent on the list. These Next and Previous buttons can save you a lot of time when reading through long lists of patent results.

By selecting the button labeled "Bottom" we are presented with the last patent on the list. By clicking on the button labeled "Hit List" we are immediately returned to our hit list summary of patent titles.

Patent number 5,183,225 issued to Dr. Forward (number 9 in our list), illustrates another truism of the PTO's patent search database; typos. The title of the patent reads: Statite: spacecraft that utilizes <u>sight</u> pressure and method of use. However, a quick read of the patent abstract reveals that the invention actually uses <u>Light</u> pressure. This is another

reason why a through patent search should include a search of the Manual of Classification, with subsequent review of all patents found in the appropriate class/ subclass. While a typo may rob you of a keyword hit, the patent should still be listed in the appropriate classification.

7. Using Wildcards

Wildcards can also be used for advanced patent searches. Let's suppose that you constructed the query:

> ISD/1/1/1991->12/31/1995 AND ABST/((Fireproof OR Firestop) AND building)

The results for searching the abstracts of patents, from the years 1991 through 1995 are shown in Figure 20 below. As you can see, there were 10 hits or occurrences of our

Results of Search in 1976 to present db for:
(ISD/19910101->19951231 AND ABST/((Fireproof OR Firestop) AND building)): 10 patents.
Hits 1 through 10 out of 10

Jump To	

Refine Search	ISD/1/1/1991->12/31/1995 AND ABST/((Fireproof OR F

PAT. NO.   Title

1 5,426,908 **T** <u>Method of construction using corrugated material</u>

2 5,425,207 **T** <u>Method of constructing buildings and other structures using corrugated material</u>

3 5,417,019 **T** <u>Passthrough device with firestop</u>

Figure 20 (Source: USPTO Website)

search query. To widen the scope of our search to include words like fireplace, firewall, and firetrap we could use a series of OR statements like the following:

> ISD/1/1/1991->12/31/1995 AND ABST/((Fireproof OR Firestop OR Fireplace OR Firewall OR Firetrap) AND building)

But a more through and efficient approach would be to use the wildcard $ to substitute for any characters occurring after the word fire. Now our search command looks like:

> ISD/1/1/1991->12/31/1995 AND ABST/(Fire$ AND building)

The results of this query are shown in Figure 21 below. As you can see, there are now 111 hits, as opposed to 10 hits for our previous search.

In Figure 21 we have actually skipped a step. Here we have taken advantage of the Refine Search box. This is the entry box shown in the center of Figure 20. For each search results listing, the PTO patent server program copies your input query into this entry box. If you want to make a slight change to the query and resubmit it, you can do it right from the results web page. Instead of using the back arrow to return to the advanced search page, just type your changes into this box and click on Refine Search.

Searcher's Secret Number 10

Use the Refine Search box to save time when making minor changes to search queries.

Results of Search in 1976 to present db for:
(ISD/19910101->19951231 AND ABST/(Fire$ AND building)): 111 patents.
Hits 1 through 50 out of 111

[Next 50 Hits]

[Jump To] [   ]

[Refine Search] | ISD/1/1/1991->12/31/1995 AND ABST/(Fire$ AND build

PAT. NO.   Title
1 5,475,364 **T** Room occupancy fire alarm indicator means and method
2 5,473,849 **T** Building wall and method of constructing same
3 5,467,565 **T** Method and apparatus for improved activation of services in an office building floor

Figure 21 (Source: USPTO Website)

B. Searching Published Patent Applications at the PTO's website

In addition to the full-text and drawings of all patents issued since 1976, the PTO's Internet site also allows you to search patent applications published since March 15th, 2001. The techniques for searching the Published Applications Full-Text database (AppFT) are almost identical to those used with the Issued Patents (PatFT) database.

1. Patent Applications Quick Search

As shown in Figure 22, below, the main search page for the Published Applications database is located at the same web address as the main search page for the Issued Patents database. Namely:

www.uspto.gov/patft

To perform a Quick Search of the AppFT database, click on the "Quick Search" link illustrated in Figure 22. Note that now we are using the links on the right hand column. You will then be presented with the webpage shown in Figure 23, below.

You can see from Figure 23 that the Quick Search pages for the issued patents and published patent applications databases are almost identical. One major difference of note is that there is only one selection of the "Select years" pull-down menu for the Published Applications database; 2001-present.

To compose a Quick Search query of published patent applications, use the same methods previously covered for a Quick Search of issued patents in Chapter 3.

Issued Patents (PatFT)
(full-text since 1976, full-page images since 1790)

- Quick Search
- Advanced Search
- Patent Number Search

- View Patent Full-Page Images
    How to View Patent Images

- Status & Event History
- Database Contents
- Help Files

Published Applications (AppFT)
(published since 15 March 2001)

- Quick Search
- Advanced Search
- Publication Number Search

- View Publication Full-Page Images
    How to View Published Application Images

- Status & Event History
- Help Files

Figure 22 (Source: USPTO Website)

Query [Help]

Term 1: fire   in Field 1: Title

AND

Term 2: protection   in Field 2: Title

Select years [Help] 2001-present   Search   Reset

Figure 23 (Source: USPTO Website)

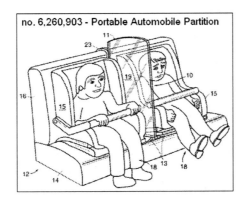

no. 6,260,903 - Portable Automobile Partition

For example, to search the Title fields of published patent applications since 2001 for the words Fire and Protection, we would fill in the Quick Search fields as shown in Figure 23. To perform the search, just click on the Search button.

The results are shown in Figure 24, below. Under the heading Results of Search in PGPUB Production Database, the system has reported 100 "hits" or patent applications in which our two search terms were found.

To view the full-text of a particular patent application, just click on the applications title or Publication Number.

Also notice, that the results are displayed in groups of 50. To see the next group of search results just click on the "Next 50 Hits" button.

The full-text of patent application 20070066165 is shown in Figure 25, below. Here, you can review the inventors name and patent abstract. By scrolling down the page, you can see the current classification, claims and description.

By clicking on the Images button at the top of Figure 25, you may review the drawings of the patent application (if you have loaded an Image Viewer program – see Chapter 3, Section D).

Searching PGPUB Production Database...

Results of Search in PGPUB Production Database for:
TTL/fire AND TTL/protection: 100 applications.
Hits 1 through 50 out of 100

Next 50 Hits

Jump To

Refine Search   TTL/fire AND TTL/protection

	PUB. APP. NO.	Title
1	20070066165	Fire protection coating for FRP-reinforced structure
2	20070051271	Composition for a fire-protection agent for materials and fire-protection method
3	20070039744	Tunnel fire protection system

Figure 24 (Source: USPTO Website)

US PATENT & TRADEMARK OFFICE
PATENT APPLICATION FULL TEXT AND IMAGE DATABASE

[Help] [Home] [Boolean] [Manual] [Number] [PTDLs]
[Hit List] [Next List] [Next] [Bottom]
[View Shopping Cart] [Add to Shopping Cart]
[Images]

(1 of 100)

United States Patent Application	20070066165
Kind Code	A1
Fyfe; Edward R.	March 22, 2007

Fire protection coating for FRP-reinforced structure

Abstract

A fire protection coating 10 includes insulation layer 20 including at least 20% free moisture. Insulation layer 20, preferably a vermiculite/gypsum mixture 26, is applied such as by spraying a water slurry of the mineral particles to structural member 85. Before the free moisture can evaporate, diffusion barrier 40, such as artificial stone formulation 44, is applied over the moist vermiculite/gypsum mixture 26. Moisture is retained within vermiculite/gypsum mixture 26 indefinitely and is released in the event of a fire to help cool and prolong the efficacy of fire protection coating 10.

Figure 25 (Source: USPTO Website)

2. Patent Applications Advanced Search

To get to the advanced search page, click on the Advanced Search link shown in Figure 22, above. The result is shown in Figure 26, below.

From Figure 26 we see that the Advanced Search pages for the issued patents and published patent applications databases are also almost identical. Again, the major difference is that the "Select years" pull-down menu for the Published Applications is limited to "2001-present."

In Figure 26 we have composed the query "Fire AND Protection AND (Building OR Structure). To see the results of this search, click on the search button shown in the figure. These results are displayed in Figure 27, below.

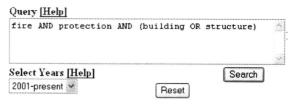

Query [Help]

```
fire AND protection AND (building OR structure)
```

Select Years [Help]   [Search]
[2001-present]   [Reset]

Figure 26 (Source: USPTO Website)

Searching PGPUB Production Database...

Results of Search in PGPUB Production Database for:
fire AND protection AND (building OR structure): 9142 applications.
*Hits **1** through **50** out of **9142***

Next 50 Hits

Jump To

Refine Search   fire AND protection AND (building OR structure)

	PUB. APP. NO.	Title
1	20070067880	Isolation of Proteins Involved in Posttranscriptional Gene Silencing and Methods of Use
2	20070067862	Chloroplast transgenic approach to express and purify human serum albumin, a protein highly susceptible to proteolytic degradation
3	20070067735	Graphical user interface
4	20070067121	Revenue class power meter with frequency rejection

Figure 27 (Source: USPTO Website)

3. Patent Applications Search by Application Number

To search by patent application number, select the Publication Number Search link in Figure 22, above. You will then be presented with the webpage shown in Figure 28 below. To review a particular patent application, just enter the application number into the query box. In the figure, we have entered patent application 20070066165. To see the results, click on Search. These results are shown in Figure 29 below.

One difference between the Patent Applications number search and the Issued Patents numbers search is that when an issued patent number is entered, the results page displays the patent immediately. In the case of the patents applications number search, an extra step is required. In Figure 29 we are presented with a Hit Summary consisting of the single patent application we were searching for. To actually review this patent application it is necessary to click on the patent application number or title. We are then shown the patent application as displayed in Figure 25, above.

Searching PGPUB Production Database...

Results of Search in PGPUB Production Database for:
DN/20070066165: 1 applications.
*Hits **1** through **1** out of **1***

Jump To

Refine Search   DN/20070066165

PUB. APP. NO. Title
1 20070066165   Fire protection coating for FRP-reinforced structure

Figure 29 (Source: USPTO Website)

Query [Help]
20070066165

Example:
Utility   : 20010000044   Search

Figure 28 (Source: USPTO Website)

Summary

Advanced Searching at the PTO Website
- Multiple Boolean operators can be combined with parenthesis to produce highly focused searches.
- Wildcards and phrase searches are allowed.
- Field Codes can be used to limit your search to specific sections of the issued patent.

- The date range operator (->) can be used to specify the range of years to be searched.
- Search results are summarized in lists. An example is all patents issued to a particular inventor. Navigation Buttons can be used to quickly move through the list.

Searching Published Patent Applications
- Published Patent Applications can be searched by Quick Search, Advanced Search and Application Number

Patent Searching at the EPO Website

So far, we have limited our Internet patent searches to the resources provided by the PTO. However, it is also important to look beyond the United States in any thorough prior art search. Prior art is not limited to inventions patented in the U.S. Patents issued in other countries are also considered valid prior art. This chapter introduces you to the patent search resources available at the Internet site for the European Patent Office.

A. Patent Searching at the EPO

To get to the EPO patent search website, you need the following address:

ep.espacenet.com

A portion of the EPO's homepage is shown in Figure 1 below. From the figure we see that there are four types of searches that can be performed: Quick, Advanced, Number and Classification. We will examine each of these search capabilities in the sections below.

1. Quick Search

To perform a quick search at the EPO website click on the "Quick Search" link shown in Figure 1, below. You will then be presented with the webpage shown in Figure 2, below.

From the figure, there are 3 steps to performing a Quick Search at the EPO website; select a search database, choose the type of search and enter your search terms. The first step is to select a search Database. The available selections are: Worldwide, EP and WIPO.

The World Intellectual Property Organization (WIPO) is a United Nations agency that administers many international treaties dealing with different aspects of intellectual property protection. This database selection enables you to search in the patent applications published by the WIPO (WO publications) in the last 24 months. Only the bibliographic data of WO patent documents can be searched and displayed.

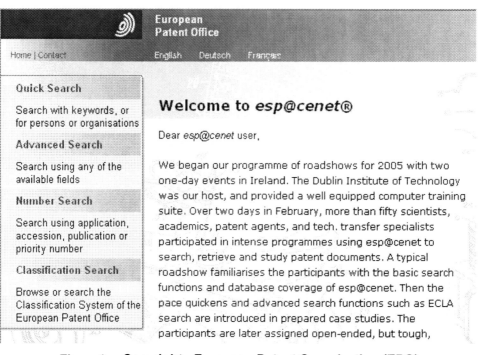

Figure 1 - Copyright : European Patent Organization (EPO)

Quick Search

1. Database

Select the patent database in which you wish to search:

Database: Worldwide

Worldwide
Patent Abstracts of Japan
EP - esp@cenet
WIPO - esp@cenet

2. Type of search

Select whether you wish to search with simple words in the titles or abstracts (where available) or with the name of an individual or organisation:

Select what to search:
⊙ Words in the title or abstract
○ Persons or organisations

3. Search terms

Enter search terms (not case sensitive):

Search term(s): fire AND protection   plastic AND bicycle

SEARCH   CLEAR

Figure 2 - Copyright : European Patent Organization (EPO)

The European Patent (EP) applications database selection enables you to search the patent applications published by the European Patent Office over the last 24 months.

In both the WIPO and the EP databases, it is not possible to perform searches either in the abstract field or using a European Classification symbol.

The default selection is the Worldwide database. The worldwide database enables you to search for information about published patent applications from 80 different countries. This database also contains abstracts of non- examined Japanese patent applications filed by Japanese applicants since October 1976 and all Japanese patent applications filed since 1998 which do not have a Japanese priority (originally filed outside Japan).

As of November 2006, this amounted to approximately 56 million patents. The list of countries covered by the worldwide database along with their corresponding Country Codes, are shown in the table to the right. The importance of these country codes will become apparent when we view our search results, presently.

It is also important to note that the content of the worldwide database varies from country to country. Some country collections have abstracts and international classification codes, while others may not even have a title. The detailed coverage of the worldwide database - as of January 2007 - is available online at:

patentinfo.european-patent-office.org/_resources/data/pdf/global_patent_data_coverage.pdf

CC	Name
AP	African Regional Industrial Property Organization
AR	Argentina
AT	Austria
AU	Australia
BA	Bosnia and Herzegovina
BE	Belgium
BG	Bulgaria
BR	Brazil
CA	Canada
CH	Switzerland
CN	China
CS	Czechoslovakia (up to 1993)
CU	Cuba
CY	Cyprus
CZ	Czech Republic
DD	Germany, excluding the territory that, prior to 3 October 1990, constituted the Federal Republic of Germany
DE	Germany
DK	Denmark
DZ	Algeria
EA	Eurasian Patent Organization
EE	Estonia
EG	Egypt
EP	European Patent Office
ES	Spain
FI	Finland
FR	France
GB	United Kingdom
GR	Greece
HK	Hong Kong
HR	Croatia
HU	Hungary
IE	Ireland
IL	Israel
IN	India
IT	Italy
JP	Japan

KE	Kenya
KR	Republic of Korea
LT	Lithuania
LU	Luxembourg
LV	Latvia
MC	Monaco
MD	Republic of Moldova
MN	Mongolia
MT	Malta
MW	Malawi
MX	Mexico
MY	Malaysia
NC	New Caledonia
NL	Netherlands
NO	Norway
NZ	New Zealand
OA	African Intellectual Property Organization
PH	Philippines
PL	Poland
PT	Portugal
RO	Romania
RU	Russian Federation
SE	Sweden
SG	Singapore
SI	Slovenia
SK	Slovakia
SU	Union of Soviet Socialist Republics (USSR)
TJ	Tajikistan
TR	Turkey
TT	Trinidad and Tobago
TW	Taiwan
UA	Ukraine
US	United States of America
VN	Vietnam
WO	World Intellectual Property Org. (WIPO)
YU	Yugoslavia
ZA	South Africa
ZM	Zambia
ZW	Zimbabwe

Table 1 – Country Codes (Source: EPO Website)

The next step is to select a Type of Search. There are two radio box selections available: (see Figure 2, above) Words in the Title or Abstract, or Persons and Organizations.

The third and final step (bottom of Figure 2) is to enter one or more search terms which may be connected by Boolean operators.

In Figure 2 we have selected the worldwide database, elected to search for words in the Title or Abstract, and entered the query Fire AND Protection. To begin the search, click on the Search button shown at the bottom of Figure 2. The results are shown in Figure 3, below.

From the summary at the top of the figure we see that there were 5100 hits returned from the worldwide database. The first three hits are shown in the figure. For each hit we are shown the Title of the document (a link which will take you to a further description of the patent), the inventor's name, the applicant (not necessarily the same as the inventor), the European Classification symbols (EC – a link to a classification description), the International Patent Classification symbols (IPC) and the Publication information (Publication Number and date).

After clicking on the patent title from hit number 1 in Figure 3 (Fire/smoke protection zone) you will see a further description of the patent illustrated in Figure 4, below.

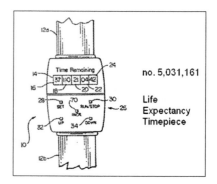

RESULT LIST
Approximately **5100** results found in the Worldwide database for:
fire AND protection in the title or abstract
Only the first **500** results are displayed.
(Results are sorted by date of upload in database)
The result is not what you expected? Get assistance ◎

1 | **Fire/smoke protection zone formation system** | in my patents list ☐

Inventor: SATOH HIROOMI (JP); KURIOKA HITOSHI (JP); (+3)
Applicant: HOCHIKI CO (JP); KAJIMA CORP (JP)
EC: A62C2/08; A62C3/02
IPC: *A62C2/08; A62C3/00; A62C3/02* (+7)
Publication info: **TW259097B** - 2006-08-01

2 | **Environmental-heatproof fireproofing composition and method** | in my patents list ☐

Inventor: LU WEN-HUA (TW)
Applicant: LU WEN-HUA (TW)
EC:
IPC: (IPC1-7): C08L1/00
Publication info: **TW259841B** - 2006-08-11

3 | **FIRE PROTECTION SYSTEM** | in my patents list ☐

Inventor: FREITAG RUDIGER (DE); PANZNER GERRIT (DE); (+2)
Applicant: SCHOTT AG (DE); FOGTEC BRANDSCHUTZ GMBH & CO K (DE)
EC: A62C2/06; A62C2/08
IPC: *A62C2/06; A62C2/08*; A62C2/00
Publication info: **KR20070004689** - 2007-01-09

Figure 3 - Copyright : European Patent Organization (EPO)

Fire/smoke protection zone formation system

Bibliographic data	Description	Claims	Mosaics	Original document	INPADOC legal status

Publication number: TW259097B
Publication date: 2006-08-01
Inventor: SATOH HIROOMI (JP); KURIOKA HITOSHI (JP); AMANO REIKO (JP); IZUSHI YOUICHI (JP); TSUJI TOSHIHIDE (JP)
Applicant: HOCHIKI CO (JP); KAJIMA CORP (JP)
Classification:
- international: *A62C2/08; A62C3/00; A62C3/02; A62C31/12; A62C35/68; A62C2/00; A62C3/00; A62C31/00; A62C35/58*; (IPC1-7): A62C2/08
- European: A62C2/08; A62C3/02
Application number: TW20040107786 20040323
Priority number(s): JP20030101077 20030404; JP20040006545 20040114

View INPADOC patent family
View list of citing documents

Report a data error here

Abstract of **TW259097B**
Fire/smoke protection zone formation system, comprising head rows formed by arranging a plurality of water curtain heads, in rows, on the ceiling surfaces or side wall surfaces of a tunnel-shaped object in the boundaries of the zones formed at specified intervals in the longitudinal direction to form water curtains by jetting water, control valves controllably opened and closed to supply pressurized water to the head rows and stop the pressurized water, and a control device controllably opening, if fire occurs, the control valves installed in the head rows positioned in the boundaries of the zones on both sides of the zones where the fire occurs to form the water curtains by spraying water from the head rows. In the head rows, the plurality of heads having the water curtain heads for spraying water with averaged particle diameters of 30 to 500 microns are disposed in rows.

Data supplied from the *esp@cenet* database - Worldwide

Figure 4 - Copyright : European Patent Organization (EPO)

In Figure 4 we see that the various sections of patent information are separated by tabs: Bibliographic data, Description, Claims, Mosaics, Original document and legal status. The default display is to show the Bibliographic data which includes the patent abstract. To review another section of the patent, just click on its corresponding tab. In the example above, these tabs are grayed out because the information is not available. An example mosaic of the patent drawings from another patent is shown in Figure 5, below. You will need the Adobe reader (freely available from www.Adobe.com) installed to view the images.

Before moving on to Advanced and Classification searching, a further discussion of classification symbols is in order. The International Patent Classification (IPC) has a hierarchical structure:

Sections	e.g. A
Classes	e.g. A47
SubClasses	e.g. A47J
Groups	e.g. A47J37
Subgroups	e.g. A47J37/06

The IPC is used by patent offices of various countries, often in addition to a national classification. The IPC classification system currently divides technology into approximately 68,000 subareas.

The European Classification System (ECLA) is an extension of the IPC. It is used by the European Patent Office (EPO) to classify patent applications. The EPO classification system adds subgroups to the IPC symbol:

| ECLS subgroups | e.g. A47J37/06**C** |
| | or   A47J37/06**C3** |

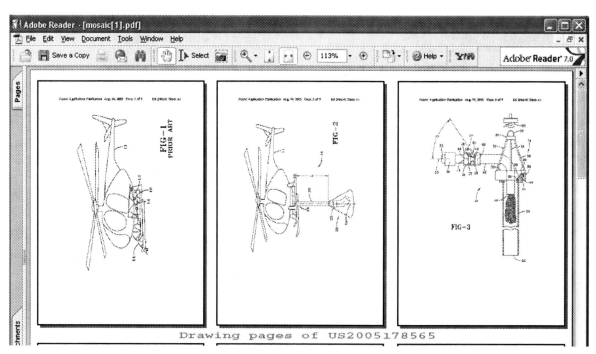

Figure 5 - Copyright : European Patent Organization (EPO)

2. Advanced Search

To perform an advanced search at the EPO website click on the "Advanced Search" link shown in Figure 1, above. You will then be presented with the webpage shown in Figure 6, below.

As seen in the figure, there are now several fields available to narrow your search results. For example, in Figure 6 we have entered the years 2006 and 2007 to limit our returned search matches to those years. In the Keywords field we have repeated the search query Fire AND Protection. Note that you are limited to a maximum of four search terms in each search field. The results of the search are shown in Figure 7, below.

As shown in the figure, the number of hits has been reduced from 5100 to 361 just by limiting the years to be searched.

Advanced Search

1. Database

Select patent database: [Worldwide ▼]

2. Search terms

Enter keywords in English

Keyword(s) in title:	[ ]	plastic and bicycle
Keyword(s) in title or abstract:	[Fire AND Protection]	hair
Publication number:	[ ]	WO03075629
Application number:	[ ]	DE19971031696
Priority number:	[ ]	WO1995US15925
Publication date:	[2006 2007]	yyyymmdd
Applicant(s):	[ ]	Institut Pasteur
Inventor(s):	[ ]	Smith
European Classification (ECLA):	[ ]	F03G7/10
International Patent Classification (IPC):	[ ]	H03M1/12

[SEARCH]   [CLEAR]

Figure 6 - Copyright : European Patent Organization (EPO)

RESULT LIST   Refine search
Approximately **361** results found in the Worldwide database for:
Fire AND Protection in the title or abstract AND **2006 2007** as the publication date
(Results are sorted by date of upload in database)
The result is not what you expected? Get assistance ◯

1 Fire/smoke protection zone formation system   in my patents list ☐

Inventor: SATOH HIROOMI (JP); KURIOKA   Applicant: HOCHIKI CO (JP); KAJIMA CORP (JP)
HITOSHI (JP); (+3)
EC: A62C2/08; A62C3/02   IPC: *A62C2/08; A62C3/00; A62C3/02* (+7)
Publication info: **TW259097B** - 2006-08-01

2 Environmental-heatproof fireproofing composition and method   in my patents list ☐

Inventor: LU WEN-HUA (TW)   Applicant: LU WEN-HUA (TW)
EC: IPC: (IPC1-7): C08L1/00
Publication info: **TW259841B** - 2006-08-11

3 FIRE PROTECTION SYSTEM   in my patents list ☐

Inventor: FREITAG RUDIGER (DE); PANZNER   Applicant: SCHOTT AG (DE); FOGTEC
GERRIT (DE); (+2)   BRANDSCHUTZ GMBH & CO K (DE)
EC: A62C2/06; A62C2/08   IPC: *A62C2/06; A62C2/08; A62C2/00*
Publication info: **KR20070004689** - 2007-01-09

Figure 7 - Copyright : European Patent Organization (EPO)

Of particular significance is the patent classification. For the first patent (Fire/smoke protection zone formation system) shown in Figure 7, there are three IPC symbols: A62C2/08, A62C3/00 and A62C3/02. Note that a maximum of three IPC or ECLA classifications will be displayed in the results. If a patent is allocated to more than three classes, this is shown by a plus sign "+" followed by the number of additional classes. In this case there are seven additional classes denoted by "(+7)." From the classification discussion in the previous section we know that the first three IPC characters (A62) signify Section A, Class 62 in the IPC Classification hierarchy.

To use the IPC classification to further limit the search results, we enter A62 in the IPC field as shown in Figure 8, below, and repeat the search. The results are shown in Figure 9.

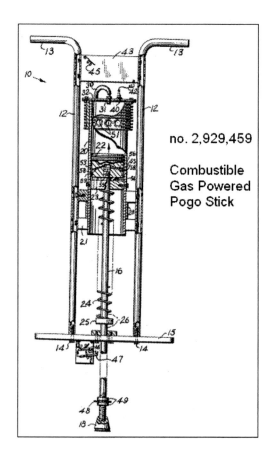

no. 2,929,459

Combustible
Gas Powered
Pogo Stick

Advanced Search

1. Database

Select patent database: Worldwide

2. Search terms

Enter keywords in English

Keyword(s) in title:		plastic and bicycle
Keyword(s) in title or abstract:	Fire AND Protection	hair
Publication number:		WO03075629
Application number:		DE19971031696
Priority number:		WO1995US15925
Publication date:	2006 2007	yyyymmdd
Applicant(s):		Institut Pasteur
Inventor(s):		Smith
European Classification (ECLA):		F03G7/10
International Patent Classification (IPC):	A62	H03M1/12

SEARCH   CLEAR

Figure 8 - Copyright : European Patent Organization (EPO)

RESULT LIST
Approximately **108** results found in the Worldwide database for:
Fire AND Protection in the title or abstract AND **2006 2007** as the publication date AND **A62** as the IPC classification
(Results are sorted by date of upload in database)
The result is not what you expected? Get assistance ◑

Refine search

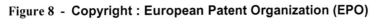

1 Fire/smoke protection zone formation system   in my patents list ☐

Inventor: SATOH HIROOMI (JP); KURIOKA HITOSHI (JP); (+3)
EC: A62C2/08; A62C3/02
Publication info: **TW259097B** - 2006-08-01

Applicant: HOCHIKI CO (JP); KAJIMA CORP (JP)
IPC: *A62C2/08; A62C3/00; A62C3/02* (+7)

2 FIRE PROTECTION SYSTEM   in my patents list ☐

Inventor: FREITAG RUDIGER (DE); PANZNER GERRIT (DE); (+2)
EC: A62C2/06; A62C2/08
Publication info: **KR20070004689** - 2007-01-09

Applicant: SCHOTT AG (DE); FOGTEC BRANDSCHUTZ GMBH & CO K (DE)
IPC: *A62C2/06; A62C2/08*; A62C2/00

3 Fire protection   in my patents list ☐

Inventor: WOBBEN ALOYS
EC:
Publication info: **AU2007200375** - 2007-02-22

Applicant: WOBBEN ALOYS
IPC: *A62C3/00; A62C3/16; A62C39/00* (+6)

Figure 9 - Copyright : European Patent Organization (EPO)

3. Classification Search

To perform a classification search at the EPO website click on the "Classification Search" link shown in Figure 1, above. You will then be presented with the webpage shown in Figure 10, below. In the figure the main European Classification sections A through H are displayed. Across the top of the display are two search boxes. The center search box allows you to search the European classification index by keyword. The box to the right of Figure 10 allows you to retrieve the class description for a specific class/subclass.

Search the european classification

View Section	Find classifications(s) for keywords		Find description for a symbol	
Index A B C D E F G H	e.g. mast sail	Go	e.g. A23C	Go

Next page: A

HUMAN NECESSITIES	A ☐
PERFORMING OPERATIONS; TRANSPORTING	B ☐
CHEMISTRY; METALLURGY	C ☐
TEXTILES; PAPER	D ☐
FIXED CONSTRUCTIONS	E ☐
MECHANICAL ENGINEERING; LIGHTING; HEATING; WEAPONS; BLASTING ENGINES OR PUMPS	F ☐
PHYSICS	G ☐
ELECTRICITY	H ☐

☐ show notes   Expand groups   Copy to searchform: Copy Clear

Figure 10 - Copyright : European Patent Organization (EPO)

The class section letters are hypertext links that lead to a breakdown of the classes contained within that section. Figure 11 shows this breakdown for Section A - Human Necessities.

From the previous section we determined that IPC codes A62C2/08, A62C3/00 and A62C3/02 were germane to our fire protection patent search. To get a further breakdown of Section/Class A62 we can click on that link as well (see Figure 11). In this manner we can keep drilling down the class hierarchy until we reach the description we need. For example, the description for A62C3/00 is shown in Figure 12.

Clicking inside the checkbox next to the A62C3/00 class designation shown in Figure 12, causes the designation to be copied into the "Copy to searchform" entry box shown at the bottom of the figure. This is actually a shortcut method for producing a list of every issued patent within that class. Clicking the "Copy" button shown at the lower right of Figure 12, causes the Advance search panel to popup, with the appropriate ELCA classification already filled in. This

View Section	Find classifications(s) for keywords	Find description for a symbol
Index A B C D E F G H	e.g. mast sail [Go]	e.g. A23C [Go]

Next page: A01

HUMAN NECESSITIES	A ☐
AGRICULTURE; FORESTRY; ANIMAL HUSBANDRY; HUNTING; TRAPPING; FISHING	A01 ☐
BAKING; EDIBLE DOUGHS	A21 ☐
BUTCHERING; MEAT TREATMENT; PROCESSING POULTRY OR FISH	A22 ☐
FOODS OR FOODSTUFFS; THEIR TREATMENT, NOT COVERED BY OTHER CLASSES	A23 ☐
TOBACCO; CIGARS; CIGARETTES; SMOKERS' REQUISITES	A24 ☐
WEARING APPAREL	A41 ☐
HEADWEAR	A42 ☐
FOOTWEAR	A43 ☐
HABERDASHERY; JEWELLERY	A44 ☐
HAND OR TRAVELLING ARTICLES	A45 ☐
BRUSHWARE	A46 ☐
FURNITURE (arrangements of seats for, or adaptations of seats to, vehicles B60N); DOMESTIC ARTICLES OR APPLIANCES; COFFEE MILLS; SPICE MILLS; SUCTION CLEANERS IN GENERAL (ladders E06C)	A47 ☐
MEDICAL OR VETERINARY SCIENCE; HYGIENE	A61 ☐
LIFE-SAVING; FIRE-FIGHTING (ladders E06C)	A62 ☐
SPORTS; GAMES; AMUSEMENTS	A63 ☐

☐ show notes   Expand groups   Copy to searchform: [   ]   [Copy] [Clear]

Figure 11 - **Copyright : European Patent Organization (EPO)**

HUMAN NECESSITIES	A ☐
LIFE-SAVING; FIRE-FIGHTING (ladders E06C)	A62 ☐
FIRE-FIGHTING (fire-extinguishing compositions, use of chemical substances in extinguishing fires A62D1/00; spraying, applying liquids or other fluent materials to surfaces in general B05; alarm arrangements G08B, e.g. fire alarms actuated by smoke or gases G08B17/10)	A62C ☐
Fire prevention, containment or extinguishing specially adapted for particular objects or places ([N: in oil wells E21B29/08, A62C35/00; in mines or tunnels E21F5/00]; for nuclear reactors G21C9/04)	A62C3 ☐
	A62C3/00 ☑

Figure 12 - **Copyright : European Patent Organization (EPO)**

Advanced Search

1. Database

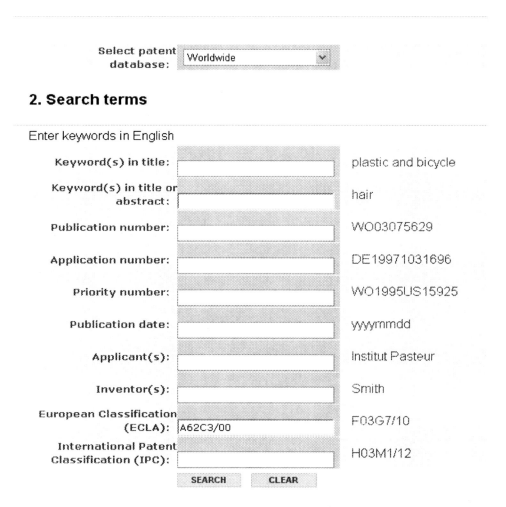

Select patent database: Worldwide

2. Search terms

Enter keywords in English

Keyword(s) in title:	plastic and bicycle
Keyword(s) in title or abstract:	hair
Publication number:	WO03075629
Application number:	DE19971031696
Priority number:	WO1995US15925
Publication date:	yyyymmdd
Applicant(s):	Institut Pasteur
Inventor(s):	Smith
European Classification (ECLA): A62C3/00	F03G7/10
International Patent Classification (IPC):	H03M1/12

SEARCH   CLEAR

Figure 13 - Copyright : European Patent Organization (EPO)

action is shown in Figure 13, above. To produce a list of all the patents within the ECLA class A62C3/00, just click the search button shown at the bottom of Figure 13. The result is shown in Figure 14.

If you already know the class symbols you can go directly to a description of that class by entering the those symbols into the description box shown at the right of Figure 15. You can also search the European Classification hierarchy by entering

keywords into the search box shown at the center of Figure 15.

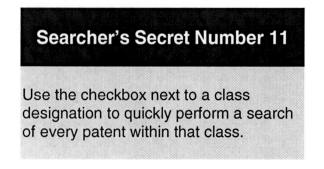

Searcher's Secret Number 11

Use the checkbox next to a class designation to quickly perform a search of every patent within that class.

RESULT LIST   Refine search

Approximately **799** results found in the Worldwide database for:
A62C3/00 as the European Classification
Only the first **500** results are displayed.
(Results are sorted by date of upload in database)
The result is not what you expected? Get assistance ○

| 1 | METHOD FOR TREATMENT OF AN ARTICLE | in my patents list ☐ |

Inventor: LUOMALA O (FI)   Applicant: CENTAUREA OY (FI)
EC: A62C3/00; B05D5/12; (+6)   IPC: *H05F1/02; A62C3/00; B05D5/12* (+15)
Publication info: **DE69836018T** - 2007-02-22

| 2 | Method and device for combatting fire in enclosed spaces aboard an aircraft | in my patents list ☐ |

Inventor: BOBENHAUSEN AXEL (DE)   Applicant: AIRBUS GMBH
EC: A62C2/06B; A62C3/00; (+2)   IPC: *A62C2/06; A62C3/00; A62C3/08* (+8)
Publication info: **ES2262056T** - 2006-11-16

| 3 | Venting device for a tunnel | in my patents list ☐ |

Inventor: VIGH ANDREAS (CH)   Applicant: VOGT AG FEUERWEHRGERAETE UND F (CH)
EC: A62C27/00; A62C3/00; (+1)   IPC: *A62C27/00; A62C3/00; A62C31/03* (+3)
Publication info: **EP1741473** - 2007-01-10

Figure 14 - Copyright : European Patent Organization (EPO)

Search the European classification

View Section	Find classifications(s) for keywords	Find description for a symbol
Index A B C D E F G H Y	[ ] Go	A62C3/00 Go

Figure 15 - Copyright : European Patent Organization (EPO)

4. Number Search

To perform a patent number search at the EPO website click on the "Number Search" link shown in Figure 1, above. You will then be presented with the webpage shown in Figure 16, below.

In Figure 16 we have selected the Worldwide database and entered the patent number "CH480276." This patent was one of the foreign patents referenced in the Sakamoto patent (5,462,805) titled, Fire-protection and safety glass panel (see Chapter 3, Figure 15). To conduct the search, click on the Search button shown at the bottom of Figure 16. The results are shown in Figure 17. To read a description of this patent, click on the patent title. This result is shown in Figure 18.

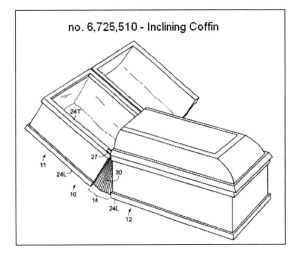

no. 6,725,510 - Inclining Coffin

Number Search

1. Database

Select the patent database in which you wish to search:

Database: [Worldwide   ▾]

2. Enter number

Enter either an application, accession, publication or priority number with country code prefix

Publication number: [CH480276   ]   WO03075629
                        [☐ Including family   ]

              [SEARCH]   [CLEAR]

Figure 16 - Copyright : European Patent Organization (EPO)

RESULT LIST
1 result found in the Worldwide database for:
CH480276 (priority or application number or publication number)
(Results are sorted by date of upload in database)
The result is not what you expected? Get assistance ⊘

1	**Verbundsicherheitsscheibe**

Inventor: PEILSTOECKER GUENTER DR (DE); DIETZEL   Applicant: BAYER AG (DE)
KARL DR (DE)
EC: B32B17/10C4; B32B27/00   IPC: C03C27/12; B32B7/12
Publication info: **CH480276** - 1969-10-31

Figure 17 - Copyright : European Patent Organization (EPO)

In Figure 18 we have clicked on the description panel. From our country code table we see that the two-letter designation "CH" refers to Switzerland. It is also apparent from the text of the patent description that it was written in German. What good does this do you if you don't happen to read German? Well, it just so happens that a number of online translation services that can solve this problem for you.

One currently free service is located at the following website address:

babelfish.altavista.com

The above link will bring you to the Babel Fish Translation website where you will find a pull-down menu that allows you to select various translations.

Verbundsicherheitsscheibe

| Bibliographic data | **Description** | Claims | Mosaics | Original document | INPADOC legal status |

Description of CH480276

Verbundsicherheitsscheibe Die handelsüblichen Verbundsicherheitsscheiben be stehen aus zwei etwa 2 bis 4, vorzugsweise etwa 3 mm dicken Glasplatten, die durch eine etwa 0,05 bis 1,0, vorzugsweise etwa 0,1 bis 0,5 mm dicke Schicht aus einem elastischen Klebemittel, in der Regel weich- macherhaltigem Polyvinylbutyral, miteinander verkittet sind.

Diese Verbundscheiben halten bei Raumtemperatur im allgemeinen Stössen mit einer Energie bis zu etwa 1,5 mkp stand. Bei stärkeren Belastungen werden sie durchstossen. In einem solchen Fall ist es der Vorteil dieser Scheiben, dass die Hauptmenge der dabei entste henden Glassplitter nicht abspringt, sondern von der Klebeschicht festgehalten wird und der Rest energielos herunterfällt. Erfolgt der Durchstoss aber durch einen menschlichen Körperteil, z. B. den Kopf, etwa bei einer Automobil-Windschutzscheibe, so besteht für diesen Körperteil dennoch die Gefahr schwerer Schnittverlet zungen, nämlich durch Bildung der sogenannten Hals krause .

Figure 18 - Copyright : European Patent Organization (EPO)

Searcher's Secret Number 12

Use an online translation service, such as Babelfish, to translate the text of Foreign patents.

Summary

Patent Searching at the EPO Website
- Use Quick Search to search through patent titles and abstracts.
- Use Advanced Search to narrow the scope of your search results.
- Use Country Codes to determine the country of origin for any foreign patents.
- Use Classification Search to determine the appropriate Class/subclass for relevant patents.
- Use Number Search if the patent number is known.
- Use a translation service to translate foreign language patents.

Chapter
6

Additional Patent Search Websites

Figure 1 - The Intellectual Property Office of Singapore Website

There are numerous additional patent search websites besides the USPTO and the EPO. Some of the searching services these websites offer are free, others services involve a fee. In this chapter we will review a number of these additional intellectual property searching resources and the services they offer.

A. SurfIP

SurfIP is a dedicated search engine that provides users with a wide range of IP related value-added services. Through SurfIP, users can retrieve IP information by using its power search features, discover new IP commercialization opportunities or even search for IP service professionals.

To get to the SurfIP patent search website, you will need the following address:

www.SurfIP.com

The SurfIP homepage is shown in Figure 1, above. SurfIP is an initiative of the Intellectual Property Office of Singapore (IPOS) - a statutory board under the Ministry of Law that advises on and administers intellectual property (IP) laws, promotes awareness and provides the infrastructure to facilitate the development of IP in Singapore. SurfIP is developed and operated by the Intellectual Property Exchange Pte. Ltd. (IPEXL), an Intellectual Property consultancy based in Singapore.

Database Coverage

The data sources covered in Patent Searches are as follows:

USPTO	covers granted patents from the US Patent and Trademark Office
EPO	covers patent applications published in the last 24 months, from the European Patent Office
IPOS	covers patent documents from the Intellectual Property Office of Singapore
SIPO	covers patent documents from the State Intellectual Property Office of the P.R.C.
CIPO	covers granted patents from the Canadian Intellectual Property Office
WIPO	covers PCT publications from the World Intellectual Property Organization
TIPO	covers patent bibliographic data provided by Chinese Taipei Patent Index
UKPO	covers patent applications published in the last 24 months, from the UK Patent Office
KIPO	covers patent documents from the Korean Intellectual Property Patent Office
TIPIC	covers patent documents from the Thailand Industrial Property Information Center
PM	covers descriptions of patent mapping and analysis reports, from Patentmaps.com

Table 1 – SurfIP Patent Search Database Coverage

At SurfIP, a user can do patent searches across multiple databases and then sort, aggregate and integrate the results. When a user enters a search query, that query is performed at the various sites using the search engines of the sites. Selection boxes are used instead of command line interfaces that require users to remember syntax and filenames. To perform a patent search at the SuftIP website, click on the Patent – Search Inventions across the Globe – link shown at the upper left of Figure 1. You will then be presented with the webpage shown in Figure 2, below.

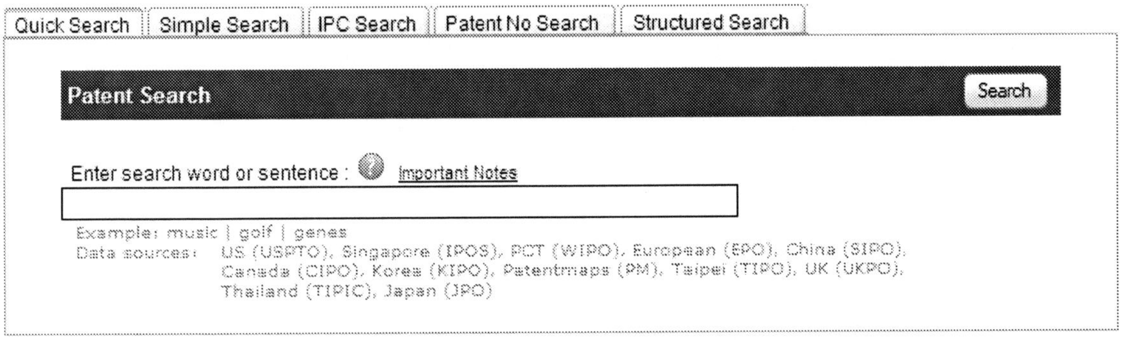

Figure 2 – SurfIP Quick Patent Search

There are five types of searches that can be performed: Quick Search, Simple Search IPC Search, Patent Number Search and Structured Search. The Quick Search (Shown in Figure 2, above) is meant to provide results with minimal user configuration. It searches all available patent data sources. The user can simply enter the search criteria and start the search.

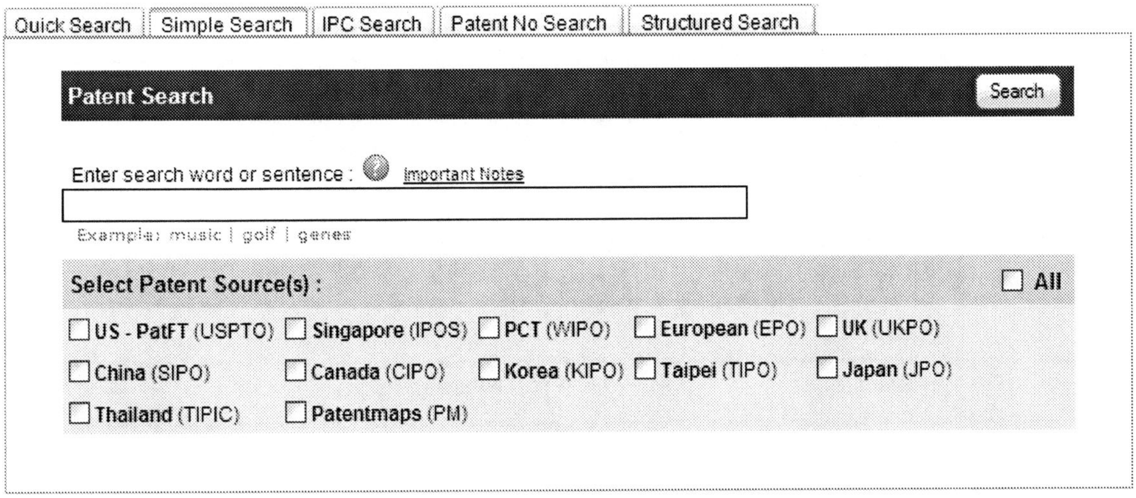

Figure 3 – SurfIP Simple Patent Search

In Simple Search, the user can search in one or more patent data sources. These data sources are selected by clicking on the appropriate box as shown in Figure 3, above. Clicking the ALL option selects all available patent sources.

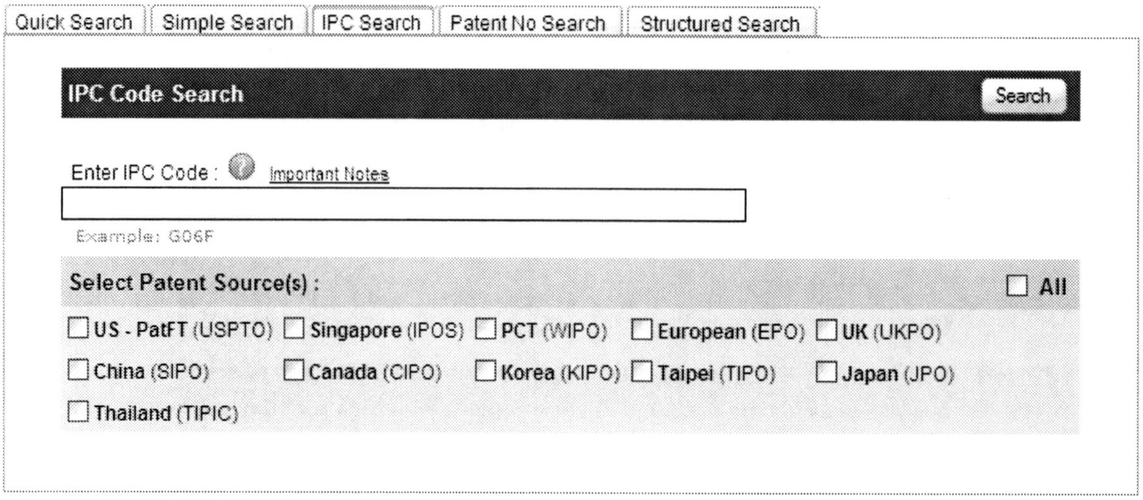

Figure 4 – SurfIP IPC Patent Search

Figure 4 shows the next Tab selected at the SurfIP website; IPC Search. In IPC Search, the user can search by International Patent Classification (IPC) codes. The results display all patent documents classified under the queried subclass, group or subgroup. For information on IPC listings, please refer to the World Intellectual Property Organization's website (www.wipo.int/portal/index.html.en) on International Classifications (www.wipo.int/classifications/fulltext/new_ipc/ipcen.html).

The table below shows the entry format for IPC search for different sources. Truncation searching is supported by some sources.

Data Source	Sub-Class Format	Group & Sub-Group Format
USPTO	G06F*	G06F 19/00
WIPO	G06F	G06F-19/00
EPO	G06F	G06F 19/00
IPOS	G06F	G06F 19/00; G06F 19*
SIPO	G06F*	G06F19/00, G06F19*
CIPO	G06F	G06F 19/00
TIPO	G06F	G06F19/00
UKPO	G06F	G06F19/00
KIPO	G06F	G06F 19/00
TIPIC	G06F	G06F19

Table 2 – IPC Entry Format

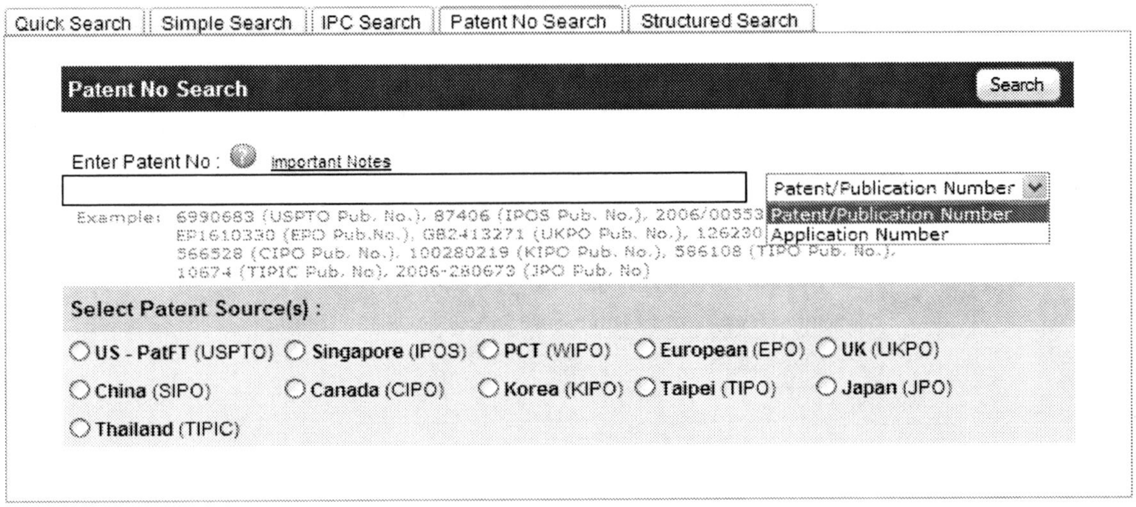

Figure 5 - SurfIP Patent Number Search

Figure 5 shows the next Tab selected at the SurfIP website; Patent Number Search. In Patent Number Search, the user can search for published patent applications and granted patents where available by entering the appropriate patent number. Please note that searching the Application Number in USPTO currently returns the Application Serial No. of US Granted Patents. Actual Application numbers search from USPTO will only be available when the US Patent Applications database (AppFT) is added.

The entry format for Application Number and Publication Number search differs from source to source. The table below illustrates the correct format that should be entered in the various data sources. Entering the number in other formats may lead to inaccurate results.

Data Source	Application Number Format	Publication Number Format
USPTO	845948	6990683
WIPO	EP/2004/008531	2005/098230
EPO	EP20020762866	EP1333613
IPOS	200507268-1	117045
SIPO	100762	1309841
CIPO	2172863	566528
TIPO	90121515	595092
UKPO	GB20040008721	GB2413271A
KIPO	1019980006278	100280219
TIPIC	13884	10674

Table 3 – Patent Number Search Formats

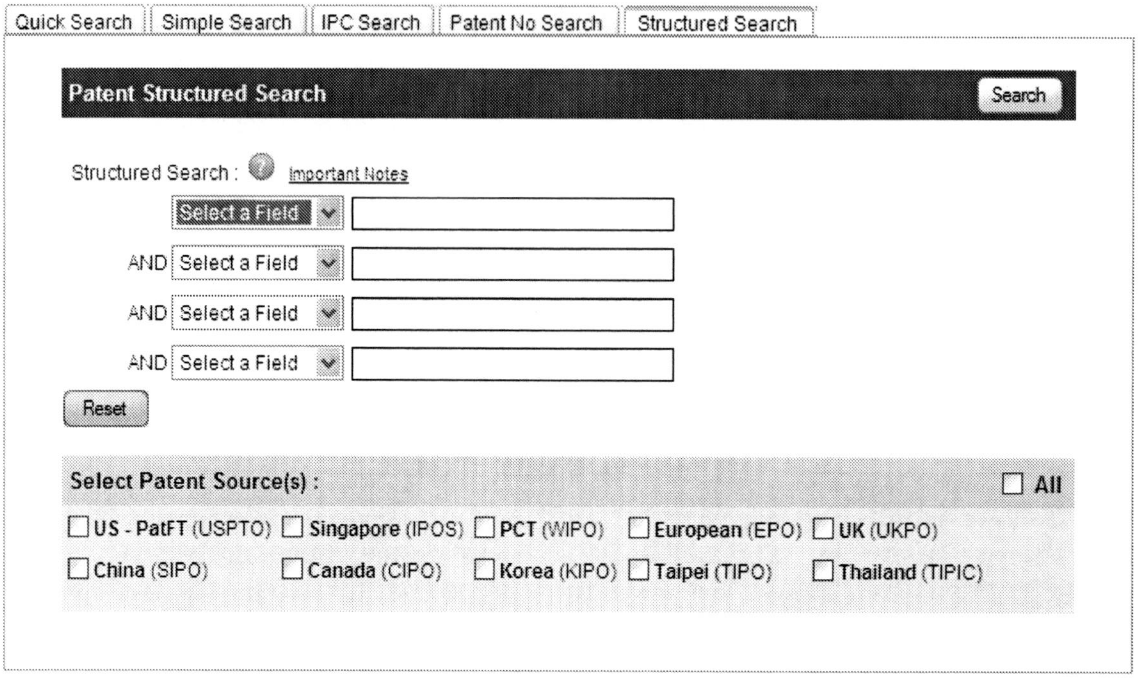

Figure 6 - SurfIP Structured Patent Search

Boolean and truncation searches are not supported for Application Number and Publication Number fields.

Figure 6 shows the next Tab selected at the SurfIP website; Structured Patent Search. In Structured Search, the user can search within individual fields of patent documents. Structured Search also provides for searching combinations of fields with the *AND* operator provided.

The same field should not be selected in more than one drop-down box. However, Patent Structured Search supports Boolean searching within the field. For instance, to search for **radio AND signal** in the **Title** field, the user should select the **Title** field **once** and enter the entire Boolean query in the corresponding text box, instead of selecting the **Title** field in two separate drop down boxes, keying **radio** and **signal** separately, and connecting them with an AND operator.

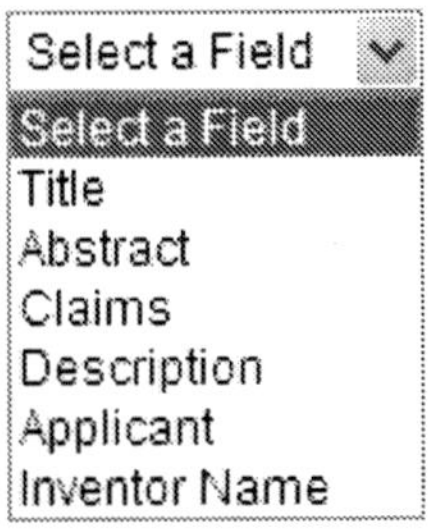

Figure 7 – Available Fields in SurfIP Structured Patent Search

Figure 7, above, shows the various fields available from the, 'Select a Field' pulldown menu. The table below shows the fields supported in Structured Search for available Patent data sources.

Data Source	Title	Abstract	Claims	Description	Applicant	Inventor
USPTO	✓	✓	✓	✓	✓	✓
WIPO	✓	✓	✓	✓	✓	✓
EPO	✓				✓	✓
IPOS	✓	✓			✓	✓
SIPO	✓	✓			✓	✓
CIPO	✓	✓	✓		✓	✓
TIPO	✓	✓			✓	✓
UKPO	✓				✓	✓
KIPO	✓	✓			✓	✓
TIPIC	✓	✓	✓		✓	✓

Table 4 – Structured Search Supported Fields

The Boolean operators available for searching include the **AND, OR** and **NOT** operators. The right truncation operator, *****, and the single truncation operator, **?,** can be used where supported. A search for **car*** will return patents containing the words: **carbon, cartel** etc., while a search for **car?** will return patents containing the words: **card, cars** etc.

A search for a phrase or a combination of words such as **motor vehicle** will return all patents containing the phrase **"motor vehicle"**. Note that putting the search phrase in quotes is not required. Phrases can also be searched in combination with Boolean searches - A search for **motor vehicle NOT car** will return all patents that contain the phrase **motor vehicle** and do not contain the word **car**.

Figure 8, below, shows the result of a Structured Search for **motor vehicle NOT car** in the abstract field of all available databases. Results from each source are displayed in separate tabs (in Figure 8 the Combined Result tab has been selected) and are presented as soon as they are returned. This ensures that the user can navigate through results and click on individual documents from a data source, even as documents from other data sources continue to load in the background in other tabs. This minimizes the waiting time before the user starts receiving results.

Results displayed from each source are presented according to relevance to the search term. At a higher level, results from all sources that have returned are combined and sorted in the Combined Results tab to allow the user a quick glance through the documents that best match the search terms among the list of documents displayed.

| Quick Search | Simple Search | IPC Search | Patent No Search | Structured Search |

Search Status and Summary: New Search

You searched for : Abstract=motor vehicle NOT car

| USPTO : 16745 | IPOS : 0 | WIPO : 9428 | EPO : Query not supported | UKPO : Query not supported |
| SIPO : 668 | CIPO : 1901 | KIPO : Network busy | TIPO : Network busy | TIPIC : Network busy |

| Combined Result | USPTO | WIPO | SIPO | CIPO |

Combined Results tab displays the first page of results from all sources that have returned. Please use the Next link in individual source tabs to browse for more results.
Displaying only 135 result(s).

S/N	App. / Pub. / Doc. No.	Title	Source Name	Relevance
1	2531139	Motor vehicle.	CIPO	★★★★
2	WO 2007/025820	Motor vehicle seat.	WIPO	★★★★
3	1272708	Motor vehicle lighting assembly.	CIPO	★★★★
4	7225695	Universally configurable motor vehicle transmission.	USPTO	★★★★
5	7229126	Motor vehicle roof with two openable covers.	USPTO	★★★
6	WO 2000/039655	Motor vehicle for educational driving.	WIPO	★★★
7	2059652	Transport apparatus.	CIPO	★★★
8	1311771	Suspension system.	CIPO	★★★
9	1255728	Electrically heatable window for motor vehicle.	CIPO	★★★
10	7222495	Motor vehicle cooling and depolluting device.	USPTO	★★★
11	88101841	Motor vehicle safeguard device and safe motor vehicle.	SIPO	★★★

Figure 8 – SurfIP Structured Patent Search Results

In addition to patent searching, by registering an account with SurfIP, users will be able to access patent search management tools that allow them to save, monitor and track their search results. Users can register an account at SurfIP using an email address and a Login ID.

B. Google Patent Search

Google is arguably the web's most popular search engine (see Chapter 7). Recently, Google has added the capability to search U.S. issued patents. One advantage that Google's patent search has over the USPTO's patent searching website is the ability to search older patents. Another advantage is that you can download a pdf document of the entire issued patent, including drawings. A disadvantage is that Google's patent database is not yet as current as the USPTO's. As of the date of this text (June 2007) the Google patent database has searchable patent documents from the 1790's through the middle of 2006. The USPTO's online patent database is updated weekly as the patents are issued. Another disadvantage of the Google site is that patent applications cannot currently be searched.

To get to the Google patent search website, you will need the following address:

www.Google.com/patents

Figure 9 – Google Patent Search Main Page

Figure 9 above shows the main page of the Google patent search website. Search terms can be typed directly into the search entry box located to the left of the 'Search Patents' button. A more precise search can be performed by clicking on the 'Advanced Patent Search' link shown to the right of the 'Search Patents' button in Figure 9. Clicking on the 'Advanced Patent Search' link brings up the webpage shown in Figure 10, below.

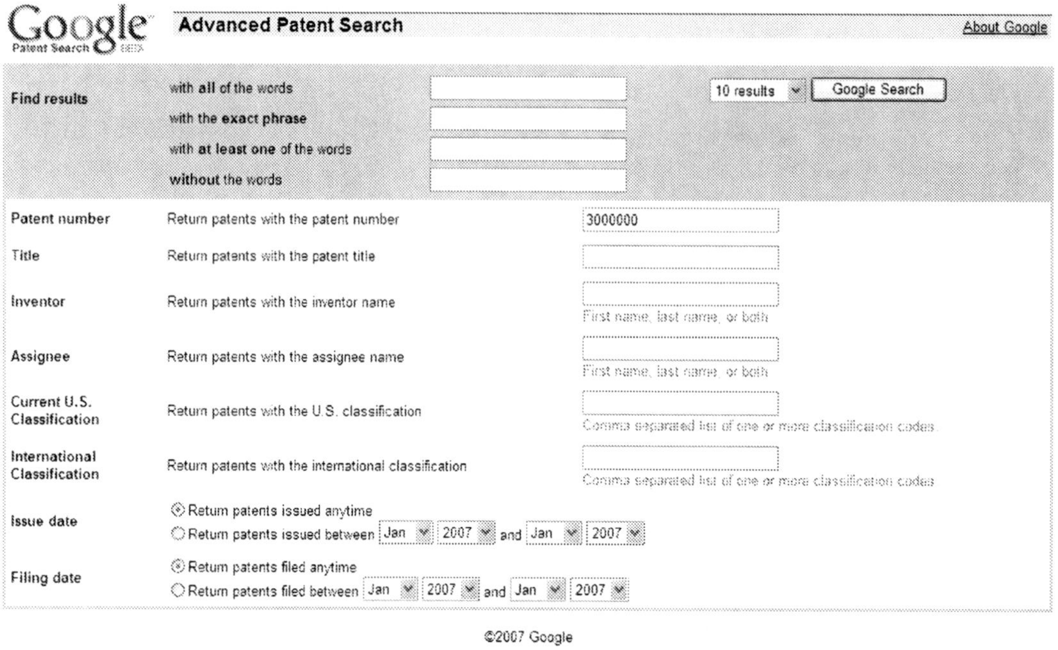

Figure 10 – Google Advanced Patent Search Webpage

On the Google Advanced Patent Search webpage, search results can be gathered in many ways. The first entry box shown in Figure 10 is labeled 'with **all** of the words.' This corresponds to the Boolean AND function covered earlier. Search terms placed in this entry box are ANDed together. The second entry box is labeled 'with the **exact phrase**.' This box allows multiple word phrases to be entered. Quotation marks are optional in this entry box. The third entry box, 'with **at least one** of the words,' corresponds to the Boolean OR function. Finally, the fourth entry box, '**without** the words,' corresponds to the Boolean NOT function and allows the user to exclude certain words from the search results.

Additionally, on the Google Advanced Patent Search webpage we can search by Patent Number, Patent Title, Inventor Name, Assignee Name, US Classification and International Classification. We can also restrict our search results to a range of Patent Issue and Filing Dates.

To illustrate some of the differences between patent searching on Google versus the USPTO website, we have constructed a simple query consisting of a single patent number (3,000,000) shown in Figure 10, above. After clicking on the 'Google Search' button, we are presented with the webpage shown in Figure 11, below.

In Figure 11 we are presented with a listing for an Automatic Reading System by K.R.Eldredge. The issue date on this patent is Sept. 12, 1961. This issue date precedes the 1976 cutoff date for full text patent searching on the USPTO website. To see the type of information available on Google's patent search website, click on the 'AUTOMATIC READING SYSTEM' link illustrated in Figure 11, below. You will then be presented with the webpage shown in Figure 12.

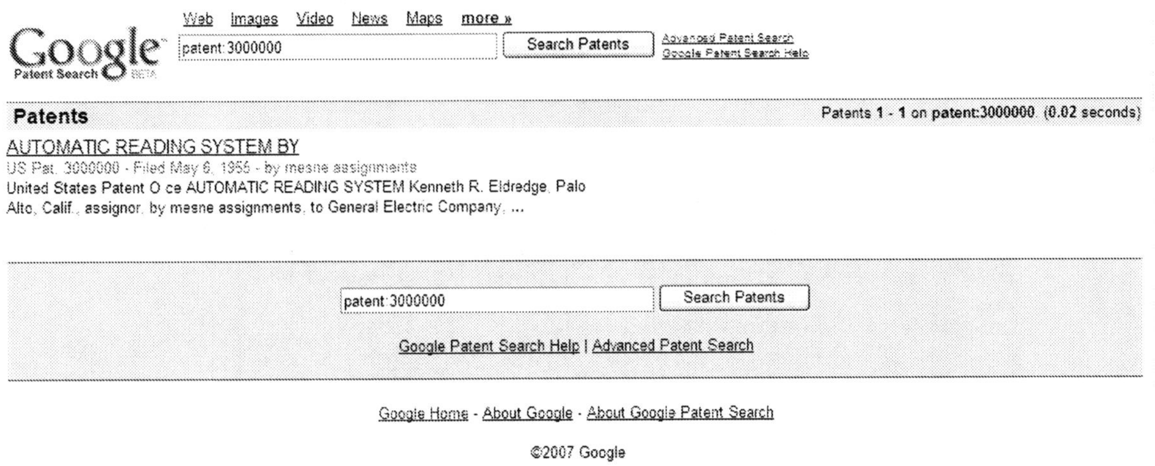

Figure 11 – Google Search By Patent Number

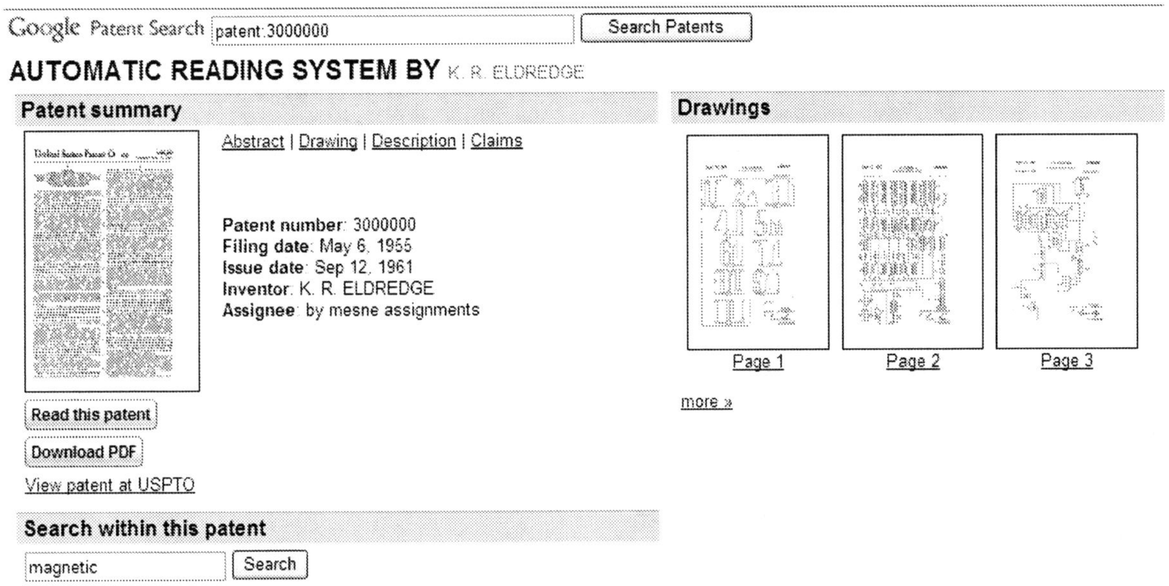

Figure 12 – Google Patent Search Result for Patent Number 3,000,000

In Figure 12 we see several links to the various sections of this 1961 patent. These links include the patent abstract, drawings, description and claims. Thumbnail sketches of the patent drawings are also displayed. Scanned images of the patent can be viewed by clicking on the patent front page image shown on the left hand side of Figure 12. Moving down the Figure we see a button labeled, 'Read this patent.' Clicking on this button will load scanned images of the patent with arrow controls right into your web browser. The next button down is labeled, 'Download PDF.' Getting a PDF copy of the complete patent is as easy as clicking on this button. Figure 13 shows the popup window that you will see if you elect to download a copy. Click 'Save' to save a copy on your computer hard disk.

A significant feature of the Google patent search website is the ability to search within these older patents. At the bottom of Figure 12 is a text search entry box labeled, 'Search within this patent. For our example the word, 'magnetic' has been entered into the search box. To perform this search, click on the adjacent button labeled, 'Search'. The results are shown in Figure 14, below.

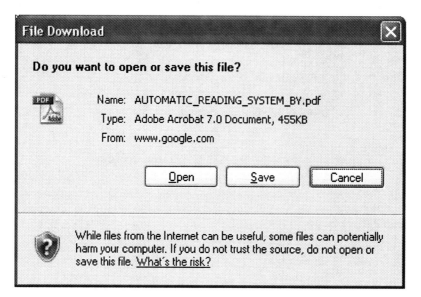

Figure 13 – Save Patent Document Popup Window

Search within this patent

magnetic   Search

Page 5
Such a writing material may be a **magnetic** ink, which is described and claimed in an application by Charles B. Clark for **Magnetic** Ink, filed 5 February, ...

Page 6
3000000 the numerals 0 through and the associated characteristic wave shapes obtained when these numerals are printed with **magnetic**-writing material, ...

Page 7
In any event, this embodiment of the invention illustrates how, from a character written with **magnetic** ink in human language, a wave shape is derived, ...

Page 8
For example, more than one **magnetic** head may be used to scan a character from different 5 directions, each of which provides a different unique wave shape ...

Page 9
3000000 of said characters is written with **magnetic** ink, each of said characters comprising a continuous distribution of **magnetic** ink on said document, ...

more »

Figure 14 – Google Search within Patent #3,000,000 Results

Figure 14 displays links to various occurrences of the search word within the patent document. To view a particular patent page of interest, click on the appropriate link. Figure 15, below, shows a typical page of the patent with the search term highlighted (also underlined for clarity) so that it can be read in the context of the rest of the patent. Google is able to accomplish this by using OCR software to search the scanned images of older patents and highlight the positions of our search words.

Performing the same patent number search on the USPTO website produces the webpage shown in Figure 16, below. Figure 16 informs us that Full text searching for patent 3,000,000 is not available. However, images of the patent pages can be viewed by clicking on the 'Images' button. After performing this action we are presented with the webpage illustrated in Figure 17. Here, we can scan the various pages of the older patent (see Chapter 3, Section D for a full discussion of the USPTO's patent image viewer program), but we cannot search within the text of the patent. The user can obtain a printout of the current displayed page of the patent by clicking on the print icon shown in the upper left of Figure 17. But the user cannot get a printout of the entire patent without viewing each patent page, one at a time.

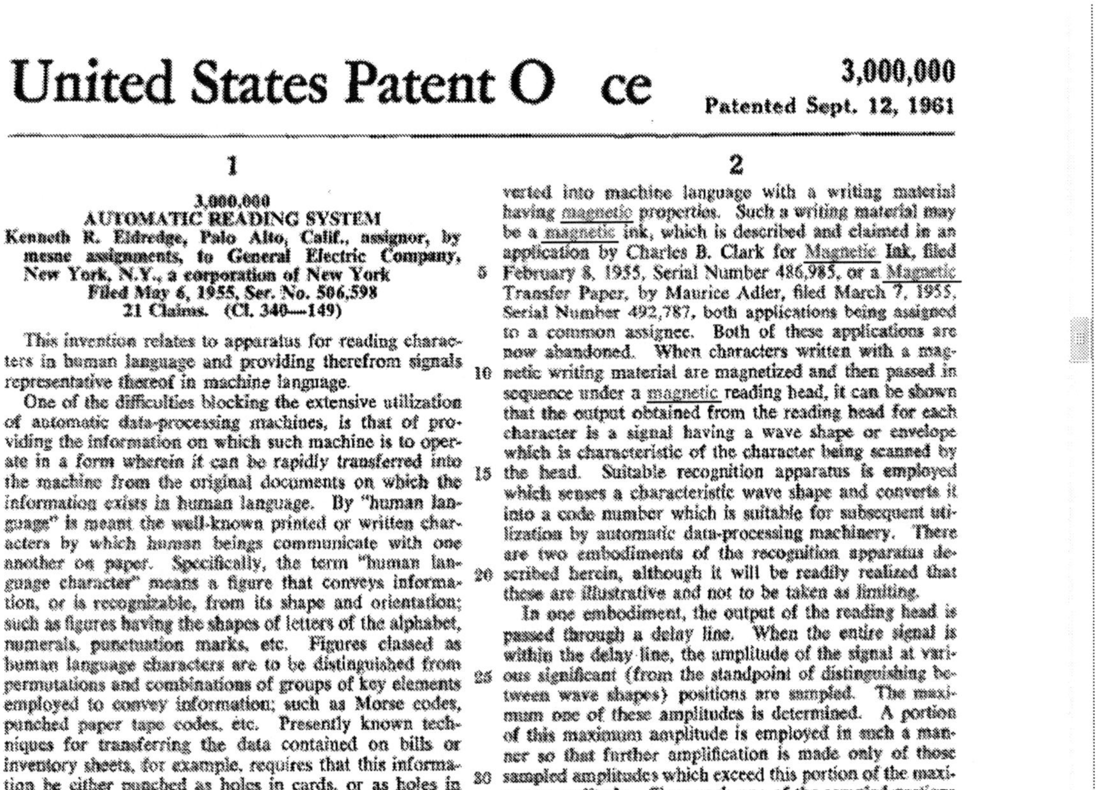

United States Patent O ce

3,000,000
Patented Sept. 12, 1961

1

3,000,000
AUTOMATIC READING SYSTEM
Kenneth R. Eldredge, Palo Alto, Calif., assignor, by mesne assignments, to General Electric Company, New York, N.Y., a corporation of New York
Filed May 6, 1955, Ser. No. 506,598
21 Claims. (Cl. 340—149)

This invention relates to apparatus for reading characters in human language and providing therefrom signals representative thereof in machine language.

One of the difficulties blocking the extensive utilization of automatic data-processing machines, is that of providing the information on which such machine is to operate in a form wherein it can be rapidly transferred into the machine from the original documents on which the information exists in human language. By "human language" is meant the well-known printed or written characters by which human beings communicate with one another on paper. Specifically, the term "human language character" means a figure that conveys information, or is recognizable, from its shape and orientation; such as figures having the shapes of letters of the alphabet, numerals, punctuation marks, etc. Figures classed as human language characters are to be distinguished from permutations and combinations of groups of key elements employed to convey information; such as Morse codes, punched paper tape codes, etc. Presently known techniques for transferring the data contained on bills or inventory sheets, for example, requires that this information be either punched as holes in cards, or as holes in paper tape, or be written magnetically in coded form on magnetic tape. Any one of these can then be fed by means of suitable input devices to an automatic data-

2

verted into machine language with a writing material having magnetic properties. Such a writing material may be a magnetic ink, which is described and claimed in an application by Charles B. Clark for Magnetic Ink, filed February 8, 1955, Serial Number 486,985, or a Magnetic Transfer Paper, by Maurice Adler, filed March 7, 1955, Serial Number 492,787, both applications being assigned to a common assignee. Both of these applications are now abandoned. When characters written with a magnetic writing material are magnetized and then passed in sequence under a magnetic reading head, it can be shown that the output obtained from the reading head for each character is a signal having a wave shape or envelope which is characteristic of the character being scanned by the head. Suitable recognition apparatus is employed which senses a characteristic wave shape and converts it into a code number which is suitable for subsequent utilization by automatic data-processing machinery. There are two embodiments of the recognition apparatus described herein, although it will be readily realized that these are illustrative and not to be taken as limiting.

In one embodiment, the output of the reading head is passed through a delay line. When the entire signal is within the delay line, the amplitude of the signal at various significant (from the standpoint of distinguishing between wave shapes) positions are sampled. The maximum one of these amplitudes is determined. A portion of this maximum amplitude is employed in such a manner so that further amplification is made only of those sampled amplitudes which exceed this portion of the maximum amplitude. Since each one of the sampled portions is preserved in what may be considered as its own channel, the last step provides a voltage pattern akin to an

Figure 15 – Google Patent Image with Search Term Highlighted

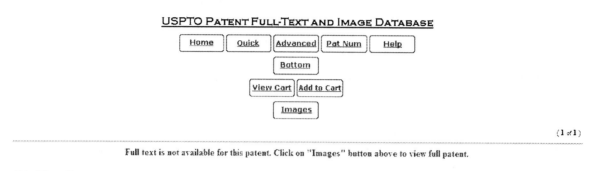

Full text is not available for this patent. Click on "Images" button above to view full patent.

United States Patent	3,000,000
Issue Date:	September 12, 1961
Current U.S. Class:	382/182 ; 235/449; 382/183; 382/320
Current International Class:	G06K 9/00 (20060101)

Figure 16 – USPTO Patent Search Result for Patent Number 3,000,000

Figure 17 – USPTO Patent Viewer Image

C. Some Fee-Based Patent Searching Websites

There are a number of Internet-based patent search systems that charge a fee for certain services. Many of these firms will perform much of the patent searching work for you, including searching foreign patent databases. Several other fee-based patent search companies are listed in Table 5, below.

Company	Web Address
Lexis / Nexis	www.lexisnexis.com
PatentCafe	www.patentCafe.com
Questel – Orbit Patent and Trademark Databases	www.questel.com
Thomson Scientific – Derwent World Patents Index	scientific.thomson.com/products/dwpi

Table 5 – Some Patent Search Service Companies

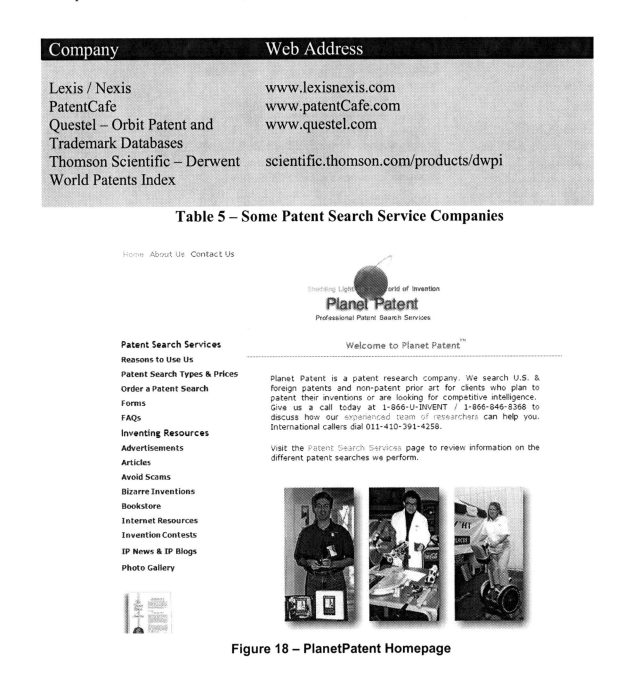

Figure 18 – PlanetPatent Homepage

Home   About Us   Contact Us

Shedding Light ... orld of Invention
Planet Patent
Professional Patent Search Services

Patent Search Services

Reasons to Use Us

Patent Search Types & Prices

Order a Patent Search

Forms

FAQs

Inventing Resources

Advertisements

Articles

Avoid Scams

Bizarre Inventions

Bookstore

Internet Resources

Invention Contests

IP News & IP Blogs

Photo Gallery

Patent Search Types and Prices

We specialize in aerospace, biomedical, biotech, business method, chemical, electrical, genetic, & mechanical patent searches.

TYPES OF PATENT SEARCHES AVAILABLE	PRICES
Novelty Search - Aerospace, Business Method, Electrical, Mechanical, & Software: Focuses on the most unique details of an invention or its most patentable qualities.	$375
Novelty Search - Chemical, Genetic, & Biotech: Focuses on the most unique details of an invention or its most patentable qualities.	$850*
Patent Collection Search: Shows the evolution of a technology over a specified period of time. Both expired and un-expired patents are included as references.	$850

Figure 19 – Partial List of PlanetPatent Services

A number of smaller patent service websites are also available. These websites will often provide custom services for a fee. One such website can be found at the following web address:

www.PlanetPatent.com

The homepage for PlanetPatent is shown in Figure 18, above. Figure 19 shows a partial list of some of the services available at this website. Mr. Glen Kotapish is the founder of Planet Patent. Mr. Kotapish is also the president of the Center for Patent Policy, www.PatentPolicy. org, a DC area patent policy think tank.

Summary

SurfIP
- Patent searches across multiple databases can be performed at the Intellectual Property Office of Singapore

Google Patent Search
- Google patent searches use OCR software to search the scanned images of older patents and highlight the positions of search words.

Some Fee-Based Patent Searching Websites
- A number of Internet-based patent search companies will perform much of the patent search work for you – for a fee.

Chapter

7

Additional Sources of Prior Art

So far in this book, we have restricted ourselves to patent searching resources. However, prior art is not limited to patented inventions. Any published information, from any corner of the globe, can prevent a patent from being granted. Even unpublished works, such as a Master's thesis, can be considered valid prior art. In this chapter, we will consider other prior art search resources. These resources include Internet search engines, government websites and industrial product and manufacturer listings. As you may recall from Chapter 1, the prior art for a given invention are those prior inventions (whether patented or not) that embody some of the same or similar elements as the current invention.

A. Internet Search Engines

To date, millions of commercial, educational and government websites have been established. These sites provide a wealth of information about current retail products and research into new product concepts. The Internet Domain Survey of January 2007 (compiled by Network Wizards (www.nw.com)) determined that there were over 433,000,000 host websites on the Internet.

So how do you search through all of this information to see if your invention idea has already been produced as a commercial product? Or, perhaps your idea is already the subject of ongoing government research. To efficiently search through millions of web pages, you make use of a program called a *search engine*. A search engine is a program that keeps track of the content of the various web pages on the Internet. The search engine then allows the user to seek specific web pages through keyword searching.

Typically, when a company creates a website, they register it with one or more of the Internet's major search engines. At a minimum, this involves providing a homepage address, contact information and some key search words. For example, if the company manufactures carbon dioxide lasers, then the search terms "laser" and "carbon dioxide" should be linked from the search engine to their webpage.

Figure 1 (Copyright Google.com – reprinted with permission)

In addition to using information supplied by registered companies, some search engines run programs called W*eb crawlers.* These programs automatically run around on the Internet, read web site information, and add it to the search engine's database.

One of the most powerful Internet search engines is called *Google*. To get to the Google search engine, you need to type the following address into your web browser:

www.google.com

Figure 1 above, shows the keyword entry section of the basic Google search page. Suppose that we have an idea for an invention that involves low-temperature physics. To search the WWW for that topic, we can type in the word Physics and the phrase "low temperature", as shown in Figure 1. At first thought, one would think that the two search terms should be connected with the Boolean operator AND. However, on the basic Google search page the AND operator is automatically applied to all search terms. We then click on the Google Search button at the lower left of the figure. The results are shown in Figure 2,

below. In the figure we see references to web pages that contain both the word Physics and the phrase "low temperature." To review any of these references in detail, just click on the title of the reference.

By clicking on the Advanced Search link at the right of Figure 1, we see the Google advanced search webpage shown in Figure 3, below. This screen gives us more options than the default AND combination of search keywords.

For example, suppose we want to find all web pages that contain the keywords Physics and Hydrogen. We would then type these two keywords into the first text entry box of Figure 3, labeled "with **all** of the words." The emphasis on all indicates that the keywords entered into this box will have the AND Boolean operator applied to them.

The text entry box directly below labeled, "with the **exact phrase**" is for entering a known search phrase. In this case we will search for "low temperature" as a phrase. Note that the quotation marks around the phrase are optional.

The next entry box labeled, "with **at**

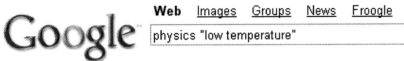

Web   Images   Groups   News   Froogle   Local   **more »**

physics "low temperature"   Search   Advanced Search
                                                         Preferences

Web   Results **1 - 10** of about **1,840,000** for **physics "low temperature"**. (0.15 seconds)

Tip: Save time by hitting the return key instead of clicking on "search"

Low Temperature Physics

Journal of Physical and Chemical Reference Data, published jointly by the National
Institute of Standards and Technology and the American Institute of ...
ltp.aip.org/ - 28k - Cached - Similar pages

Journal of **Low Temperature Physics**

Fundamental theoretical and experimental research developments in all areas of
cryogenics and **low temperature physics**.
www.kluweronline.com/issn/0022-2291 - Similar pages

> www.kluweronline.com/issn/0022-2291/contents
> Similar pages
> [More results from www.kluweronline.com]

Journal of **Low Temperature Physics**

Journal of **Low Temperature Physics** ... We are particularly interested in information
that would be useful to the **low temperature** community. ...
www.phy.duke.edu/~hm/JLTP/ - 2k - Cached - Similar pages

Figure 2 (Copyright Google.com – reprinted with permission)

Google   **Advanced Search**   Advanced Search Tips | Hurricane Katrina Resources - About Google

Find results	with **all** of the words	physics hydrogen		10 results ▾	Google Search
	with the **exact phrase**	"low temperature"			
	with **at least one** of the words	cryogenics cryogeny			
	without the words	nitrogen			
Language	Return pages written in		English ▾		
File Format	Only ▾ return results of the file format		any format ▾		
Date	Return web pages updated in the		anytime ▾		
Occurrences	Return results where my terms occur		anywhere in the page ▾		
Domain	Only ▾ return results from the site or domain		_e.g. google.com, .org More info_		
SafeSearch	◉ No filtering ○ Filter using SafeSearch				

Figure 3 (Copyright Google.com – reprinted with permission)

least one of the words," replicates the Boolean OR function. In this case, let us search for the word Cryogenics or cryogeny, as shown in the figure.

The fourth entry box labeled, "**without the words,**" is for excluding keywords from the search and duplicates the Boolean NOT operator. In our case, let us exclude the word nitrogen.

Other options on the Google advance search page allow you to specify the Language, File format, Date and other search criterion. For this search we will set the language to English (as shown in Figure

3) and leave the other settings at their default values.

To proceed with this search, click on the Google Search button shown to the upper right of Figure 3. The results are shown in Figure 4, below. From the top of Figure 2 we can see that 1,840,000 hits were returned as a result of our basic search. The top of Figure 4 shows that with the Google advanced search web page we have quickly reduced this by several orders of magnitude to 11,600.

Other popular Internet search engines include Yahoo and MSN search, as well as, a host of others.

Google

Web   Images   Groups   News   Froogle   Local   **more »**

physics hydrogen cryogenics OR cryogeny "low | Search | Advanced Search / Preferences

○ Search the Web ⦿ Search English pages

Web Results **1 - 10** of about **11,600 English** pages for **physics hydrogen cryogenics** OR **cryogeny "low temperature" -nitrogen**.

Tip: Save time by hitting the return key instead of clicking on "search"

Useful Reference Books in **Cryogenics**
various. **Low Temperature Physics**. various. Progress in **Cryogenics**. various ...
Selected Properties of **Hydrogen** (Engineering Design Data), NBS ...
www.yutopian.com/Yuan/References.html - 121k - Cached - Similar pages

Open Directory - Science: Technology: Cryotechnology
About Temperature - A good general discussion of the **physics** and concept
of "temperature ... **Cryogenics** (journal) - International journal of **low temperature** ...
dmoz.org/Science/Technology/Cryotechnology/ - 14k - Sep 13, 2005 - Cached - Similar pages

ScienceDaily -- Browse Topics: Science/Technology/Cryotechnology
Cryogenics (journal) - International journal of **low temperature** engineering
including applied ... The Nobel Prize in **Physics** 1996 - Awarded to David M. Lee, ...
www.sciencedaily.com/directory/ Science/Technology/Cryotechnology - 69k - Sep 13, 2005 - Cached - Similar pages

Oxford **Physics** - Library
6.3/COD, Codlin, Ellen M. **Cryogenics** and refrigeration: a bibliographical guide,
300794147 ... 6.3/GOR, Progress in **low temperature physics**, 300794158 ...
www.**physics**.ox.ac.uk/library/ list.asp?CID=6.0-6.9&lib=cl - 56k - Sep 13, 2005 - Cached - Similar pages

Figure 4 (Copyright Google.com – reprinted with permission)

B. The Thomas Register

In the previous section we looked for companies, products and research facilities that have published information on the WWW. But what about all those companies that don't have web pages? The Thomas Register industrial database has contact information for over 100,000 American and Canadian companies. Some of these companies have websites, but many do not. When a listed company has an established website, the Register provides a link to that Internet address. When a website does not exist, the Register provides contact information such as a physical address, telephone and fax number.

To get to the Thomas Register website, you need to type the following address into your web browser:

www.ThomasNet.com

The homepage for the Thomas Register is shown in Figure 5, below. Searching is a simple three-step process. First, we decide if we want to search for a product or service, company name, brand name or Industrial Web by selecting the appropriate tab from the top of Figure 5. Second, we enter a search keyword or keywords. Finally, we select the geographical area in which we wish to search.

Now let's suppose that we have an invention idea for a pneumatic (air-powered) motor. To search for similar products, we enter the keywords Pneumatic and Motor, select Product/Service from the central pull-down menu and for the widest possible geographical coverage we select All States/ Provinces from the Where pull-down menu. These selections are illustrated in Figure 5. Finally, we click on the search button, and the results are shown in Figure 6.

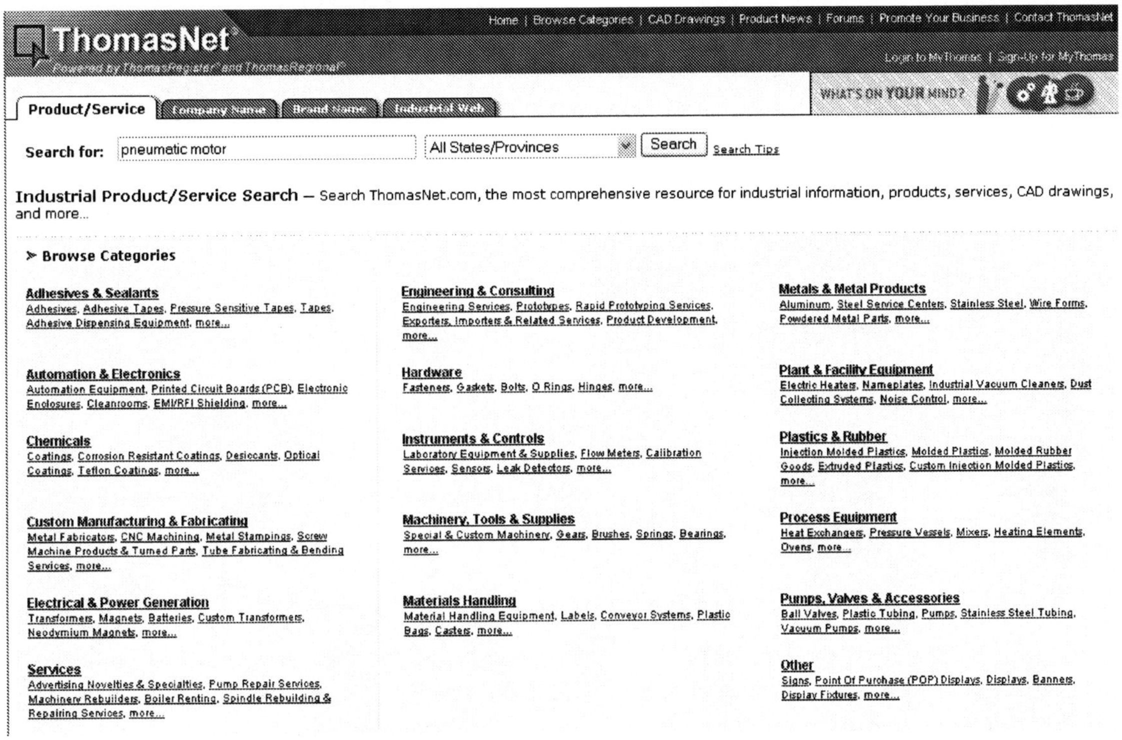

Figure 5 (Copyright ThomasNet - reprinted with permission)

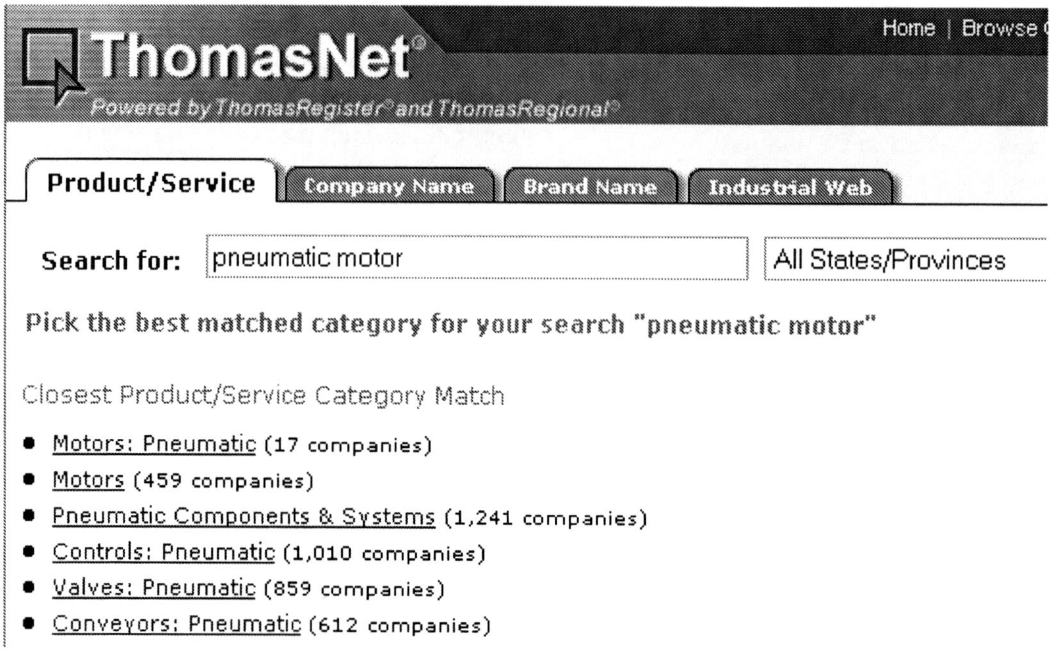

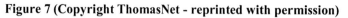

Figure 6 (Copyright ThomasNet - reprinted with permission)

Figure 7 (Copyright ThomasNet - reprinted with permission)

At the top of figure 6, seventeen (17) companies matching our product description (Motors: Pneumatic) were found. Other relevant category matches are listed below.

To get a listing of these companies, click on the 'Motors: Pneumatic' link. The results are shown in Figure 7, above.

Company Profile | News & Press Releases

Ingersoll-Rand Productivity Solutions
1467 Rte. 31 S., P.O. Box 1776
Annandale, NJ 08801
Phone: 908-238-7000
http://www.irtools.com
Website Links: Online Catalog | Site Map

Worldwide manufacturer of tools & equipment. Products include air & electric power tools, material handling equipment, fluid handling products, vehicle service tools & dispensing systems. Services include ergonomics consulting, installation, preventive maintenance, system monitoring, repair service, assembly solutions, aftermarket parts/service & industrial productivity. Assembly services include tools & systems design, precision fastening, ergonomic handling, engine starting & dispensing. Industry services include garage/vehicle service, automotive assembly, shipbuilding, appliance assembly & woodworking/furniture making. Markets served include aerospace, textile, pharmaceutical, special machine, vehicle service, government, automotive production, warehousing, electronics, transportation, manufacturing, construction & agriculture.

Activity: Manufacturer

Motors: Pneumatic Information

Manufacturer of pneumatic & air motors available in direct drive multivane, in-line planetary gear, gear drive piston, spur gear, milling & sawing models. Motors available in ranges from 0.11 hp to 30 hp. Available in speed ranging from 92 rpm to 26000 rpm. Available with 0.10 ft-lb. to 1090 ft-lb. torque ratings & 150 degree to 300 degree temperature range. Industries served include transportation, manufacturing, construction & agriculture.

- http://www.irtools.com/products/airmotors/index.asp

Figure 8 (Copyright ThomasNet - reprinted with permission

The listing shown in Figure 7 gives a brief company profile for each entry. To get further details, click on the Company Profile link. For example, to extract the contact information for the second listed company, Ingersoll-Rand, just click on the corresponding company profile link. The resulting webpage is shown in Figure 8.

From the company information we see that Ingersoll-Rand offers a wide range of air motors. Sometimes the simplest way of determining the uniqueness of your invention idea is simply to see what is already on the market.

C. Government Websites

The U.S. Government spends billions of dollars on research annually. It is quite possible that some of this research could be directly related to your invention ideas. Most government agencies support at least one website, and much of their research information is unclassified and accessible.

One of the most useful of these government websites is run by the Defense Technical Information Center (DTIC). DTIC contributes to the management and conduct of defense-related research, development and acquisition efforts by providing access to, and exchange of, scientific and technical information. DTIC's Scientific and Technical Information Network (STINET) Service provides scientific and technical information to the public. To get to the STINET website, you need to type the following address into your web browser:

stinet.dtic.mil

Take special note of the ".mil" at the end of the website address.

Figure 9 shows a section of the STINET homepage. Let's suppose that your invention is related to recent developments in the field of Nuclear

Public STINET
(Scientific & Technical Information Network)

Home	Collections	Find It	Contact Us	Help

About STINET

What's New

DTIC Collections

Special Collections

MultiSearch

Journals

Other Resources

MCTL

The Defense Technical Information Center (DTIC)'s Scientific and Technical Information Network (STINET) Service helps the DoD community access pertinent scientific and technical information to meet mission needs effectively.

Perform a simple search of DTIC's Technical Reports Collection

Search for :

Nuclear Propulsion

[Search] [Clear Query]   Search Help

Limit search to technical reports with **Full Text** links available: ☐

Other Search Options	Quick Search	Guided Search	Advanced Search

Figure 9 (Source: Defense Technical Information Center)

Rocket Propulsion. To search for any related research we enter the keywords, Nuclear propulsion, into the Search for text box shown in Figure 9. To start the search, click on the Search button below the text entry box. A portion of the results are shown in Figure 10.

From Figure 10, we see that there were 448 matches for our search query. To view the text of the first matching search result, click on the link labeled, "View Full Text pdf -297 KB" as shown in the top of the figure. The result is shown in Figure 11, below. Here, you can read a study comparing Nuclear Thermal and Nuclear Electric rocket propulsion. You will need to have the adobe page reader program installed on your computer (which can be freely downloaded from www.adobe.com) in order to read the document.

Advanced searching is also available at the STINET web site. To get to STINET's advanced search page, click on the Advanced Search link at the extreme lower right of Figure 9. The resultant web page is shown in Figure 12, below.

In Figure 12 we have decided to limit our search to studies that involved Nuclear propulsion and Mars. To that end we have added the Boolean operator "<and>" (see Figure 12) to require all search terms to be present in the search results. Note the use of the less-than (<) and greater than (>) syntax at the STINET web site. The results of our advanced search are shown in Figure 13, below.

Public STINET

Home | Collections

Your search for **nuclear propulsion** matched **448** out of **851920** documents from the collection(s): **tr**.

Results list navigation: 1|2|3|4|5|6|7|8|9 [NEXT]

1. View TR Citation | View Full Text pdf - 297 KB
   Title: A Comparison of Nuclear Thermal and Nuclear Electric Propulsion for Interplanetary Missions
   AD Number: ADA431030 *Corporate Author:* AIR FORCE ACADEMY COLORADO SPRINGS CO DEPT OF ASTRONAUTICS *Personal Author:* Osenar, Michael J. *Report Date:* March 21, 2005 *Media:* 13 Pages(s) *Distribution Code:* 01 - APPROVED FOR PUBLIC RELEASE 26 - NOT AVAILABLE IN MICROFICHE *Report Classification:* (Not Available). *Source Code:* 433039 From the collection: Technical Reports

2. View TR Citation | View Full Text pdf - 1 MB
   Title: Nuclear Thermal Rocket Propulsion Systems
   AD Number: ADA430931 *Corporate Author:* AIR FORCE ACADEMY COLORADO SPRINGS CO DEPT OF ASTRONAUTICS *Personal Author:* Lawrence, Timothy J. *Report Date:* March 18, 2005 *Media:* 17 Pages(s) *Distribution Code:* 01 - APPROVED FOR PUBLIC RELEASE 26 - NOT AVAILABLE IN MICROFICHE *Report Classification:* (Not Available). *Source Code:* 433039 From the collection: Technical Reports

Figure 10 (Source: Defense Technical Information Center)

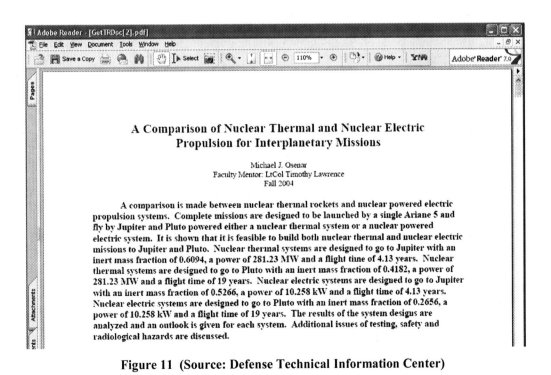

Figure 11 (Source: Defense Technical Information Center)

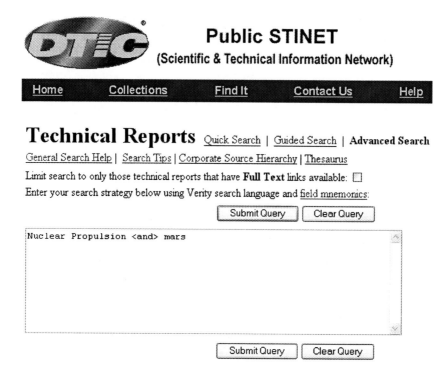

Figure 12 (Source: Defense Technical Information Center)

Your search for **nuclear propulsion <and> mars** matched **15** out of **851920** documents from the collection(s): **tr**.

1. View TR Citation | View Full Text pdf - 1 MB

   Title: Nuclear Power Systems for Manned Mission to Mars
   AD Number: ADA429836   *Corporate Author:* NAVAL POSTGRADUATE SCHOOL
   MONTEREY CA   *Personal Author:*   McGinnis, Scott J.   *Report Date:*
   December 01, 2004   *Media:* 105 Pages(s)   *Distribution Code:*   01 - APPROVED
   FOR PUBLIC RELEASE   26 - NOT AVAILABLE IN MICROFICHE   *Report
   Classification:* (Not Available).   *Source Code:* 251450   From the collection:
   Technical Reports

2. View TR Citation

   Title: Entry Velocities at Mars and Earth for Short Transit Times.
   AD Number: ADA272591   *Corporate Author:* INSTITUTE FOR DEFENSE
   ANALYSES ALEXANDRIA VA   *Personal Author:*   Finke, Reinald G.   *Report
   Date:* July 01, 1993   *Media:* 43 Pages(s)   *Distribution Code:*   01 - APPROVED
   FOR PUBLIC RELEASE   *Report Classification:* (Not Available).   *Source Code:*
   179350   From the collection: Technical Reports

Figure 13 (Source: Defense Technical Information Center)

U.S. Dept. of the Interior	www.doi.gov
USDA Forest Service	www.fs.fed.us
Department Of Commerce	www.commerce.gov
Department of Energy	www.doe.gov
NASA Commercial Technology Network	www.nctn.hq.nasa.gov
Dept. of Health and Human Services	www.os.dhhs.gov
Department of Education	www.ed.gov
National Technology Transfer Center	www.nttc.edu
Environmental Protection Agency	www.epa.gov
Dept of Transportation	www.dot.gov
National Science Foundation	www.nsf.gov
US Army Corps of Engineers	www.usace.army.mil

Table 1 - Websites of Selected Government Agencies

As you can see from the top of Figure 13, the number of matching hits has been reduced from 448 to 15 by adding the requirement for the presence of the keyword Mars in the search result.

In addition to DTIC, there are a large number of other government websites which offer valuable information for prior art searches. Selected government websites are listed in Table 1, above.

D. Usenet Newsgroups

Unlike the WWW where websites all over the world are connected through hypertext links, the Usenet is a collection of thousands of individual newsgroups. Several million people from all over the world *subscribe* to these newsgroups. Each newsgroup is devoted to a certain topic or subject. With so many topics covered, the odds are that one or more newsgroups will be relevant to your field of invention.

Messages of interest to each group are *Posted* or written to that group. Newsgroup messages are then read via a newsreader program. To access the Usenet via Microsoft Windows Outlook Express (also an email program), click on the Tools menu and select Newsgroups, as shown in Figure 14, below.

If you have not setup the newsreader service, it will be necessary to add and configure a news host. The properties popup window will ask you for certain configuration inputs. This window has tabs across the top labeled, General, Server, Connection and Advanced. Most of the inputs you are likely to deal with are entered with the General and Server tabs.

Figure 14

Microsoft product screen shot(s) reprinted with permission from Microsoft Corporation

Figure 15

Microsoft product screen shot(s) reprinted with permission from Microsoft Corporation

Figure 15 shows some typical settings for the General tab. Here, we have entered News1 as a News Account name. At a minimum, under User Information, you will need to enter your User Name and Email address. Under the Server tab (see Figure 16) we have entered our news server name, account name and password. You may have to contact your Internet Service Provider (ISP) to get the correct news server name. Typically, the news service names are something like: news.(ISP name).(com or net).

Once you have successfully connected to your ISP's newsreader service you will be prompted to download a list of current newsgroups. At last count there were more than 15,000, so this download may take a few seconds.

There are topics ranging from aviation (newsgroup name: aus.aviation) to Zenith computer systems (newsgroup name: comp.sys.zenith). There are so many newsgroups that it is helpful to search for a particular topic with the search box show at the top of Figure 17, below.

For example, suppose you have an idea for a new circuit board design. You could enter the search term Electronics, as shown in Figure 17. The display instantly lists all the newsgroups with the word electronics in the title. There is no need to click on a search button. In figure 17 we have selected the newsgroup:

alt.electronics.manufacture.circuitboard

To see a list of messages recently posted to this newsgroup, click the Go to button shown at the bottom of the figure. To read a particular message, just double-click on it.

News1 Properties

General | Server | Connection | Advanced

Server Information

Server name: news.BigISP.com

☑ This server requires me to log on

Account name: JohnDoe@BigISP.com

Password: ●●●●●●

☑ Remember password

☐ Log on using Secure Password Authentication

OK | Cancel | Apply

Figure 16

Microsoft product screen shot(s) reprinted with permission from Microsoft Corporation

alt.electronics.manufacture.circuitboard - Outlook Express

File Edit View Tools Message Help

New Post | Reply Group | Reply | Forward | Print

alt.electronics.manufacture.circuitboard

Figure 18

Microsoft product screen shot(s) reprinted with permission from Microsoft Corporation

New Message

File Edit View Insert Format Tools Message Help

Send | Cut | Copy | Paste | Undo | Check | Spelling | Attach | Sign | Offline

Newsgroups: alt.electronics.manufacture.circuitboard

Cc:

Subject:

Figure 19

Microsoft product screen shot(s) reprinted with permission from Microsoft Corporation

Newsgroup Subscriptions

Account(s): News1

Display newsgroups which contain:

electronics

☐ Also search descriptions

All | Subscribed | New

Subscribe
Unsubscribe
Reset List

Newsgroup	Description
alcatel.microelectronics	
alcatel.microelectronics.general	
alcatel.microelectronics.vhdl	
alt.binaries.schematics.electronics	
alt.electronics	
alt.electronics.analog	
alt.electronics.analog.vlsi	
alt.electronics.manufacture	
alt.electronics.manufacture.circuitboard	
alt.electronics.maplin-electronics	

Go to | OK | Cancel

Figure 17

Microsoft product screen shot(s) reprinted with permission from Microsoft Corporation

To post a message to the group, just click on the New Post button in Outlook Express shown at the upper left-hand corner of Figure 18. A message window will then popup as shown in Figure 19. Notice that the newsgroup name, alt.electronics. manufacture.circuitboard has already been added to the newsgroup destination line. Simply type in a subject line, and the body of your message. To post the message to the selected newsgroup, click on the send button.

The Usenet has millions of readers who like to participate in interesting discussions and answer questions. But they don't like to answer the same questions over and over again. For this reason a "frequently asked questions" (FAQ) list of questions and answers is often posted to each group. Before you post a question to a newsgroup, please read any FAQ postings. Often you will find that your question has been anticipated and the answer already provided.

There are certain rules and conventions for posting messages to Usenet newsgroups. These are generically referred to as *Netiquette*. Some of the most important rules of Netiquette are summarized below.

Rules of Netiquette

1. Post your question or message only to the newsgroup that is the most appropriate. Sending messages to multiple newsgroups is called "spamming" and is very frowned upon.
2. Put a short, descriptive header into the Subject line of your posting. People use these headers to select which messages to respond to.
3. Keep your message short and concise.
4. If you reply to a previous posted message, include the essential parts of the original message in your response, but not the entire original message.
5. Don't use the net for sending nasty messages (called "flames"), advertising or chain letters.

E. Trade Magazines, Books and Stores

Another good place to search for prior art is in trade magazines. Trade magazines are often very specific to one topic and can provide a wealth of information for inventors in that subject area. For example, let's suppose that your invention has something to do with mining equipment.. Then the magazines *Dimensional Stone*, *Stone Review* and *Stone World* may very well contain highly relevant information.

How do you find out what magazines are out there? Well, there are several journals that list magazine titles and subjects. One of the most useful is called *Writer's Market*. Written mainly for freelance writers, this volume contains the names, descriptions, and contact information for thousands of trade magazines. Other useful directories are:

1. Burrells Media Directory Magazine and Newspapers
2. Directory of Book, Catalog and Magazine Printers
3. The Directory of Small Press & Magazine Editors & Publishers

In addition to magazines, there are an endless number of books published on every conceivable subject. You can check your local bookstore or one of the large book store chains. There are also a number of bookstores accessible via the Internet. One particularly useful resource is Amazon.com.

Stores are another fruitful place to look for prior art. Consult your local yellow pages for listings. For example; if your invention is a new type of tool, it might be useful to visit your local Sears. If you find your invention is already on the store shelves, you've saved yourself a lot time, money, and heartache.

Summary

Internet Search Engines

- Internet search engines, such as Google, can be used to efficiently search through millions of web pages.

The Thomas Register

- The Thomas Register industrial database has contact information for over 100,000 American and Canadian companies.

Government Websites

- The U.S. Government spends billions of dollars on research annually. Most government agencies support at least one website, and much of their research information is unclassified and accessible.

Usenet Discussion Groups

- The Usenet is a collection of thousands of individual discussion newsgroups. Each newsgroup is devoted to a certain topic or subject. One or more newsgroups may be relevant to your field of invention.

Trade Magazines, Books and Stores

- Thousands of magazines and books exist around certain trades or subjects.
- Stores that cater to your future customers are good places to look for prior art.

Part 3

PTDL-Based Patent Searches

I n this part of the book, we cover the resources available at the nationwide network of Patent and Trademark Depository Libraries (PTDLs). These resources include:

- Chapter 8 - Using the following printed manuals: the *Index to the U.S. Patent Classification*, *Manual of Classification* and *Classification Definitions*.

- Chapter 9 - Using the Classification And Search Support Information System (CASSIS) computer system.

- Chapter 10 - Using the Examiner Assisted Search Tool (EAST) and the Web-based Examiner Search Tool (WEST).

Chapter

8

Hitting the Books

In this chapter we leave behind the Internet and the World Wide Web and enter the world of the Patent and Trademark Depository Library (PDTL). Every PTDL has patent information available in several formats, printed manuals, microfilm and computerized databases. See Appendix A to locate the PDTL nearest you.

The printed manuals we will be using are the *Index to the U.S. Patent Classification, Manual of Classification* and *Classification Definitions*. In this chapter, you will learn how to use these manuals to determine which classes and subclasses apply to your invention. Once you have identified the appropriate class/subclass, you can then obtain a listing of every patent that has been issued within that class by using one of several methods. As you will see, this method of patent searching is far more efficient than randomly searching for matching keywords within issued patents.

A. Index to the U.S. Patent Classification

Let's start with a hypothetical new idea you want to check out for possible patentability.

A common occurrence for people who drive is to see a vehicle with its turn signal stuck in the "on" position. This happens occasionally when automobiles negotiate gentle curves or during lane changes. This is a problem because other drivers can't tell if the signaling car is about to change direction or remain traveling straight ahead. While seeing this happen during your drive to work one day, you come up with an idea for a turn signal timer. This device would automatically cancel the turn signal after a given period of straight-ahead travel time.

After locating the nearest Patent and Trademark Depository Library, you decide to do a patent search for your idea. As discussed in Chapter 3, Section B, the most efficient way to start is to search for the class and subclass of your invention. Then proceed to search through the patents issued under each of the relevant classes.

Your first task is to come up with a list of words that describe your idea. Then use the *Index to the U.S. Patent Classifications* to look for those words. The *Index to the U.S. Patent Classifications* contains two very useful resources:

1) An alphabetical listing of all of the classes used by the PTO.
2) A cross-reference list of all known subject areas of invention, along with the appropriate class and subclass.

CLASSES ARRANGED IN ALPHABETICAL ORDER -- Continued

Class	Title of Class	Class	Title of Class
271	Sheet Feeding or Delivering	505	Superconductor Technology: Apparatus, Material, Process
413	Sheet Metal Container Making	248	Supports
270	Sheet—Material Associating	312	Supports: Cabinet Structure
114	Ships	211	Supports: Racks
116	Signals and Indicators	128	Surgery
117	Single—Crystal, Oriented—Crystal, and Epitaxy Growth Processes; Non—Coating Apparatus Therefor	600	Surgery
		604	Surgery
508	Solid Anti—Friction Devices, Materials Therefor, Lubricant or Separant Compositions for Moving Solid Surfaces, and Miscellaneous Mineral Oil Compositions	606	Surgery
		601	Surgery: Kinesitherapy
		602	Surgery: Splint, Brace, or Bandage
241	Solid Material Comminution or Disintegration	607	Surgery: Light, Thermal, and Electrical Application
206	Special Receptacle or Package	520	Synthetic Resins or Natural Rubbers — — Part of the Class 520 Series
75	Specialized Metallurgical Processes, Compositions for Use Therein, Consolidated Metal Powder Compositions, etc.	521	Synthetic Resins or Natural Rubbers — — Part of the Class 520 Series
		522	Synthetic Resins or Natural Rubbers — — Part of the Class 520 Series
267	Spring Devices	523	Synthetic Resins or Natural Rubbers — — Part of the Class 520 Series
365	Static Information Storage and Retrieval	524	Synthetic Resins or Natural Rubbers — — Part of the Class 520 Series
249	Static Molds	525	Synthetic Resins or Natural Rubbers — — Part of the Class 520 Series
52	Static Structures (e.g., Buildings)	526	Synthetic Resins or Natural Rubbers — — Part of the Class 520 Series
428	Stock Material or Miscellaneous Articles	527	Synthetic Resins or Natural Rubbers — — Part of the Class 520 Series
125	Stone Working	528	Synthetic Resins or Natural Rubbers — — Part of the Class 520 Series
126	Stoves and Furnaces		
127	Sugar, Starch, and Carbohydrates		

A-9

Figure 1 (Source: USPTO)

Let's suppose that you have selected the following words to describe your invention:

Car
Turn Signal
Timer
Electrical

These descriptive terms are arranged in order, from the general to the specific. In other words, the term "car" describes the general product that uses our invention. The term "turn signal" refers the device upon which our invention will operate. Finally, the terms "timer" and "electrical" pertain to the type of turn signal and the timer function used to turn the signal off.

The classification system used by the PTO also flows from the general to the specific. By using this strategy we will attempt to capture all of the classes related to your invention.

The alphabetical listing of all of the classes used by the PTO is at the beginning of the *Index to the U.S. Patent Classification*. You will use the alphabetical listing of classes to find a class for each of the words on your list. Since there are only about 430 classes, it is quite possible that you will not find a match for each of your descriptive terms. For this reason, it is helpful to come up with a few synonyms for your descriptive terms. For example, in addition to the word "car," you can add the following two descriptive terms:

1. Automobile
2. Vehicle

Figure 1, above, shows a typical page from the alphabetical listing of classes in the *Index*. Here we have boxed class 116, Signals and Indicators. You should write down the class name and number for any

classes that match your descriptive words. The search results from the alphabetical list of classes are shown in Figure 2 below.

The next section of the *Index to the U.S. Patent Classification* (right after the alphabetical listing of classes) is the cross-reference list of all known subject areas of invention. This cross-reference list makes of the bulk of the *Index*.

Here, you look up each of the classes found from Figure 2 and write down the class and subclass of any matching references. For example, from Figure 2 you found Class 340 while searching for the term "Electrical." A section from the *Index* cross-reference for Class 340 is shown in

Search Results from Listing of Classes

General Terms Used for Cars

Term	Class Found
Car	None
Automobile	None
Vehicle	Motor Vehicles: Class 180, Land Vehicles: Class 280

More Specific Terms Pertaining to Turn Signals

Term	Class Found
Turn Signal	None
Turn	(Turning): Class 82
Signal	Signals and Indicators: Class 116

Terms Pertaining to the Type of Turn Signal

Term	Class Found
Timer	None
Electrical	Communications: Electrical: Class 340 Electricity: Electrical Systems and Devices: Class 361

Figure 2

Surgical	607	1+
Therapeutic application	607	115+
Trawl net fish control	43	9.6
Signaling, electric (see signal)	340	
Noise suppression in signal	128	901*
Radio	455	
Railway	246	
Telegraph	178	
Telephone	379	
Television transmission	348	469+
Vehicle mounted	340	425.5+
Socket (see socket, electric)		
Soldering	219	129
Iron	219	245+
Iron design	D08	30
With pressure	219	85.1

Figure 3 (Source: USPTO)

Figure 3. Here we see a small section of the listings under the topics Electric & Electricity. These results would indicate that class 340, subclass 425.5+, was highly relevant to vehicle mounted electric signals. The plus sign (+) following the subclass 425.5 indicates there are subclasses that further differentiate vehicle mounted electric signals.

The search results for all our descriptive terms are summarized in Figure 4, below. For the general terms "Car," "Automobile" and "Vehicle," the most relevant class/ subclass would appear to be Class 340, subclass 425++ (as shown in figure 3). The more specific terms, "Turn signal," "Turn" and "Signal," lead us to Class 116 Subclass 28R+ for Signals and Indicators. Finally, the most specific terms, "Timer" and "Electrical," again lead us to class 340, subclass 425.5+. Clearly, class/subclass 116/28R+ and 340/425.5+ warrant further examination.

B. Manual of Classification

We have now proceeded as far as we can in the *Index to the U.S. Patent Classification*. Next we turn to the *Manual of*

Search Results from Cross-Reference List of Inventions

General Terms Used for Cars: Car, Automobile and Vehicle

Subject Area	Class	Subclass
Land Vehicle	280	
Vehicle Mounted	340	425.5+

More Specific Terms Pertaining to Turn Signals: Turn Signal, Turn and Signal

Subject Area	Class	Subclass
Signals & Indicators	116	28R+

Terms Pertaining to the Type of Turn Signal: Timer and Electrical

Subject Area	Class	Subclass
Electrical	340	425.5+

Figure 4

Classification. This manual has an indented list of all the subclasses to be found under each main class. The classes are listed in numerical order. Each class is covered by its own page or group of pages. Here we can easily look up each of the class/subclass numbers found in the *Index to the U.S. Patent Classifications*.

Why should we look up the class/ subclass numbers in this manual? Don't we already have our class/subclass information from the Index? Well, yes and no. What we have so far are a few individual class/ subclass combinations. By using the *Manual of Classification*, we can see all of the subclasses within each major class. Furthermore, this listing of subclasses is indented. This gives you a visual aid towards understanding how the various subclasses are related. By reviewing this indented list of subclasses, you may find further classifications of interest.

Figure 5, below, is a page from the *Manual of Classification* for class 340. The figure shows a partial listing of the indented list of subclasses under the subclass 425.5— Land Vehicle Alarms or Indicators. The dots or periods to the left of the subclass title indicate how specific that subclass is. The more dots there are, the more specific the subclass. For example, subclass 442 has two dots to the left of the title and refers to tire deflation or inflation. Subclass 443 has three dots to the left and refers to a particular measurement means of deflation or inflation, namely, tire height.

From a close examination of the indented list of subclasses, it would appear that subclass 465—Turning or Steering would be the most relevant for our turn signal canceling invention. Figure 6, below, shows the appropriate section from the

no. 6,637,447 - Beerbrella

```
425.5    LAND VEHICLE ALARMS OR INDICATORS
426      .Of burglary or unauthorized use
427      ..Of motorcycles or bicycles
428      ..Responsive to changes in voltage or current in a vehicle
             electrical system
429      ..Responsive to inertia, vibration, or tilt
430      ..With entrance/exit time delay
431      .For trailer
432      .For bicycle
433      .For school bus
434      .For taxi
435      .Of relative distance from an obstacle
436      .Of collision or contact with external object
437      ..Curb
438      .Internal alarm or indicator responsive to a condition of the
             vehicle
439      ..Operation efficiency (e.g., engine performance, driver
             habits)
440      ..Tilt, imbalance, or overload

441      ..Speed of vehicle, engine, or power train
442      ..Tire deflation or inflation
443      ...By indirect detection means (e.g., height measurement)
444      ....Relative wheel speed
445      ...With particular telemetric coupling
```

Figure 5 (Source: USPTO)

indented list of subclasses. Here we see that subclass 463 refers to the general topic of External Alarms or Indicators of Movement, and subclass 465 limits those movements to turning or steering.

The process of finding the appropriate subclass moves from the general to the specific. Figure 7 summarizes this process for class 340, subclass 465. First, we start with the general topic, "Communications: electrical." Then we proceed to electrical communications that are used for land vehicle alarms or indicators. Then we further limit the topic to external alarms or indicators of movement. Finally, the patents issued under subclass 465 are limited to electrical signals that are used on land vehicles for the purpose of external indicators of turning or steering.

```
463        .External alarm or indicator of movement
464        ..Plural indications (e.g., go, slow, stop)
465        ..Turning or steering
466        ..Speed
467        ..Acceleration or deceleration
```

Figure 6 (Source: USPTO)

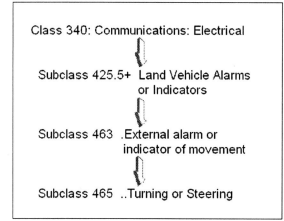

Figure 7

C. Classification Definitions

Now we proceed to our third manual, *Classification Definitions*. The *Classification Definitions* manual contains a written description for every class and subclass used by the PTO. Here we can look up each of our class/subclass numbers and determine their relevance.

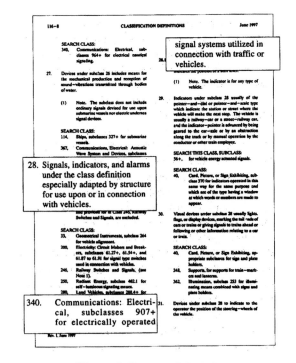

Figure 8 (Source: USPTO)

Figure 8, above, shows page 116-8 of the *Classification Definitions*. That is, the 8th page for the class 116. About halfway down the left-hand column is the description for subclass 28 (boxed in). Reading the definition, we see that this subclass pertains to signals that are especially adapted for use upon, or in connection with, vehicles.

Below each subclass definition is a "Search Class Cross Reference." This section contains a listing of additional classes that are related to the subject matter. In the figure, we see that class 340 is referenced for signal systems utilized in connection with traffic or vehicles.

Figure 9, below, shows page 116-9 from the *Classification Definitions*. Here, we see that Class 116, subclass 35 relates to "Devices under subclass 28 placed upon a vehicle for indicating to others than the operator, the motion of any change, either actual or intended, in the rate or direction of the motion of the vehicle." This definition tells us that subclass 28 is for signaling devices used only on vehicles and only for the purpose of indicating a change of direction (a turn) or a change in rate of travel (brake lights) to persons other than the driver.

In the search class cross-reference below this definition, we again see a reference to Class 340. Clearly, Class 340, along with the referenced subclass 463, is highly relevant to vehicle turn signals.

In Figure 10, below, we see page 340-23 from the *Classification Definitions*. Subclass 463 includes signals for turning, braking and backing. However, subclass 465 (shown boxed), "Subject matter under subclass 463 in which the external signal indicates that the vehicle is executing a turning movement," is specifically limited to electronic signals used to indicate vehicle turning.

By using the *Index to the U.S. Patent Classifications*, the *Manual of Classification* and the *Classification Definitions*, we have

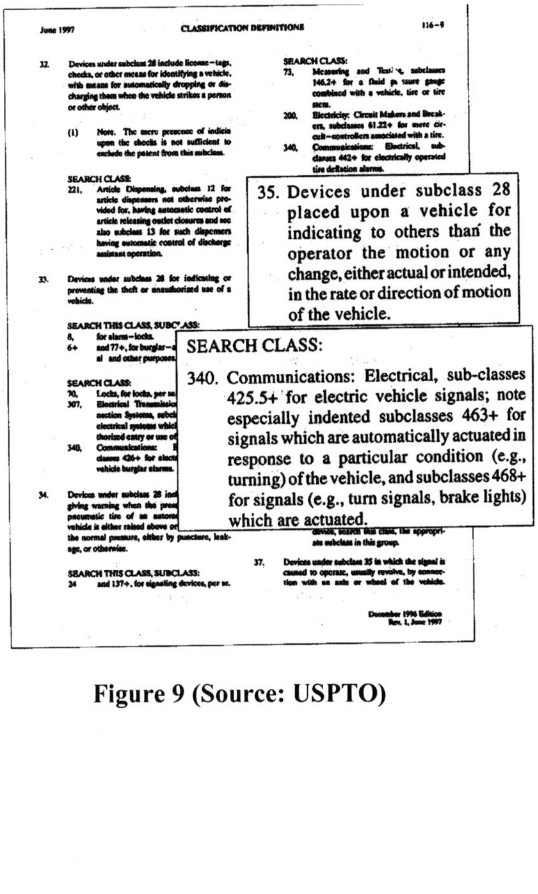
June 1997 CLASSIFICATION DEFINITIONS 116-9

35. Devices under subclass 28 placed upon a vehicle for indicating to others than the operator the motion or any change, either actual or intended, in the rate or direction of motion of the vehicle.

SEARCH CLASS:

340. Communications: Electrical, sub-classes 425.5+ for electric vehicle signals; note especially indented subclasses 463+ for signals which are automatically actuated in response to a particular condition (e.g., turning) of the vehicle, and subclasses 468+ for signals (e.g., turn signals, brake lights) which are actuated.

Figure 9 (Source: USPTO)

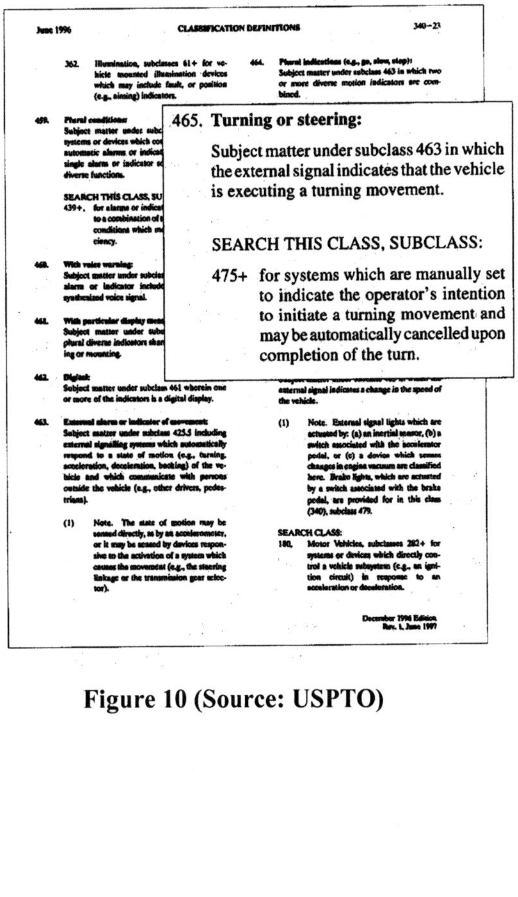
June 1996 CLASSIFICATION DEFINITIONS 340-23

465. **Turning or steering:**

Subject matter under subclass 463 in which the external signal indicates that the vehicle is executing a turning movement.

SEARCH THIS CLASS, SUBCLASS:

475+ for systems which are manually set to indicate the operator's intention to initiate a turning movement and may be automatically cancelled upon completion of the turn.

Figure 10 (Source: USPTO)

identified class 340, subclass 465, as a highly likely place to find patents related to turn signals for vehicles. Class/subclass 340/465 is a good place to check to see if our idea for an automatic turn signal canceling device has been anticipated. The process for using the classification manuals is summarized in the flow chart shown in Figure 11, below.

Figure 12, below, shows a handy worksheet you can take with you to the PTDL. You'll find a blank worksheet form in Appendix B. We've filled out a portion of the worksheet sample here to show you how it would be used in the context of our turn signal invention. The first column (Column A) is used to list your descriptive words. In the next column, Column B, you record the class numbers of any matching class names you find in the alphabetical listing of classes from the *Index to the U.S. Patent Classification*. Multiple rows are provided in case more than one matching class is found. In our case we have filled in Turn Signal and Vehicle for the first two descriptive terms. The corresponding classes were determined to be 116 (Signals & Indicators) and 340 (Vehicle).

The rest of the worksheet is used to determine the subclasses for which you want to get listings of all issued patents. You might remember from our discussion of how to search through the manuals at the PTDL that to determine this, you would consult the cross-reference list of all known subject areas of invention from the *Index to the U.S. Patent Classification*. In Column C, you would record the subclass of any matching references. For Class 116 in our turn signal example, this turned out to be subclasses 28 and 35. For Class 340, the referenced class was 425.5 (as shown in Figure 3).

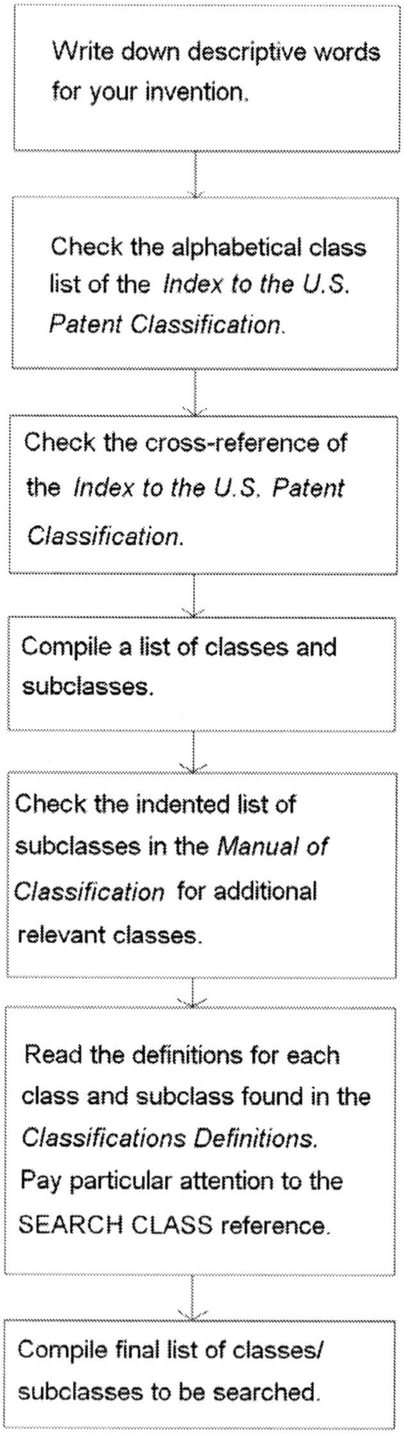

Figure 11

Classification Search Sheet						
A. Descriptive Words	B. Class Nos.	C. Subclass from Index	D. Subclass from Man. of Class.	E. Get List	F. Search Class	G. Get List
1.Turn Signal	116	28		X	340	
		35		X	340	
2.Vehicle	340	425.5+	465	X	340/475	X

Figure 12

Next, you would proceed to the indented list of all the subclasses in the *Manual of Classification*. From our example, it was determined that subclass 465—Turning or Steering—was the most relevant. So we recorded Class 465 under Column D, Subclass from Man. of Class.

From here, you would proceed to the third manual, the *Classification Definitions*. Here you would read the written description for each of your classes and subclasses and decide if you wanted a listing of every patent issued in that classification. For the description of Class 166, subclass 28, we determined that this subclass pertains to signals that are especially adapted for use upon, or in connection with, vehicles. So we marked an "X" in Column E, the "Get List" column next to subclass 28, which reminds us to get a list of patents issued in that class/subclass. The search class cross-reference for subclass 28 (right below the subclass definition—see Figure 9) contained a reference to Class 340. So we note that in the "Search Class" column, Column F.

From the description of Class 340, subclass 465—Turning or Steering—it would appear that this subclass is very relevant to our turn signal canceling invention, so we mark an "X" in Column G (the corresponding "Get List" column). The

search class cross-reference for subclass 465 (see Figure 10) contained a reference to subclass 475. So we note that in Column F and mark the Get List column, Column G, for this subclass as well.

The Classification Search Sheet is helpful because as you proceed from left to right, filling out the sheet, you can see exactly where you found your classification information. Also, referencing the search class information (far left column) helps in two ways. First, as discussed previously, it leads you to other places to search. Second, it can give you a feel for the quality of the search results. In the above case, each of our subclass descriptions told us to search Class 340. This is a further indication that we are on the right track.

Finding the correct classification(s) for your invention is the key to a successful patent search. This is because, once you have identified a given class, it is a relatively simple matter to obtain a listing of every issued patent within it. As mentioned, this technique is superior to randomly searching the text of patents for matching keywords (as explained in Chapter 3, Section A). This is because keyword search results depend entirely on the keywords used. If different words are used to describe similar, patented inventions, you

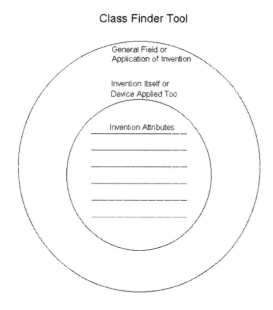

Figure 13

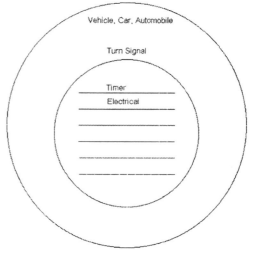

Figure 14

will miss many related patents and never know it.

In fact, relevant prior art is often missed by inexperienced patent searchers, who simply fail to identify the appropriate category(s). Also, this search for patent classification is still dependent upon the words you use to describe your invention. The "Class Finder Tool" is a visual aid to help you with your patent classification search. The Class Finder Tool is shown in Figure 13, above.

The outer circle of the diagram represents the general field or application of the invention. You can think of it as all the relevant factors surrounding your idea. The inner circle represents the invention itself. If the invention is a new application applied to an existing device, then the inner circle is the device that the invention is directly applied to. The blank lines within the inner circle are where you write down the specific attributes of the invention.

Figure 14 is an example of the class finder tool filled out for our turn signal

canceling device. First, we label our inner circle. Since our idea is to cancel a turn signal after a given period of time, our invention is directly applied to a turn signal. This also gives us our most general application of the invention. For example, if we had labeled our inner circle "An astable, multivibrator timer circuit for canceling turn signals," we would be limiting ourselves to just one manifestation of a much wider concept.

Next, we try to find words that will encompass the most general aspects of our invention. Originally, we thought of turn signals applied only to cars. So we write down the word "car" and the word "automobile." However, the circle around the turn signal device reminds us that there are other devices that use turn signals. Examples are such things as boats and bicycles (can you think of others?). So, we use the general term vehicle to describe bodies in motion that need to signal a change of direction

Class Finder Tool: Bathroom Nightlight

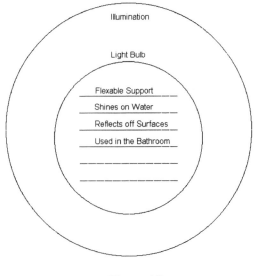

Figure 15

Next, we move to the inside of our invention and write down the specific aspects of our idea. In the case of our turn signal, we know that the signal is electrical, as opposed to mechanical, and that a timer is involved to cancel the signal.

As a further example, Figure 15 shows the Class Finder Tool filled out for the bathroom nightlight invention of Chapter 3. Here, the major aspect of the invention is a lamp/nightlight which uses a standard light bulb. Since there are many ways to cast light (for example, fireplaces, arc lamps and reflected sunlight), the general field is illumination. Finally, the specific attributes include a flexible support and use in the bathroom. See Appendix B for a blank Class Finder Tool form.

Summary

Index to the U.S. Patent Classification
- Use the *Index to the U.S. Patent Classification* to find class and subclass names that correspond with the descriptive words for your invention

Manual of Classification
- Use the *Manual of Classification* to find further subclasses that may be related to your invention

Classification Definitions
- Use the *Classification* Definitions to review the descriptions of classes and subclasses and determine which apply to your invention.

Chapter

9

Using Cassis

In addition to printed format, the PTO publishes a great deal of patent and trademark information on DVD. The PTO has developed a special computer search program to retrieve this information. This program is known as CASSIS (Classification And Search Support Information System). Every PTDL has a least one computer set up to run the CASSIS program. Furthermore, PTDLs have personnel on hand who are willing and able to help you get started on the system. It's a good idea to call ahead and make an appointment.

The CASSIS computer system is based on a series of DVDs. Each DVD in the series is devoted to a certain topic. The DVD labeled "Patents BIB" contains bibliographical data for utility patents issued from the year 1969 to the present. This includes the date of issue, state/country of first listed inventor's residence, assignee at time of issue, patent status (withdrawn, expired, etc.), current classifications and patent title.

The DVD labeled "Patents CLASS" contains the current classification of all utility, design and plant patents issued from Patent Number 1 to the present.

The DVD labeled "Patents ASSIST" contains an electronic version of the manuals used in Chapter 7; that is, the *Index*

to the U.S. Patent Classification, Manual of Classification and the *Classification Definitions*. Other electronic manuals on the Patents ASSIST DVD include: the *Classification Orders Index* (provides a list of classifications abolished and established since 1976, with corresponding classification order number and effective date); the *IPC-USPC Concordance* (the *U.S. Patent Classification to International Patent Classification Concordance* is a guide for relating the U.S. Patent Classification System to the *International Patent Classification System*, published by the World Intellectual Property Organization); the *Manual of Patent Examining Procedure* (provides patent examiners and patent applicants with a reference work on the practices and procedures related to prosecution of patent applications in the U.S. Patent and Trademark Office); a listing of attorneys and agents registered to practice before the PTO; and the *Patentee-Assignee Index* (shows ownership at time of issue for utility patents 1969 to present, for other types of patents 1977 to present, and inventors' names from 1975 to present).

The DVD labeled "USAApp" contains facsimile images of patent application publications filed on, or after, November 29, 2000.

The "USAPat" DVDs contain facsimile images of U.S. patents from 1994 to the present. The operative word here is DVDs. The current USAPat back file project is capturing the image data for all patent grants since 1790 on a set of approximately 400 DVD-ROMs.

The welcome screen of the Cassis2 (Cassis version 2) computer program is shown in Figure 1 below. The Cassis databases are grouped in four divisions: Main, Patents CLASS, Patents ASSIST and Trademarks ASSIST. Clickable buttons representing these divisions are shown to the left of Figure 1. To access the data on a particular CASSIS DVD you select one of these buttons with the mouse and load the appropriate DVD.

Clickable tabs are used (see Figure 1) to select from five search and display screens. These selections are:

1. Short Form Search
2. Form Search
3. Command Search
4. Results
5. Sort

In Sections A – C we will be using the Short Form Search.

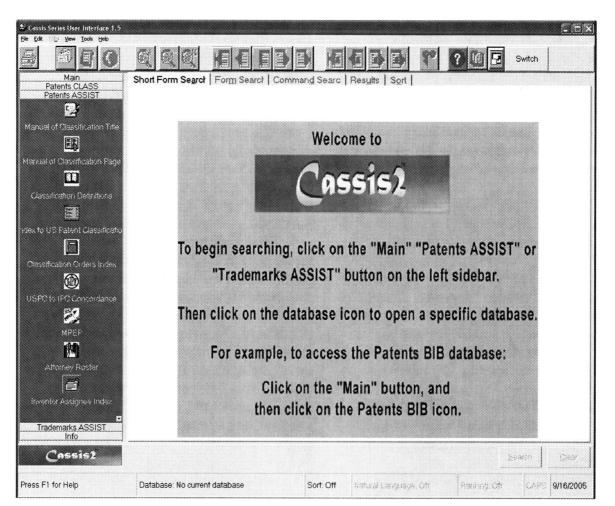

Figure 1 (Source: Cassis2 – USPTO)

A. Index to the U.S. Patent Classification

The CASSIS version of the *Index to the U.S. Patent Classifications* is found on the 'Patents ASSIST' DVD. To access this document, click on the Patents ASSIST button as shown in Figure 1, above. Then click on the icon for the *Index* (about halfway down the figure.) After a few seconds delay (while the appropriate DVD database loads) you will see a popup window that will display the contents information for the DVD loaded into your computer. To continue, just click on the OK button.

After clicking OK, you will see the screen shown in Figure 2, below. This is the Basic Search screen under tab #1. At this screen we can search for class titles that match our descriptive keywords. For example, to search for an index term that matches the word Vehicle, under the Select Field label, use your mouse to select "Index Term" as shown in the figure. Then, enter Vehicle in the adjacent blank entry field (labeled: Enter Search Terms). To begin the search, click on the Search button shown in the lower right of the figure.

The results of this search are shown in Figure 2 as well. To the left of the "Hits"

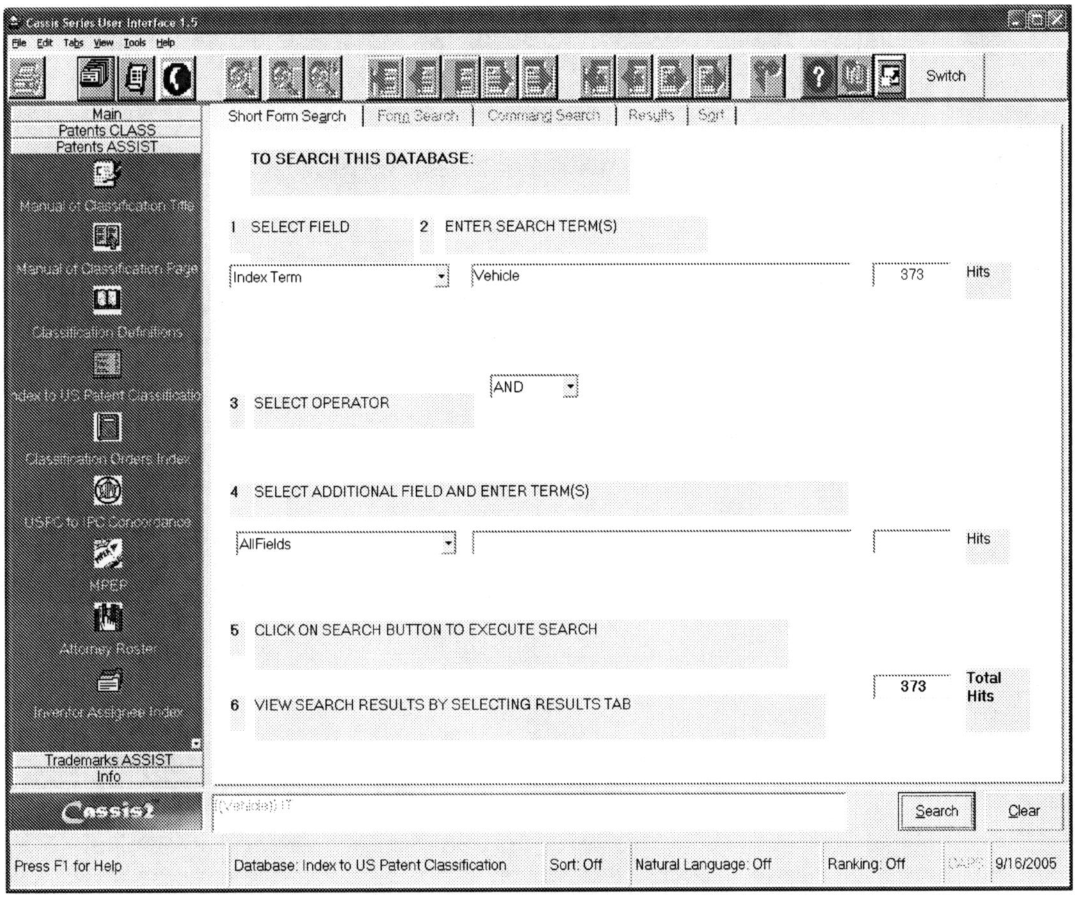

Figure 2 (Source: Cassis2 – USPTO)

label, the number 373 indicates that there were 373 occurrences of the search word Vehicle in the *Index*. To review the search hits, click on the Results tab (fourth tab – see Figure 2.)

The Results screen has two display windows. In the upper window we have our alphabetical cross reference listing of invention subject area to search keyword. To see how our search term is referenced in any given invention subject area, we click on that subject area. For example, in Figure 3 we have scrolled down to "Turn Indicators" and clicked on the adjacent selection box (note the check mark in the figure.)

The lower display window on Figure 3 shows that Class 166, subclass 28R+ is referenced. This is the same result we obtained from our manual search of the Index.

To get a printout of the display shown in Figure 3, just click on the printer icon shown at the upper left of the figure.

If you have selected more than one invention subject area you can choose which results to print by going to the File main menu option and selecting Print (see Figure 4.) You will be given a choice to print the selected list items, the entire list, the current document, the selected documents, or all of the documents.

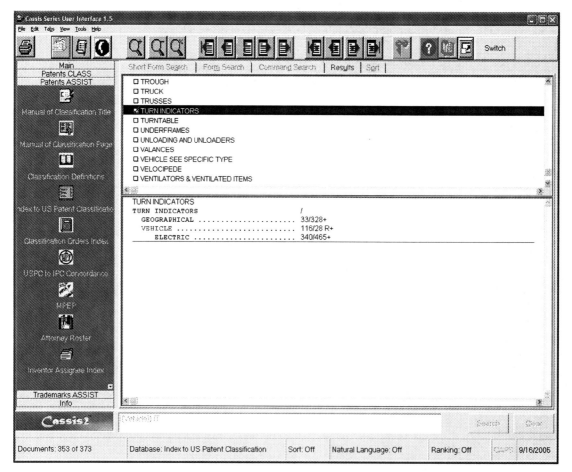

Figure 3 (Source: Cassis2 – USPTO)

Figure 4 (Source: Cassis2 – USPTO)

Figure 5 (Source: Cassis2 – USPTO)

To save your search results, click on the File main menu option and select Save. The options are displayed in Figure 5, above. You are given the choice of saving the current item from the results list, selected list items, the entire list, the current document, selected documents, or all of the documents. Insert a floppy disk into the floppy drive, enter a file name and click on OK.

B. Manual of Classification

From here, we can look at our next reference volume, the *Manual of Classification*. To see a page from this manual, click on the "Manual of Classifications-Page" icon, as shown to the left of Figure 3. After a few seconds delay (while the appropriate DVD database loads) you will see a popup window that will display the contents information for the DVD loaded into your computer. To continue, just click on the OK button.

After clicking OK, you will see the Basic Search screen for the *Manual of Classification* (see Figure 6, below). Under the Select Field label, we now have three search fields to choose from. We can search for a class number, a class title or a subclass title/number.

For example, to obtain the indented list of all the subclasses under class 340, under the Select Field label, use your mouse to select "Class Number" as shown in Figure 6. Then, enter 340 in the Enter Search Terms field, and click on the Search button.

The results of this search are shown in Figure 6 as well. This is very similar to the result screen obtained from the search of the *Index of the US Patent Classification*, as shown in Figure 2. In Figure 2, there were 373 occurrences of the search word Vehicle. For the *Manual of Classifications*, the number 1 to the left of the "Hits" label indicates that one indented list of subclasses for Class 340 was found. To view the indented list of subclasses under class 340, click on the Results tab (fourth tab – see Figure 6.)

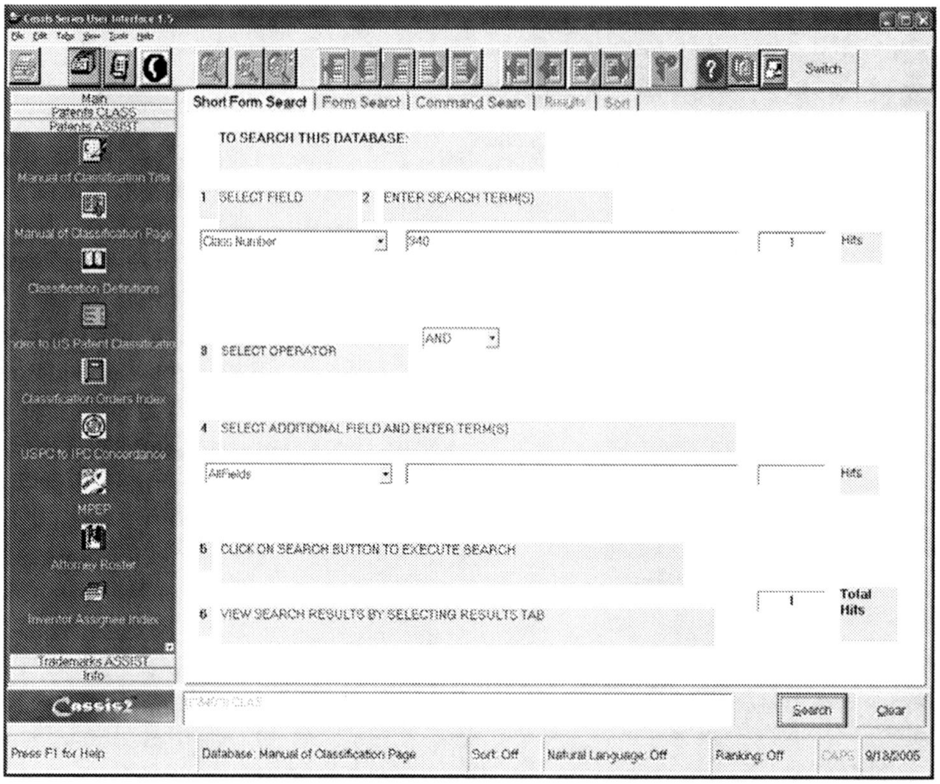

Figure 6 (Source: Cassis2 – USPTO)

Figure 7 (Source: Cassis2 – USPTO)

The resulting display (see Figure 7) is similar to the indented list shown in Chapter 7, Section B. A printout or electronic copy of a page from the *Manual of Classifications* can also be obtained by use of the methods described in the previous section.

C. Classification Definitions

The *Classification Definitions* manual can be accessed by clicking on the "Classifications Definitions" icon, as shown to the left of Figure 7. After a few seconds delay (while the appropriate DVD database loads) you will see a popup window that will display the contents information for the

DVD loaded into your computer. To continue, just click on the OK button.

After clicking OK, you will see the Basic Search screen for the *Classification Definitions* (see Figure 8, below). Under the Select Field label, we now have two search fields to choose from. We can search for a classification or a class title.

During our search of the Index to the U.S. Patent Classification (Figure 3) under the classification "Turn indicators—vehicle—electric," we identified the classification 340/465. To obtain the definition for class 340, subclass 465, use your mouse to select "Classification" as

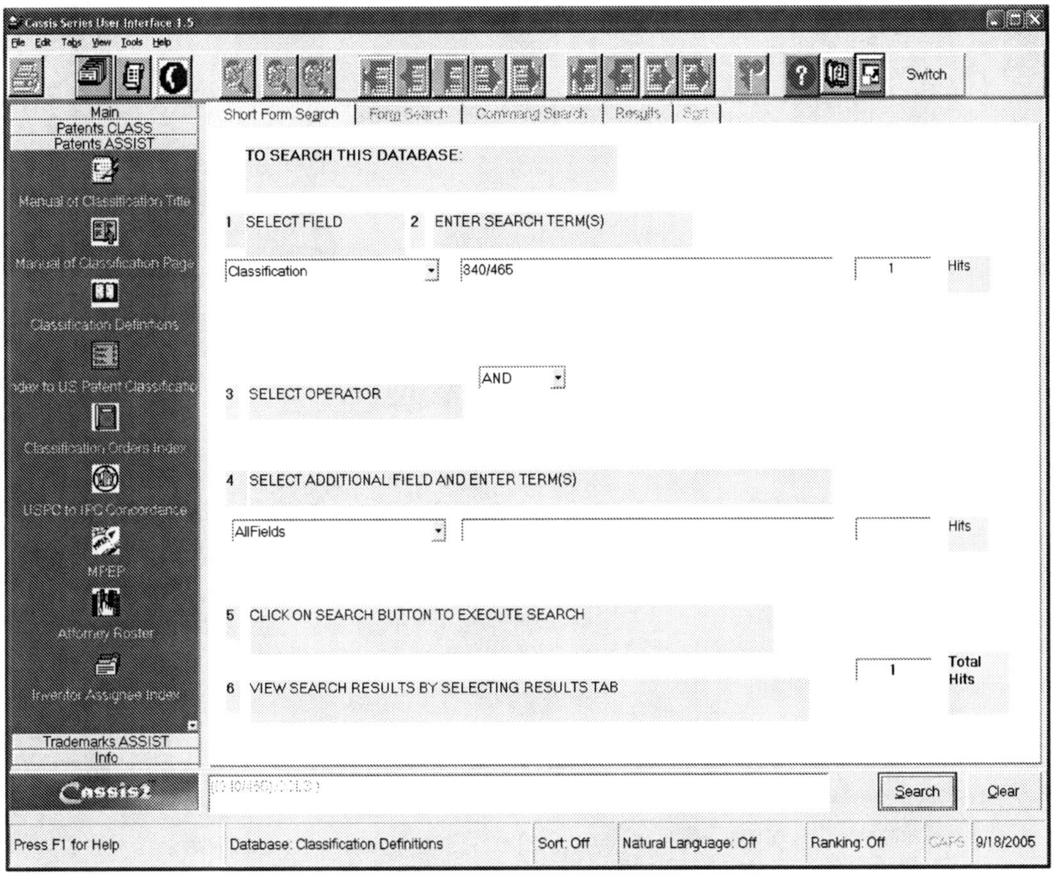

Figure 8 (Source: Cassis2 – USPTO)

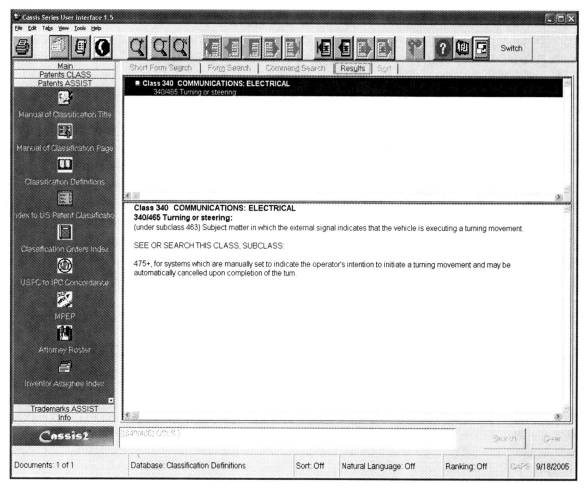

Figure 9 (Source: Cassis2 – USPTO)

shown in Figure 8. Then, enter 340/465 in the Enter Search Terms field, and click on the Search button.

The results of this search are shown in Figure 8 as well. The results show the number 1 to the left of the "Hits" label. This indicates that the program has found one class/subclass definition in its search.

To view the class/subclass definition, click on the Results tab. The resulting display (see Figure 9) is similar to the indented list shown in Chapter 7, Section C. A printout or electronic copy of this definition can also be obtained by previously described methods.

D. Form Search

Referring to Figure 10, below, the Form Search screen is located under tab #2. With this form we select the specific field from a drop-down list in the left column. Search terms are then typed into the text entry box adjacent to the selected field. Next, a Boolean or Proximity operator (more about these shortly) can be applied.

For example, suppose we have an idea for a foam-filled fender. To search the Manual of Classification we could use the query shown in Figure 10. In the figure we

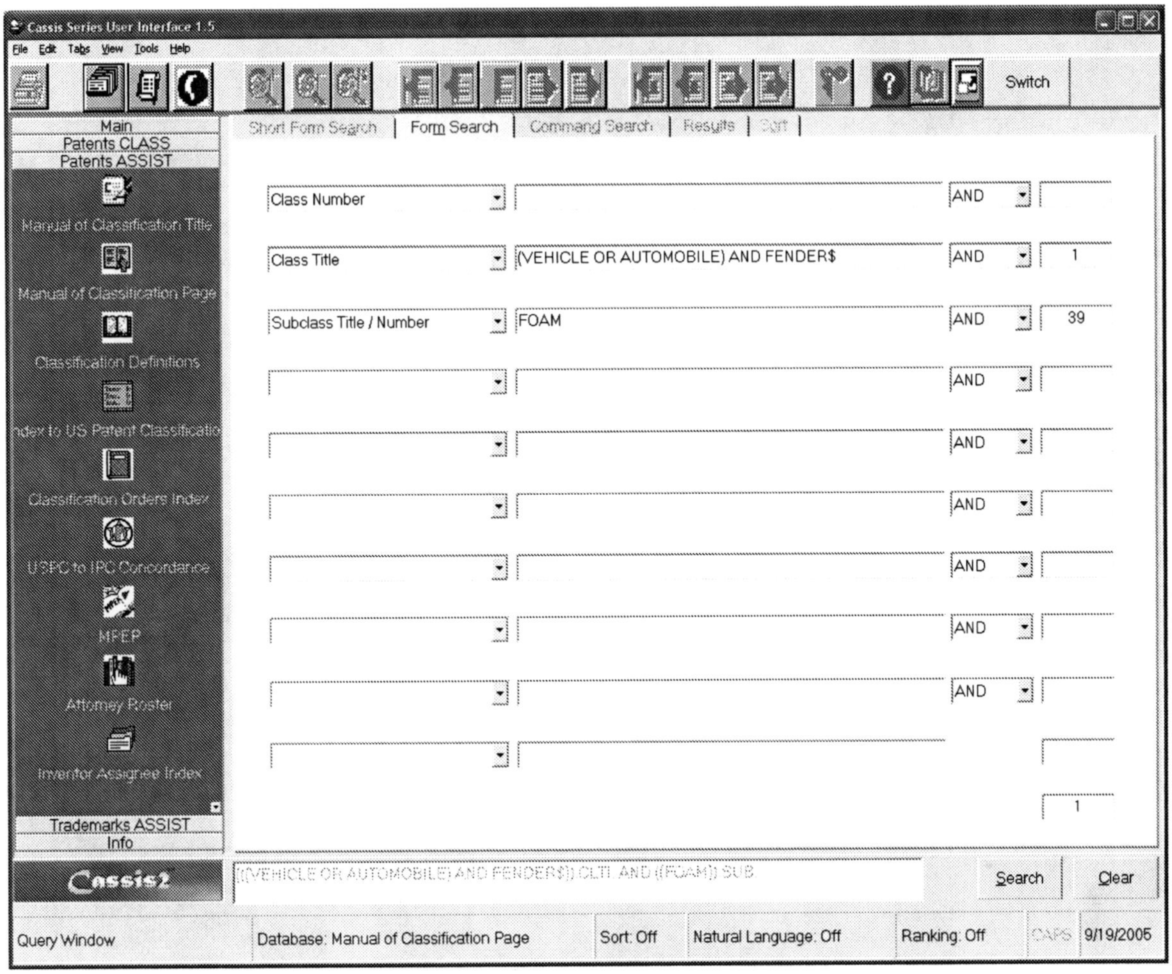

Figure 10 (Source: Cassis2 – USPTO)

have decided to search for the terms Vehicle OR Automobile AND Fender$ in the class title, as well as the term Foam in the subclass title. Notice that the wildcard ($) has also been used for the search term Fender$. This is to insure that we capture the singular and plural forms of the word. Also notice that the pull-down of column 3 has been set to the default AND operation. This ensures that both the Class Title and Subclass Title search results must match our queries for a hit to be returned. To conduct this search we click on the Search button shown at the bottom of Figure 10.

The results of this search are shown in Figure 10 as well. The results show the number 1 to the left of the "Hits" label for our class title search (row 2 – Figure 10). We also have 39 hits for our Subclass Title search for the word Foam. At the bottom right of the form these two results are ANDed together to produce a single combined hit. This indicates that the program has found one class/subclass definition in its search.

Also notice at the bottom of Figure 10, that our combined search query has been reproduced (parsed) for our review. This is given as:

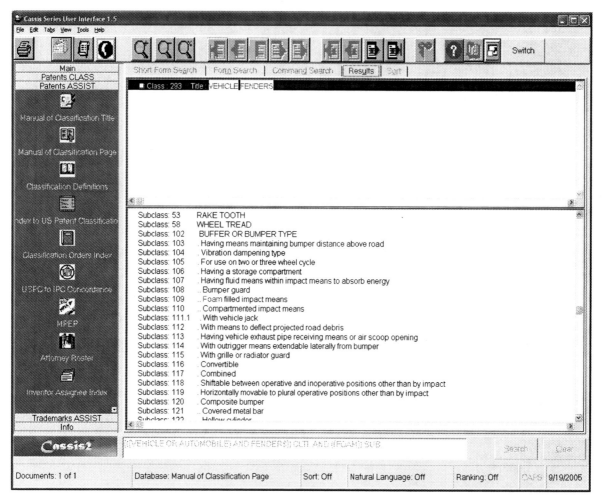

Figure 11 (Source: Cassis2 – USPTO)

(((VEHICLE OR AUTOMOBILE)
AND FENDER$)).CLTI.AND
((FOAM)).SUB

Here, we can verify that the proper search terms have been applied to the Class Title (CLTI) field and the Subclass Title (SUB) field.

Figure 11 shows the results (after clicking the results tab.) In the upper window we see Class 293—Vehicle Fenders. In the lower window is the class breakdown. Toward the middle of this window is subclass 109—Foam filled impact means.

E. Command Search

Referring to Figure 12, below, the Command Search screen is located under tab #3. With this form we have additional flexibility in combining information from different search fields using Boolean and Proximity operators, wildcards and phrases.

In Figure 12 we have changed search documents from the *Manual of Classification – Page* to the *Classification Definitions*. In the figure, we have decided to search for the terms Inlet and Valve. We have used the NEAR proximity operator (see Table below) to specify that the two

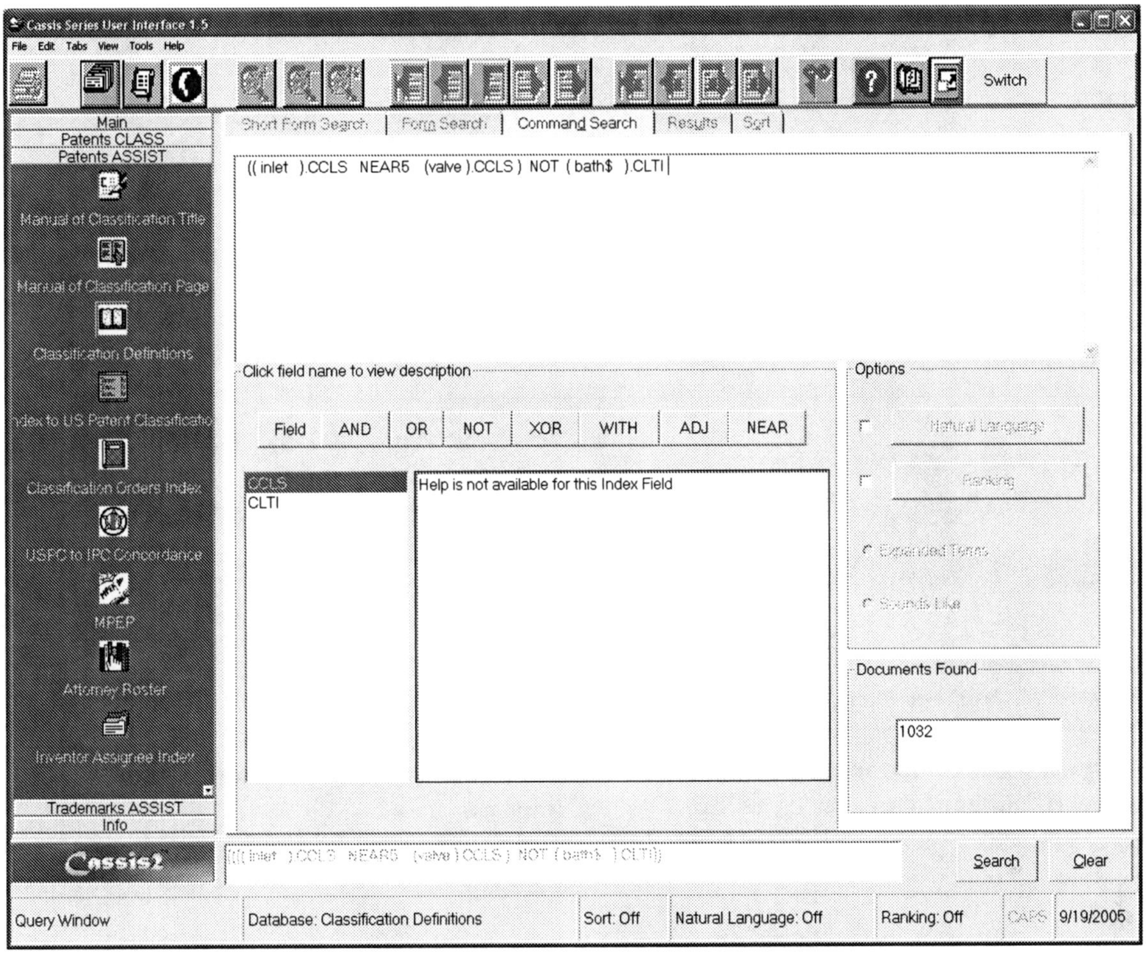

Figure 12 (Source: Cassis2 – USPTO)

Operator	Description	Examples
ADJ	Indicates that the search terms must appear next to each other in the order specified.	Inline ADJ Skate
	Additional separation can be allowed by including an optional number.	Inline ADJ5 Skate
NEAR	Indicates that the search terms can appear in either order with up to one word between.	Inlet NEAR valve
	Additional separation can be allowed by including an optional number.	Inlet NEAR5 valve
WITH	Indicates that the search terms must appear in the same sentence. The search terms can appear in any order.	Valve WITH fluid

Table 1 (Source: Cassis2 – USPTO)

search terms must be within 5 words of each other, in any order.

We have also specified that the term bath$ cannot occur in the classification title of the search result. This is useful for excluding bathroom applications.

To conduct this search we click on the Search button shown at the bottom of Figure 12. Also notice at the bottom of Figure 12, that our combined search query has been reproduced (parsed) for our review. This is given as:

((((inlet).CCLS NEAR5 (valve). CCLS) NOT (bath$).CLTI))

F. Additional Cassis Features

Additional features of the Cassis system include Natural language searching, customized displays, saving and loading frequently used search queries and searching for a listing of all the patents issued within a given class/subclass (patents CLASS DVD).

Summary

Index to the U.S. Patent Classification
- Use Cassis to search the *Index*.
- Print and Save search results.

Manual of Classification
- Use Cassis to search the *Manual of Classification.*

Classification Definitions
- Use Cassis to search the *Classification Definitions.*

Form Search
- Select Search Fields and use Boolean and Proximity operators.
- Verify correctness of parsed search query.

Command Search
- Combine information from different search fields using Boolean and Proximity operators, wildcards and phrases.
- Verify correctness of parsed search query.

Additional Cassis Features
- Natural Language queries, customized displays, saving and loading Queries.
- Extract a list of all patents issued within a class.

Chapter

10

EAST Meets WEST

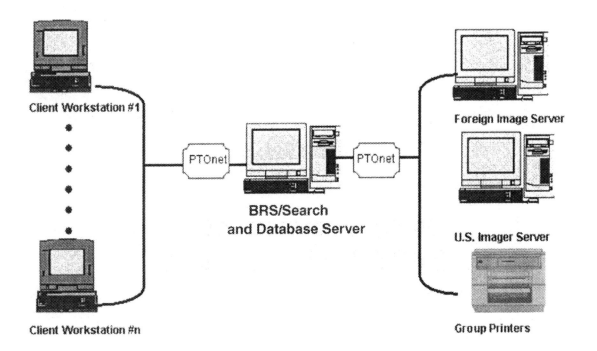

Figure 1 (Source: EAST Training Manual – USPTO)

This chapter introduces you to the EAST and WEST software interfaces to the PTO database files. The search language used with these databases is the BRS Search engine language (BRS is named after the former search company Bibliographic Retrieval Services.)

At the USPTO public search facility in Alexandria, Virginia, computer workstations provide access to the EAST and WEST search systems. Both EAST and WEST use a 'middle-ware translator' (see Figure 1) to convert user search commands into a form that the BRS search engine understands.

A. Web based Examiner Search Tool (WEST)

In order to use the WEST search interface you will need USPTO personnel to login with a user ID and password. Once logged in, WEST opens up in a default freeform search window (see Figure 2, below.) One of the major advantages to using WEST is the wealth of patent data that can be searched. A summary of these searchable databases is shown in Table 1.

Database	Description
USPT	Contains, at a minimum, bibliographic information (patent number, publication date and current classification information) for patents from the 1790's to the present.
USOCR	Scanned images file of patents issued from 1920 to 1970. Contains minimal index information such as patent number, title (utility), publication date and current classification information. No text editing performed.
PGPub	Utility applications that have been pending for 18 months.
JPAB	English language abstracts of unexamined Japanese patent applications starting with October, 1976.
EPAB	Published documents from the European Patent Office (EPO) and selected member countries.

Table 1
(Source: WEST Training Manual – USPTO)

As an example, a simple search for the keyword Sugar is shown in Figure 2. The default USPT database is selected and the keyword Sugar is typed into the search box labeled Term. The results display is limited to 10 results per page by entering a 10 in the window labeled Display. Finally, the output is displayed in the CIT (Citation) format. This format includes the patent number, issue date, title, first inventor and class/subclass. To perform this search, click on the Search button shown at the bottom of Figure 2. The results are shown in Figure 3, below.

The results of a WEST search are often referred to as a Posting. A Posting consists of:

- The Term(s) searched
- The total number of records containing the search terms
- A unique L-number label applied to each search result answer set.

In Figure 3 we see that there were 85,546 hits for the keyword Sugar. This group of results makes up what is called an "answer set." To the left of our answer set is the L-number (see bottom of Figure 3.) The answer set L-number is a numbered label that is applied to each search that we perform. The L-numbers will increase sequentially throughout your search session. The numbers will range from 1 to 999.

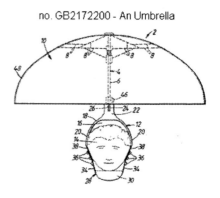

no. GB2172200 - An Umbrella

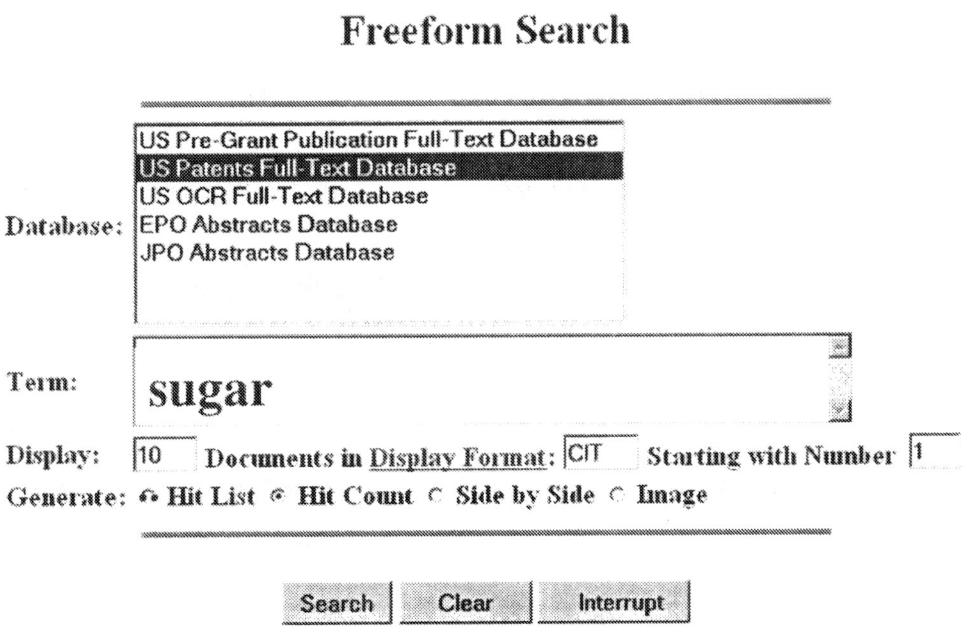

Freeform Search

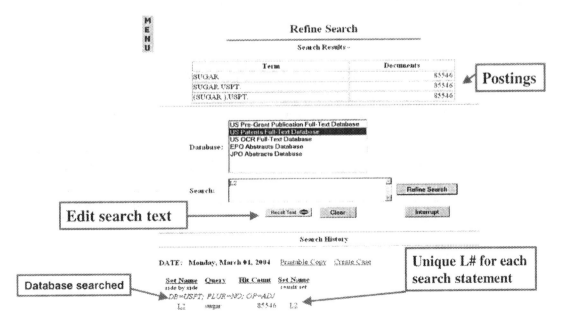

Figure 2 (Source: WEST Training Manual – USPTO)

Hit Screen Results

Figure 3 (Source: WEST Training Manual – USPTO)

Multiple search words can be combined with Boolean Search terms as shown in Table 2, below. See Chapter 1 for a detailed discussion of Boolean Searching.

Multiple search words can also be combined with Proximity operators. The allowed Proximity operators are shown in Table 3, below. Note that:

- All the proximity operators can be combined with NOT
- The ADJ and NEAR operators can be followed by a number (1-99) that represents the maximum "words apart" the search terms can be

- The default separation of 1 is used if no number is specified.

Some example proximity searches are:

- Electrical not with wire
- Electrical adj wire
- Electrical near wire

In the second example above, the BRS system will interpret Wire as being separated from Electrical by 1 term (default). Chapter 8 also has a discussion of Proximity operators and examples.

If you click on the L-number that was generated as a result of your search, you are taken to the Hit List (Figure 4.) Here, the patents are numbered and listed based on the issue date with the most recently issued displayed first.

Boolean Operator	Description
AND	Search for documents that contain both of the specified search terms with no restriction as to where the terms are found in relation to one another.
OR	Search for documents that contain one or more specified search terms with no restriction as to where the terms are found in relation to one another.
NOT	Search for documents that contain the first term you specify, but NOT the second term.
XOR	Search for documents that contain EITHER the first term or the second term, both NOT both terms..

Table 2
(Source: WEST Training Manual – USPTO)

Proximity Operator	Description
ADJ	Searches for adjacent terms occurring in the same sentence, in the order specified.
NEAR	Searches for adjacent terms occurring in the same sentence, in any order.
WITH	Searches for terms occurring in the same sentence, in any order.
SAME	Searches for terms occurring in the same paragraph, in any order.

Table 3
(Source: WEST Training Manual – USPTO)

To see how the search keyword is used in the context of the patent, click on the KWIC (KeyWord In Context) button indicated by the arrow at the Bottom of Figure 4. The result is shown in Figure 5.

By clicking on the KWIC button, the entire paragraph that each search term is located in will be displayed. The search term will also be highlighted and underlined to indicate that it is a clickable link. By clicking on the highlighted term, BRS/WEST moves to the next occurrence of the search term.

no. WO9939598 - Substance Dispensing Headgear

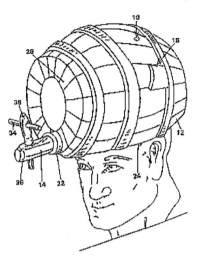

Hit List Results

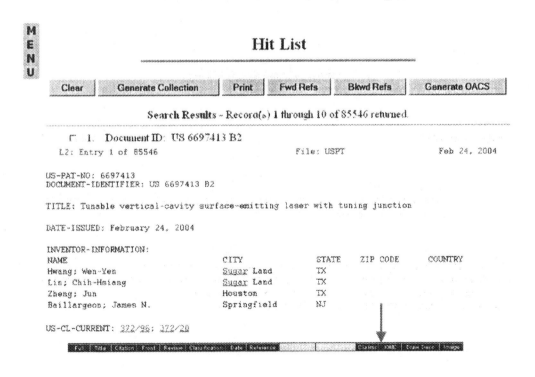

Figure 4 (Source: WEST Training Manual – USPTO)

KWIC in Text

```
M
E
N   First Hit    Fwd Refs
U

                          ┌   [ Generate Collection ]  [ Print ]

      L2: Entry 4 of 85546              File: USPT         Feb 24, 2004


   DOCUMENT-IDENTIFIER: US 6696607 B2
   TITLE: Use of phenethyl acrylamides, novel phenethyl acrylamides, method for the production
   thereof and agents containing the same


   Brief Summary Text (70):
   They are especially important for controlling a large number of fungi on a variety of crop
   plants such as wheat, rye, barley, oats, rice, maize, grass, bananas, cotton, soya, coffee,
   sugar cane, grapevines, fruit species, ornamentals and vegetables such as cucumbers, beans,
   tomatoes, potatoes and cucurbits, and on the seeds of these plants.
```

Figure 5 (Source: WEST Training Manual – USPTO)

Images of the patent document can also be viewed using WEST. At the extreme lower right of Figure 4 is a clickable button labeled image. To view an image of the displayed patent, click on this link. A close up of the link is shown in Figure 6, below.

Figure 6
(Source: WEST Training Manual – USPTO)

A representative patent image is shown in Figure 7, below.

Wildcard (truncation) characters are also allowed in WEST search queries to replace character(s) within a search term or keyword. Table 4 lists these wildcards. See Chapter 1 for a discussion on the role of Wildcards in Boolean searching.

Wildcard	Description
$	Replaces for any number (including 0) of characters.
$n	Specifies the definite number of wildcard characters to be replaced.
?	Replaces exactly one (1) character.

Table 4
(Source: WEST Training Manual – USPTO)

View Image

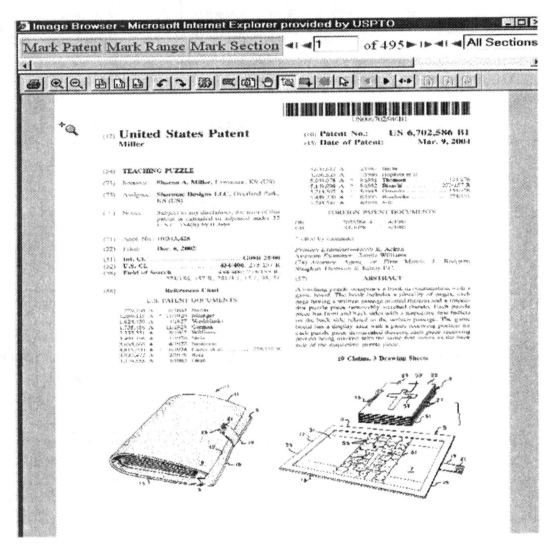

Figure 7 (Source: WEST Training Manual – USPTO)

B. Examiner Automated Search Tool (EAST)

At the USPTO public search facility in Alexandria, Virginia, the EAST search interface is available. In order to use EAST you will need PTDL personnel to login with a user ID and password. Once logged in, EAST opens up in the default workspace shown in Figure 8, below. A workspace is a window of an application that has sub-windows within it.

The default EAST workspace has three frames (Sub-windows):

- The Tree View contains various folders associated with the active session

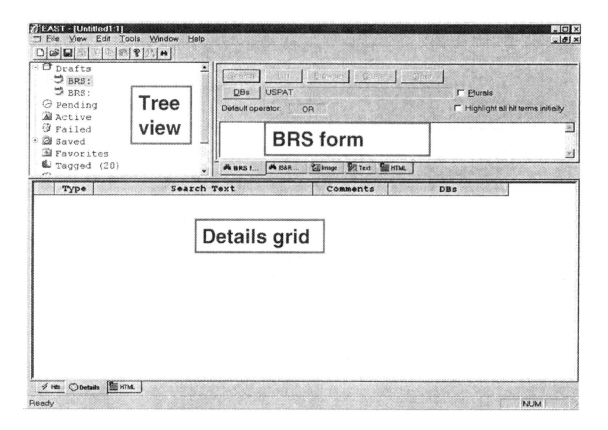

Figure 8 (Source: EAST Training Manual – USPTO)

- The BRS Form window is where you enter your search queries.
- The Details Grid displays the results of your search.

EAST supports the same Boolean Operators as WEST (see Section A - Table 2.) EAST also supports Proximity Operators (Section A - Table 3) and Wildcards (Section A - Table 4.)

The searchable databases available with EAST are virtually identical to those available with WEST, but the names are different. Also, there is the caveat that the USOCR database cannot be combined with other databases while performing multiple database file searching. These databases are summarized in Table 5, below.

To select a database to search, click on the DBs button shown in Figure 9, below.

You will then see the popup window shown in the figure. Available databases are added or deleted by clicking on the appropriate checkbox. Click OK to confirm the database selection.

EAST processing can be monitored via the Tree View. The most relevant folders in the Tree View (upper left – Figure 8, above) are:

- Drafts Folder: As you type in a search statement, the words appear here.
- Pending Folder: Contains queries that have been submitted to the BRS server for processing.
- Active Folder: Contains search results.
- Failed Folder: If a query encounters an error during a search or the search is aborted, the query will be marked with a red icon.

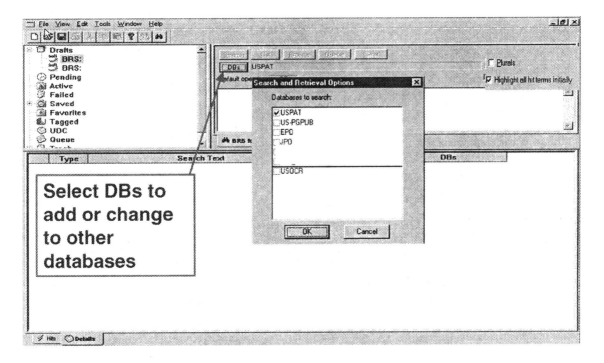

Figure 9 (Source: EAST Training Manual – USPTO)

- Saved Folder: Search collections from the Active Folder are saved here.
- Tagged Folder: Allows users to easily identify all patents having a user-defined Tag.
- Queue Folder: Draft queries can be placed in this folder for execution at a later time.
- Trash Folder: Deleted items are moved here.

Database	Description
USPAT	Contains, at a minimum, bibliographic information (patent number, publication date and current classification information) for patents from the 1790's to the present.

Database (cont.)	Description (cont.)
USOCR	Scanned images file of patents issued from 1920 to 1970. Contains minimal index information such as patent number, title (utility), publication date and current classification information. No text editing performed.
US-PGPUB	Utility applications that have been pending for 18 months.
JPO	English language abstracts of unexamined Japanese patent applications starting with October, 1976.
EPO	Published documents from the European Patent Office (EPO) and selected member countries.

Table 5
(Source: EAST Training Manual – USPTO)

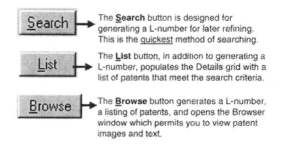

Figure 10 (Source: EAST Training Manual – USPTO)

A close up of the BRS Form window is shown in Figure 10, above. The BRS Form permits the searcher to enter simple and complex searches. When composing a search you can right-click inside the window to get the dropdown menu shown in Figure 10. Then simply select the desired operator with your mouse to add it to the search query you are constructing.

There are five clickable buttons that are grayed out in Figure 10, above. Once you begin entering your search query these buttons will become active. A summary of the most relevant buttons is shown in Figure 11, below. To perform a quick search, click the Search button.

Figure 12, below, shows the EAST workspace after several queries have been executed. As shown in the figure, the Active folder has been populated with several queries and the Details Grid has been filled with L-labeled search results. These L labels

work in a similar fashion to their WEST counter parts.

In order to view the text or image results of your search, select the Browse button (see Figure 11). Figure 13, below, shows an example browser window view of a patent. Use the tabs across the bottom of the browser to switch between text and image views.

Selecting a Button for Text Searching

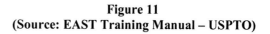

**Figure 11
(Source: EAST Training Manual – USPTO)**

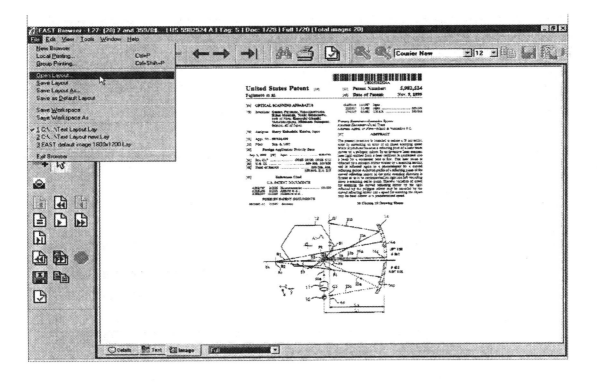

Note how the postings in the **Active** folder reflect **EAST**'s interpretation of the search. However, displaying your search history (Hint: click on the **Active** folder in the Tree View and then look at the **Details** grid) shows the search as you *actually entered it*.

Figure 12 (Source: EAST Training Manual – USPTO)

Figure 13 (Source: EAST Training Manual – USPTO)

C. Additional EAST/ WEST Features

Additional features of the EAST/ WEST search interfaces include customized displays, saving and loading frequently used search queries and searching classification definitions.

Summary

Web based Examiner Search Tool (WEST)
- Access multiple databases.
- Supports Boolean and Proximity operators.
- Supports Wildcard symbols.
- View patent images.
- L-labeled search results.

Examiner Automated Search Tool (EAST)
- Access multiple databases.
- Supports Boolean and Proximity operators.
- Supports Wildcard symbols.
- View patent images.
- L-labeled search results.
- Workspace (multi-windowed) interface.

Part 4

Where Do I go from Here?

In this part of the book, we help you assess the results of your search in terms of their effect on the patentability of your invention.

.

Chapter

11

What's Next?

If you used the techniques in this book to search for patents similar to your idea at the PTDL and/or on the Internet you probably have come up with at least a half dozen prior art patents.

Searcher's Secret Number 13

If you haven't found any prior art for your invention idea, you haven't looked hard enough.

So where do you go from here? The next step is to decide if you should go through the effort and expense of filing a patent application in light of your search results.

A. Has Your Invention Been Anticipated by the Prior Art?

In order to get a utility patent (as opposed to a design patent), your patent application has to satisfy four legal criterion. (For a detailed description of what is patentable, as well as the entire patent application process, we

highly recommend *Patent It Yourself* by David Pressman (Nolo).)

1. Your invention has to fit into an established Statutory Class.
2. Your invention must have some Utility. In other words, it has to be useful.
3. Your invention must have some Novelty. It must have some physical difference from any similar inventions in the past.
4. Your invention must be Unobvious to someone who is skilled in the appropriate field.

Let's look at each of these requirements. The first is fairly simple. In order to get a patent, your invention must be either a Process, a Machine, an Article of Manufacture, a Composition of Matter or a New Use invention. Let's look at a few examples:

- *Process.* A process is just the performance of a series of operations on something. Electroplating is an example of a process.
- *Machine.* A machine is a device consisting of a series of fixed or

moving parts that direct mechanical energy towards a specific task. An example of a machine with no moving parts would be a screwdriver. A more complex machine would be an automobile engine.

- *Article of Manufacture.* An article of manufacture can be made by hand or machine. As opposed to machines, articles of manufacture are inventions that are relatively simple, with few or no moving parts. Blue jeans and other clothes are good examples.

- *Composition of Matter.* A composition of matter is a unique arrangement of items. Chemical compositions such as glue and plastics are good examples of compositions of matter.

- *New Use Process.* A new use process is simply a new way of using an invention that fits in one of the first four statutory classes.

Virtually all inventions that have some use also fit into one or more of these classes. It's not necessary to decide which class applies to your invention as long as it is arguably covered by at least one of them.

The second criterion your patent application has to satisfy is that it must be useful. Fortunately, any new use will satisfy this requirement. In general if your invention is operable (if it functions), it will satisfy this requirement. Perpetual motion machines or other devices that violate an established law of physics are examples of inventions that fail this requirement.

The third criterion is novelty. In order to

meet this requirement, your invention must be somehow different from all previous inventions. This includes both non-patented, as well as patented, inventions.

Generally, there are three types of difference categories:

- physical differences
- combinatorial differences
- new uses

An example of a physical difference between your invention and a previously patent product would be the elimination, replacement or functional modification of a component of the previous device.

As an example of elimination of a component, consider the invention shown in Figure 1 below. The figure shows a side and front view of a fire safety glass window. It consists of four elements.

1. Element #1. Left-hand side glass segment.
2. Element #2. A thermal conduction film.
3. Element #3. Right-hand side glass segment.
4. Element #4. Heat-conducting metal frame.

For this invention to work, a heat-conducting film is sandwiched between two glass plates. When a sharp temperature rise occurs on either side of the glass, the film conducts the heat away from the window to the metal frame.

Now consider the invention shown in Figure 2 below. This figure is also a side and front view of a safety glass window. In this case there are three elements.

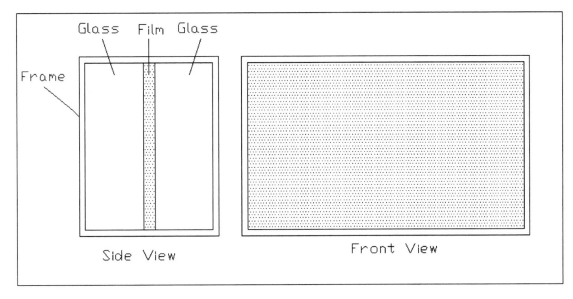

Figure 1

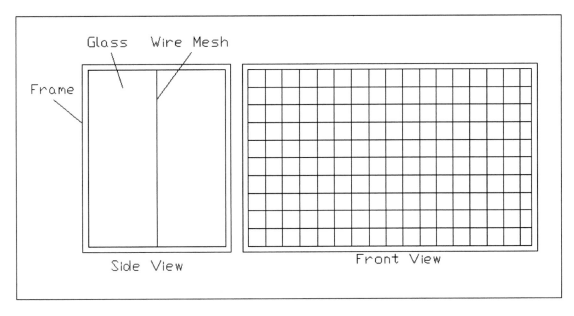

Figure 2

1. Element #1. Thermal-conducting wire mesh.
2. Element #2. Glass segment enclosing the wire mesh.
3. Element #3. Heat-conducting metal frame.

The wire mesh conducts heat away from the glass and into the frame, just as the first invention does. But now, instead of two separate glass elements, there is only one continuous glass element (in which the wire grid is embedded).

As an example of a replacement physical difference, consider the centrifugal water pump shown in Figure 3 below. Centrifugal pumps use impellers to impart energy to the water. For the sake of simplicity, we will identify four essential elements.

1. Element #1. Pump intake.
2. Element #2. Impeller.
3. Element #3. Pump casting.
4. Element #4. Pump discharge.

Let us suppose that the impeller is made out of metal. You design a new impeller for this pump that performs as well, but is made out of plastic. This replacement physical difference would satisfy the novelty requirement.

As an example of a functional modification, suppose our water pump vibrates at high pressure (high impeller speed) due to water turbulence. You redesign the blades of the impeller by increasing their pitch. This solves the turbulence problem and allows the pump to operate at high pressure. You have therefore made a functional modification.

A new combination of two different inventions can also be used to satisfy the novelty requirement. An example would be the combination of a hot air balloon (an old invention) and a new high strength lightweight fabric. The lightweight fabric replaces the older balloon material, making the balloon lighter. This provides more lift and lets the balloon carry more cargo.

A new use of an old invention can also satisfy the novelty requirement. As an example, suppose during World War II a sonar engineer developed a sonar receiver that detects the sound of a ship's propeller. Several years later an independent inventor designs a pool alarm that uses the same technology to sound an alarm if a child accidentally falls into a pool. Even though the pool alarm uses the same electronics, it would pass the new use test.

A systematic approach can be made for assessing novelty (except if you publish or publicly use your invention more than one year prior to applying for a patent, then it's no longer novel).

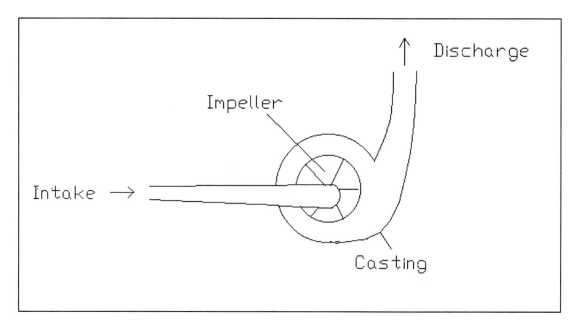

Figure 3

1. Analyze your invention for elements.
2. Analyze each prior art reference for its elements.
3. Compare the elements of each prior art reference to the elements of your invention.
4. If no one prior art reference contains all of the same elements used in the same way and for the same purpose as your invention, then its novel.

The forth criterion is unobviousness. This is the toughest of the patent requirements. Essentially, it means your new concept must be a significant step forward in the field of the invention. In other words, if a skilled worker who is thoroughly familiar with developments in the area of your invention would consider the idea obvious, you would fail this test. As an example, consider the balloon made with new lightweight fabric from the previous paragraph. While this invention qualifies as novel, it would be obvious to a person skilled in the art of balloon making to try using new lightweight materials.

The Prior Art Aspect of a Previously Issued Patent is Larger Than the Patent's Claims

Novice inventors often confuse the claims of a patent with the concept of prior art anticipation. Don't make the mistake of thinking that if an aspect of your invention hasn't been "claimed" in a prior patent, you can claim it. The claims of the patent only define the legal scope of the inventor's intellectual property. If a claim is violated (infringed upon), an inventor has offensive legal rights. He can sue the infringer. See Chapter 1 for a description of the purpose of each section of a patent.

In general, incremental changes are considered obvious since the results could be easily predicted by someone skilled in the related field, whereas, changes that produce *new and unexpected results* are considered unobvious.

Oftentimes, new inventions combine elements from two or more previous inventions. Here, the end result must also produce a new and unexpected outcome. For example, electrical circuits can carry alternating currents. A square piece of iron has certain magnetic field properties due to its composition. By combining the two via electrical windings on opposite legs of the iron square, you can create a transformer. By varying the number of turns in the primary and secondary windings (the primary winding is on the voltage supply side of the iron core) you obtain either a voltage increase or decrease (a step-up or a step-down transformer). This is a new and unexpected result.

B. First to File vs. First to Invent and Pending Patent Applications

One of the pitfalls of any patent search is that there is no way to search pending patent applications prior to 18 months from filing (see Chapter 4, Section B). Another inventor may have already filed a patent application on essentially the same invention as you. Because pending patent applications are kept confidential (prior to 18 months), if the patent hasn't been issued yet you have no way of knowing about it. This is one of the occupational hazards involved in applying for a patent.

If you have a patent application pending, and a patent is issued that covers the essential aspects of your idea, you may still be able to get a patent. How? You do it by proving that you conceived of the invention prior to the inventor listed in the opposing patent.

While most of the world uses what is known as a first to file system (the first person to file a patent application is legally recognized as the inventor), we in the U.S. use a first to invent system. This means that the inventor who can prove to have conceived of the idea first, gets the patent.

To prove when you first conceived of your invention idea, you have to keep legally acceptable records. Nolo publishes an excellent workbook called *The Inventor's Notebook*, where you can record the conception, building and testing of your invention. The notebook walks you through the due diligence process and help's you

prove the earliest possible date of invention. It can also help you if your first to invent status is ever challenged by another inventor.

C. Conclusion

In closing, we hope that you have found the information and techniques illustrated in this book both useful and enlightening. By using this resource, the Internet and the nationwide network of PTDLs, the independent inventor can indeed perform a reasonably accurate, preliminary patent search.

Summary

Has Your Invention Been Anticipated by the Prior Art?
- If you haven't found any prior art, you haven't looked hard enough.
- In order to get a Utility Patent, your patent application has to satisfy four legal criterions: fit into a Statutory Class, have some Utility, have some Novelty and be Unobvious.

- The Prior Art aspect of a previously issued patent is larger than the patent's claims.

First to File vs. First to Invent and Pending Patent Applications
- Can't search Pending Patent Applications prior to 18-months from filing.
- U.S. has a First-to-Invent as opposed to First-to-File patent system.

Patent and Trademark Depository Libraries

(source: Patent and Trademark Depository Library Program website: current as of May 2007

Alabama
Auburn	Ralph Brown Draughon Library, Auburn	334 844-1737
Birmingham	Birmingham Public Library	205 226-3620

Alaska
Anchorage	Loussac Public Library, Municipal Libraries	907 562-7323

Arkansas
Little Rock	Arkansas State Library	501 682-2053

California
Los Angeles	Los Angeles Public Library	213 228-7220
Sacramento	California State Library, Courts Bldg.	916 654-0069
San Diego	San Diego Public Library	619 236-5813
San Francisco	San Francisco Public Library	415 557-4500
Sunnyvale	Sunnyvale Public Library	408 730-7300

Colorado
Denver	Denver Public Library	720 865-1711

Delaware
Newark	University of Delaware Library	302 831-2965

District of Columbia
Washington	Founders Library, Howard University	202 806-7252

Florida
Fort Lauderdale	Broward County Main Library	954 357-7444
Miami	Miami-Dade Public Library	305 375-2665

Orlando	University of Central Florida Libraries	407 823-2562

Georgia
Atlanta	Georgia Institute of Technology	404 894-1395

Hawaii
Honolulu	Hawaii State Library	808 586-3477

Idaho
Moscow	University of Idaho Library	208 885-6584

Illinois
Chicago	Chicago Public Library	312 747-4450
Springfield	Illinois State Library	217 782-5659

Indiana
Indianapolis	Indianapolis-Marion County Public Library	317 269-1741
West Lafayette	Siegesmund Engineering Library, Purdue	765 494-2872

Iowa
Des Moines	State Library of Iowa	515 242-6541

Kansas
Wichita	Ablah Library, Wichita State University	800 572-8368

Kentucky
Louisville	Louisville Free Public Library	502 574-1611

Louisiana
Baton Rouge	Troy H. Middleton Library, LSU	225 578-8875

Maine
Orono	Raymond H. Fogler Library, University of Maine	207 581-1678

Maryland
Baltimore	University of Baltimore Law Library	410 837-4554
College Park	Engineering and Physical Sciences Library, University of Maryland	301 405-9157

Massachusetts
Amherst	W.E.B. Du Bois Library, UMass	413 545-2765
Boston	Boston Public Library	617 536-5400, Ext. 2226

Michigan

Ann Arbor	Art, Architecture & Engineering Library, University of Michigan	734 647-5735
Big Rapids	Ferris Library for Information, Technology and Education (FLITE), Ferris State University	231 591-3602
Detroit	Detroit Public Library	313 833-1450

Minnesota

Minneapolis	Minneapolis Public Library	612 630-6000

Mississippi

Jackson	Mississippi Library Commission	601 432-4111

Missouri

Kansas City	Linda Hall Library	816 363-4600, Ext. 724
St. Louis	St. Louis Public Library	314 241-2288, Ext. 390

Montana

Butte	Montana Tech Library of the University of Montana	406 496-4281

Nebraska

Lincoln	Engineering Library, Nebraska Hall, 2nd Floor West, University of Nebraska-Lincoln	402 472-3411

Nevada

Las Vegas	Clark County Library District	702 507-3421
Reno	University Library, University of Nevada-Reno	775 682-5593

New Jersey

Newark	Newark Public Library	973 733-7779
Piscataway	Library of Science and Medicine, Rutgers University	732 445-2895

New Mexico

Albuquerque	Centennial Science and Engineering Library, The University of New Mexico	505 277-4412

New York

Albany	New York State Library	518 474-5355

Buffalo	Buffalo and Erie County Public Library	716 858-8900
New York	Science, Industry and Business Library, New York Public Library	212 592-7000
Rochester	Central Library of Rochester and Monroe County	585 428-8110
Stony Brook	Melville Library, Room 1101, SUNY at Stony Brook	631 632-7148

North Carolina

Charlotte	University of North Carolina at Charlotte	704 687-2241
Raleigh	D. H. Hill Library, North Carolina State University	919 515-2935

North Dakota

Grand Forks	Chester Fritz Library, University of North Dakota	701 777-4888

Ohio

Akron	Akron-Summit County Public Library	330 643-9075
Cincinnati	The Public Library of Cincinnati & Hamilton Cty	513 369-6932
Cleveland	Cleveland Public Library	216 623-2870
Columbus	Ohio State University	614 292-3022
Dayton	Wright State University	937 775-3521
Toledo	Toledo/Lucas County Public Library	419 259-5209

Oklahoma

Stillwater	Edmon Low Library, Oklahoma State University	405 744-7086

Oregon

Portland	Paul L. Boley Law Library, Lewis & Clark College	503 768-6786

Pennsylvania

Philadelphia	The Free Library of Philadelphia	215 686-5331
Pittsburgh	The Carnegie Library of Pittsburgh	412 622-3138
University Park	PAMS Library, Pennsylvania State University	814 865-7617

Puerto Rico

Bayamón	Learning Resource Center, Bayamón Campus, University of Puerto Rico	787 993-0000 Ext. 3222
Mayagüez	General Library, Mayagüez Campus,	787 832-4040 Ext. 2307

University of Puerto Rico

Rhode Island
Providence   Providence Public Library   401 455-8027

South Carolina
Clemson   R. M. Cooper Library, Clemson University   864 656-3024

South Dakota
Rapid City   Devereaux Library, South Dakota School of   605 394-1275
Mines and Technology

Tennessee

Nashville   Stevenson Science & Engineering Library,   615 322-2717
Vanderbilt University

Texas
Austin   McKinney Engineering Library, ECJ 1.300,   512 495-4500
The University of Texas at Austin
College
Station   Texas A&M University   979 845-2111
Dallas   Dallas Public Library   214 670-1468
Houston   Fondren Library - MS 225, Rice University   713 348-5483
Lubbock   Texas Tech University Library   806 742-2282
San Antonio   San Antonio Public Library   210 207-2500

Utah
Salt Lake City   Marriott Library, University of Utah   801 581-8394

Vermont
Burlington   Bailey/Howe Library, University of Vermont   802 656-2542

Virginia
Richmond   James Branch Cabell Library, Virginia   804 828-1101
Commonwealth University

Washington
Seattle   Engineering Library, University of   206 543-0740
Washington

West Virginia
Morgantown   Evansdale Library, West Virginia University   304 293-4695, Ext.
5113

Wisconsin

Madison	Kurt F. Wendt Library, University of Wisconsin-Madison	608 262-6845
Milwaukee	Milwaukee Public Library	414 286-3051

Wyoming

Cheyenne	Wyoming State Library	307 777-7281

Appendix

B

Forms

Classification Search Sheet

Class Finder Tool

Classification Search Sheet

A. Descriptive Words	B. Class Index-Alpha	C. Subclass Index-Xref	D. Subclass Man.of Class.	E. Get List	F. Search Class	G. Get List
1.						
2.						
3.						
4.						
5.						
6.						
7.						
8.						
9.						
10.						

Class Finder Tool

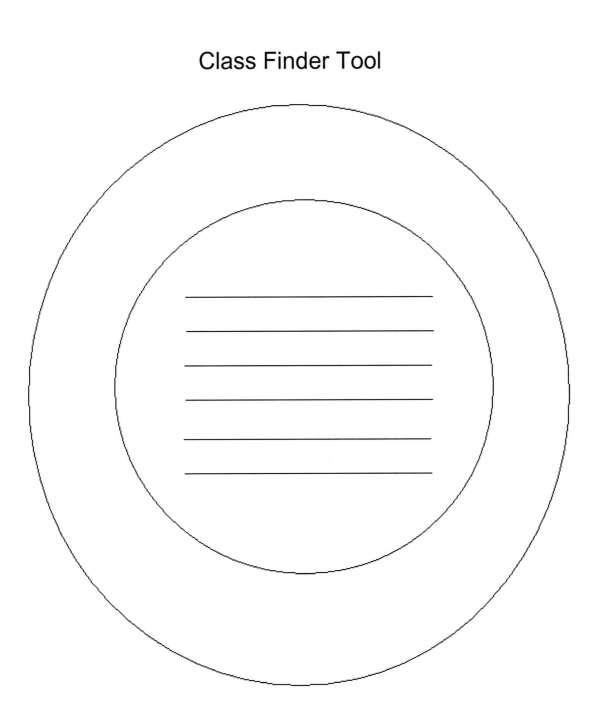

Summary of Searcher's Secrets

1. The more keywords used with the AND operator, the smaller the number of matches obtained and the more meaningful each match is to the searcher.

2. The OR operator is used to widen the scope of the search results.

3. One, and only one, of the keywords combined with the XOR operator will appear in each of the patents in the search results.

4. The ANDNOT operator is used to exclude specific keywords from the search results.

5. The PTO may use a term you don't expect for a class/subclass title. Use a thesaurus as necessary to find alternative descriptive words for your class titles.

6. Find the most relevant classes and subclasses for your invention. Then review all of the issued patents within those classes.

7. When in doubt about the order of evaluation in complex patent search commands, use parentheses to explicitly set the order. Then check the output command at the top of the results report.

8. By placing a Field Code outside a set of parentheses in complex Boolean queries, you apply that field code to every keyword in the contained expression.

9. To apply the Issue Date field code (ISD) to a range of dates use the (->) operator. For example:

   ISD/1/1/2003->12/31/2005

10. Use the Refine Search box to save time when making minor changes to search queries.

11. Use the checkbox next to a class designation to quickly perform a search of every patent within that class.

12. Use an online translation service, such as Babelfish, to translate the text of Foreign patents.

13. If you haven't found any prior art for your invention idea, you haven't looked hard enough.

Glossary

Abstract. One or two paragraphs appearing on the front page of an issued patent, summarizing the invention.

ANDed Search Commands. The process of combining multiple keywords in a Boolean argument together with AND operators. An example would be: Fire AND Protection AND (Building OR Structure), where Fire, Protection, and the keywords within the parentheses are ANDed.

Boolean Logic. Logic used to combine keywords into more powerful searches. There are four Boolean logical operators that we need to understand; AND, OR, XOR and ANDNOT.

Browser. A computer program that provides a way to look at information on the World Wide Web.

CASSIS. The Classification And Search Support Information System.

Class and Subclass. These are the categories that the PTO uses to classify or sort the various types of inventions.

Class Finder Tool. A visual aid used for finding the relevant classes of an invention.

Click. Pressing the left mouse button down once, and then releasing it.

Copyright. Copyrights are used to protect the expressive works of authors, computer programmers, movie producers and other artistic creators.

Double Click. Pressing the left mouse button down and releasing it twice, in rapid succession.

FAQs. A list of frequently asked questions, along with the corresponding answers.

Field Codes. At the PTO website, these are characters that precede a keyword. The characters are used to limit the search for that keyword to certain sections of the patent.

Hard Disk. Used for long-term storage of programs and information. This data remains with your computer after the power has been turned off.

Hit. A match reported by a computer search program, between a keyword and a database. The document that the word occurred in and sometimes the location of the word are returned to the user.

Homepage. Electronic documents that are published on the www. For multiple documents at the same location, the homepage is the top-level document.

HTML Document. A document that has special codes in it that allow the browser programs (Netscape Navigator,

Microsoft Internet Explorer, etc.) to display and link the document with other documents on the Internet.

Hypertext Link. Electronic documents that are published on the WWW are linked together through hypertext links. Usually a word or words on a homepage are highlighted and/ or underlined. By clicking on the highlighted word, you move from one document to another.

Intellectual Property. A product of the human mind. Patents, trademarks, trade secrets and copyrights fall under the category of Intellectual Property.

Internet. A worldwide network of interconnected government, business, university and scientific computer networks.

ISDN. An acronym for the Integrated Services Digital Network. It is a numerical phone network.

ISP. Internet Service Provider. A company that provides dialup telephone number and broadband access to the Internet.

Keyword Search. The search process carried out by a computer program, where entered keywords are matched with words stored in a database. When the program finds a match, the program will report back the document in which the word was found, and in some cases, the location of the word within the document.

MB. A contraction of the words mega and byte. It stands for one million bytes. A byte is just a word of computer data.

Modem. A device that converts digital computer data into analog data for transmission and reception over standard telephone lines.

Netiquette. Generally accepted rules and conventions used for posting messages to Usenet newsgroups.

Optical Character Recognition Program. A computer program that can extract words from a digital image.

Pneumatic. Air operated.

Posting Messages to a Newsgroup. Writing messages of interest to a particular newsgroup.

Preferred Embodiment. Inventor's "best guess" version of the invention configuration, at the time the patent application was written.

Prior Art. Previous inventions that are in the same field, or a closely related field, as the current invention.

Proximity Operators. These operators allow you to search for two or more keywords within a specified number of words of each other. An example would be searching for the words Fire and Protection in any order within a sentence or a paragraph.

Scroll Bar. A scroll bar is a Windows feature that lets you use the mouse to see objects that are outside the normal viewing area.

Search Class Cross-Reference. A listing of additional classes that are related to the current subject matter. Located below the current subclass definition in the *Classification Definitions*.

Search Engine. A program that keeps track of the content of the various Web pages on the Internet. The search engine then allows users to seek specific Web pages through keyword searching.

Trade Secret. Generally described as any information that, if kept secret, gives its owner a competitive business advantage. The formula for Kentucky Fried Chicken is one example.

Trademark. A symbol or word associated with a particular product, or a family of products. Examples are Diet Coke and Mr. Coffee.

TXT Document. A document in text format, a common format that any word processor can read.

Usenet. A collection of over 15,000 Internet newsgroups,

Venn Diagram. Graphical representation of Boolean logic.

Web Crawler. A program that automatically accesses website information. Usually called from an Internet search engine.

Web Page. Generic term for any document published on the www.

Website. Used to refer to a particular Web page on the WWW .This term is usually accompanied by a WWW location address, such as www.upsto.gov.

Wildcard. An asterisk (*), a dollar sign ($) or a question mark (?) that can be used to replace one or more characters (letters) in a keyword.

World Wide Web (WWW). A part of the Internet. Computers on the WWW host websites, where information can be read by browser programs and displayed on the home user's computer monitor.

Index

Printed in the United States
108058LV00006B/131/A